# Secretary's Standard Reference Manual and Guide

# Secretary's Standard Reference Manual and Guide

### Mary A. De Vries

PARKER PUBLISHING COMPANY, INC.
WEST NYACK, NEW YORK

**Library of Congress Cataloging in Publication Data**

De Vries, Mary Ann.
    Secretary's standard reference manual and guide.

    Includes index.
    1.  Secretaries--Handbooks, manuals, etc.
2.  Office practice--Handbooks, manuals, etc.
I.  Title.
HF5547.5.D47     651.4       77-21888
ISBN 0-13-797712-3

# WHAT THIS BOOK
## CAN DO FOR YOU ...

Every secretary needs a reliable guide to the latest and best secretarial practices. *Secretary's Standard Reference Manual and Guide* combines the most essential reference material in this field with practical, time-saving techniques and procedures and realistic solutions to troublesome problems. Indeed, the assistance of many experienced and knowledgeable individuals in businesses and other organizations has resulted in a desk reference that the secretary can consult confidently, with the assurance that it provides the most widely recognized, standard techniques and practices for handling every aspect of her duties. The data has been refined and organized with three principal objectives in mind:

1. To examine each facet of secretarial work you will find in the modern business office, for example:

- Receiving visitors
- Using the telephone properly
- Processing the mail
- Coping with problems among co-workers
- Applying successful typing and dictation techniques
- Setting up a dependable, time-saving file system
- Keeping accurate insurance and other personal records
- Making travel arrangements
- Writing effective business letters

2. To illustrate techniques and procedures that will save you time and effort in handling your secretarial duties, for example:

- Planning your work load
- Selecting and using time-saving office machines and systems
- Using typing shortcuts

5

- Sorting and routing mail efficiently
- Working with forms
- Filing and finding rapidly
- Applying effective data-processing procedures
- Saving time with special dictation and transcription techniques
- Streamlining your office

3. To give you easy-to-find, easy-to-understand answers to the many questions and problems that confront a secretary each day, for example:

- Introducing an important visitor to the manager
- Handling a difficult caller
- Helping an assistant improve her skills
- Serving refreshments at a director's meeting
- Arranging accommodations when you travel with the manager
- Avoiding misunderstandings about the use of petty cash
- Typing the address of a person who has several academic degrees

This book is intended to be kept on your desk, readily available for frequent reference. That means it is necessary for the contents to be arranged so information can be located in a moment. Thus, the data is presented not only in the usual manner, by chapter and topic, but also by section number. For instance, if you want to know how to type a telegram, and the table of contents or a cross-reference in the text refers you to section 1.15, you simply turn to the fifteenth section of chapter 1. The numbered paragraphs will make it much easier for you to spot items in an instant.

To present material in the clearest, most concise way, *Secretary's Standard Reference Manual and Guide* offers you 246 fact-filled sections arranged among 14 chapters:

1. Effective Business Communication
2. A Guide to Office Etiquette
3. Handling Personnel Problems
4. Mastering Office Efficiency
5. Successful Typing and Dictation Techniques
6. The Key to Rapid Filing and Finding
7. Processing Business Information
8. Keeping Company Books and Personal Records
9. Preparing for Business Meetings
10. Preparing for Business Trips
11. The Art of Written Communication

12. Using Correct English
13. Preparing Material for Publication
14. Letters, Charts, and Tables for the Secretary

Every effort has been made to insure that each section presents the latest techniques and procedures, covering nearly every conceivable task or situation you might encounter. These are but a few of the wide range of topics included:

**1.8** Do's and Don'ts When Answering the Phone

**2.3** Getting Along with Co-Workers

**2.10** Business-Related Social Occasions

**3.1** Working with the Manager

**4.2** Typing and Dictation Shortcuts

**4.11** Information Storage and Retrieval Equipment

**5.7** Typing Numbers and Fractions

**6.12** Ordering and Requisitioning

**7.1** Basic Data-Processing Procedures

**7.17** Typing the Report

**8.9** Keeping Office Payroll Accounts

**9.10** Parliamentary Procedure

**10.2** How and When to Use a Travel Agency

**11.9** Addressing Women

**12.43** Sentence Structure

**13.7** Copy Preparation

**14.17** Glossary of 100 Common Business Terms

*Secretary's Standard Reference Manual and Guide* is designed to fill all your needs for a standard reference work in this field. Since it covers the full range of secretarial duties, from answering the telephone to keeping the company books, secretaries at all levels of work, in almost any type of business, can benefit from using it regularly. As the information avoids superfluous detail, you can find what you need to know fast, and to put an additional supply of facts and figures at your fingertips, the final chapter consists solely of a collection of the most useful charts and forms for quick, easy reference.

I am grateful to the many businesses and other organizations that supplied up-to-date material for evaluation in preparing this book, and to the secretaries and business executives who generously provided helpful suggestions and practical information.

**Mary A. De Vries**

# CONTENTS

**9**

**KEEPING COMPANY BOOKS AND PERSONAL RECORDS**
(*Continued*)

### Tips on Keeping Office and Company Records   118

## 9   PREPARING FOR BUSINESS MEETINGS  .................... 124

### Making Preliminary Arrangements   124

### Procedures at the Meeting   128

### Taking and Typing Minutes   129

## 10   PREPARING FOR BUSINESS TRIPS  ....................... 134

### Planning the Trip   134

### Domestic Travel   137

**PREPARING FOR BUSINESS TRIPS (Continued)**

### USING CORRECT ENGLISH (*Continued*)

### Guide to Capitalization   184

### Dictionary of Correct Word Usage   192

### A Review of the Parts of Speech   205

# Secretary's Standard Reference Manual and Guide

# 1

# *EFFECTIVE BUSINESS COMMUNICATION*

## Receiving Visitors at the Office

In many offices the secretary is also a receptionist. Your role in communicating with the public is vital to the company's efforts to build a good image. Greeting visitors in a friendly and efficient manner requires poise, good judgment, tact, understanding, and patience. The manager will expect you to give all visitors courteous attention and to convey an attitude that will help the company develop and maintain goodwill.

### 1.1. How to Greet a Caller

No matter what your impression of the visitor is, approach him with a smile. Greet him with "Good morning," or "Good afternoon." If he does not offer information about the purpose of his call, ask, "May I help you?"

You need not rise if your desk is in a convenient location for visitors, unless the caller is an older person or someone of particular importance. Let the visitor make the first gesture toward shaking hands.

## 1.2. Find Out the Purpose of the Call

A secretary is expected to find out tactfully why a caller wants to see the manager, whether the caller telephones for an appointment or appears in person without an appointment. Of course, his intent may be clear from previous visits or correspondence or from his business card.

Most visitors will be happy to state their names and business, and will either produce their cards or tell you what they wish to see the manager about. If a visitor fails to volunteer this information, you may ask, "May I tell Mr. Jensen what you would like to see him about?"

*Greeting a caller who enters the office or reception room.* Ask the visitor if you can be of help.

"Good morning, Mrs. Brown. I'm Miss Davis, Mr. Hughes' secretary. May I help you?"

Or: "Good morning, Mr. Hall. I'm Mr. Hughes' secretary. He's not in his office right now, but is there anything I can do for you?"

*Greeting a caller who refuses to state his business.* You will have to be firm if the visitor does not have an appointment.

"I'm sorry, Mrs. Brown, but Mr. Hughes' schedule is so full that he can see people only by appointment. Could you tell me what you would like to discuss with him?"

If she still refuses: "I'm very sorry, Mrs. Brown, but I'm afraid I can't schedule an appointment without knowing what you want to discuss with Mr. Hughes. Perhaps you would prefer to write him a confidential note."

## 1.3. Making a Caller Comfortable

Show a caller where to leave his hat, coat, briefcase, and other articles. Offer to hang up the caller's coat.

If the caller will have to wait for the manager, see that he has a comfortable chair, a newspaper or magazine, an ash tray, and sufficient light. If he would like to use a telephone, show him to a private phone if one is available. Do not show any unnecessary interest in his conversation.

If the visitor wants to open a conversation with you, reply in a friendly manner. Avoid discussion on controversial subjects such as politics and do not argue when you differ with him. Never discuss company business or personal problems.

If a caller arrives while you are having coffee, offer him or her refreshments also. If the caller refuses, wait to have your own refreshments, but serve the manager.

## 1.4. Receiving a Visitor with an Appointment

When a caller with an appointment arrives, notify the manager immediately unless he or she is in conference and cannot be interrupted. If the caller has to be kept waiting, explain the delay. If the delay will last for any length of time, tell the caller the approximate time he will have to wait. He can then judge whether he wants to wait or make a later appointment.

*Interrupting a conference.* Try to avoid interrupting a conference, but if you have an understanding with the manager that he or she is to be interrupted for certain callers, do so quietly and unobtrusively. Enter the conference room without knocking on the door. Slip the manager a typed message and leave—unless, of course, he or she signals you to wait. If a visitor overstays his appointment, call the manager on the telephone and notify him or her of another appointment.

If there is a telephone call for a visitor during a conference, and the caller insists on speaking to the visitor, type a message and quietly hand it to the visitor. Wait for a reply, if the visitor wants to relay a message, or indicate which telephone to use, if the visitor wants to take the call.

*Making introductions.* When the visitor is someone the manager has not met, it is your duty to escort him into the office and perform the introductions. If the visitor is there for the first time and has given you a card, hand the card to the manager to make it easier for him or her to remember the caller's name.

If the manager does not know the caller, show him or her into the office and, mentioning the manager's name first, say, "Mr. Hughes, this is Mr. Adams." If the caller is an older person, a dignitary, or a woman, mention the caller's name first: "Mrs. Jones, this is Mr. Hughes."

## 1.5. Receiving a Caller without an Appointment

If you decide, after questioning the visitor, that the manager would like to see him, you might say:

"Mr. Hughes might be able to see you now. If you'll wait a moment, I'll ask him."

Or: "Mr. Hughes will be in a staff meeting the whole day. Will Thursday at ten o'clock be convenient for you?"

Or: "Mr. Hughes has another appointment in 15 minutes, but I know he would like to see you for a few minutes now."

*Callers merely looking to kill time.* More than likely there is an associate of the manager who is frequently coming over just to pass the time of day. If the manager has no time to pass, transform yourself into a polite barricade by saying, with a smile, "Oh, Mr. Hughes is extremely busy right now. May I take a message?"

You might also have to deal with people who drop in to see the manager because they "just happened to be in the neighborhood." Use your best judgment when handling this type of situation. If the visitor is a good customer, or indicates he might become one, let him talk with the manager. If he is just looking to kill time, suggest that he drop in some other time.

But if a good friend of the manager stops by, and the manager is free, announce the visitor and escort him or her into the office right away.

*When the manager does not want to see the caller.* When you know the manager is not interested in the purpose of the visit or is too busy to see the caller, you might say:

"I wish I could be more helpful, Mr. Smith, but Mr. Hughes is going to be busy for some time. The only thing I can suggest is that you take your matter up with him in writing. I know he'll read your letter as soon as it arrives."

If the caller persists, your only reply can be, "I'm very sorry, Mr. Smith, but there's nothing else I can do."

*Sending a caller elsewhere.* If a caller can be best served by someone other than the manager, tell him so and guide him to the person he should see. You might say, "Mr. Johnson of our sales department knows all about the particular machine you're interested in. Shall I call him and find out if he can see you this morning?"

## 1.6. Dealing with Office Personnel

If the manager has an "open-door" policy to office personnel, do not ask the purpose of a call. However, if a new, young employee wants to see the manager, and you believe it may be about a routine matter, you might say: "Mr. Hughes is busy at the moment. Is there anything I could do?" If the employee insists upon seeing the manager, don't argue. Announce him if the manager is free, or make an appointment for him as soon as possible.

## 1.7. When the Caller Leaves

Your greeting *and* farewell should be accompanied by a smile. A closing light remark, such as, "I hope you'll have a pleasant trip back to Nashville," is always appropriate. Also make sure the visitor has left nothing behind. Try to remember his name; it will flatter him when you address him properly the next time you see him. If the building is large and the caller has not been there before, offer to escort him or her to the elevator or lobby.

---

## USING THE TELEPHONE

The correct use of the telephone is an important skill that can create invaluable goodwill toward your company. Whether you use the phone a little or a lot, you should know how to use it well. This requires clear and thoughtful communication, as well as a thorough knowledge of available equipment and services.

### 1.8. Do's and Don'ts When Answering the Phone

A few simple *do's and don'ts* when answering the telephone will help you make a favorable impression.

1. Answer the phone promptly, after the first ring if possible.
2. Be courteous and friendly, and speak clearly and distinctly.
3. If you must leave your desk, arrange for someone to take your calls. Leave word where you can be located and when you will return.
4. Keep paper and pencil handy for taking messages.
5. If you must leave the telephone to get information, ask the caller if he can hold the line and thank him for waiting when you return. If the interruption will take some time, offer to call back.
6. If a second extension rings, let the caller finish what he is saying and then ask if he would mind holding the line for a minute. Press the hold button and answer the second extension: "Mr. Hughes' office. I have a caller on another extension. Will you please hold the line a minute?"
7. Give the caller your undivided attention, and do not interrupt when he is speaking.
8. If your telephone does not have a hold button, and you must speak to someone else in the room, cover the receiver with the palm of your hand.

9. If it is necessary to transfer a call, explain why, and remain on the line until the operator has answered and has been given the correct extension.

10. End your call graciously, saying, "Thank you, Mr. Lewis," or "Goodbye," and replace the receiver gently. Let the caller hang up first.

### 1.9. Answering and Screening Calls for the Manager

Most executives do not have the time or desire to talk to everyone who calls. Thus, their secretaries must screen their telephone calls to find out who is calling and why.

A legitimate caller seldom objects to giving his or her name and business. However, if a caller does not immediately volunteer this information, simply ask, "May I tell Ms. Davis who is calling?" If the caller insists upon withholding his name you might say, very politely, "I'm very sorry, but Ms. Davis has someone with her at the moment. If you prefer not to give me your name, I'd suggest you write to her and mark your letter 'personal.' I'll be glad to see that she gets it at once."

If a person gives you his name, but refuses to tell you what he is calling about, you might tell such a caller, "I'm sorry, but Ms. Davis has instructed me to announce what her callers want to discuss before I connect them." If the caller persists, suggest that he write a "personal" letter. If he does not want to do that, you can suggest that he leave his number, but do not promise that the manager will call back.

When the manager is away, try to handle as many calls as you can yourself. Some calls you may be able to transfer to other offices. When the caller can be satisfied only by speaking to the manager, you should offer to have the manager call back when he or she returns. Always have some idea of when the manager is expected back in the office.

### 1.10. Placing Calls for the Manager

The trend today is for executives to place their own calls, especially when direct-distance dialing is used, eliminating the secretary as a go-between. Some executives, if they want their secretaries to dial, will stay on the line and be ready to talk as soon as the called party answers. However, a secretary can save time for the manager in placing calls, particularly those requiring operator assistance. The following procedure is recommended:

Your employer, Mr. Dean, asks you to place a call to Mrs. Morse. If you reach Mrs. Morse directly, say, "Mr. Dean of Dean Laboratories is calling, Mrs. Morse. Here he is."

If, instead, you reach Mrs. Morse's secretary, say, "Is Mrs. Morse there, for Mr. Dean of Dean Laboratories?" Mrs. Morse's secretary will put her employer on the phone and trust you to see that Mr. Dean comes on the line promptly. As Mrs. Morse may not immediately be available, you would waste the manager's time if you put him on the phone as soon as you had spoken to Mrs. Morse's secretary. If Mrs. Morse is available and does come on the line, simply say, "Here is Mr. Dean, Mrs. Morse."

There is another procedure that the manager may prefer, especially when you call a close friend of his, or someone to whom special deference is due, such as a senior executive in the company. Connect the manager as soon as you speak to the secretary at the other end of the line. Say to the manager, Mrs. Morse will be on the line in a minute, and then connect him before Mrs. Morse comes on the phone.

### 1.11. Making Long-Distance Calls

*Long-distance calls.* These may be either station-to-station (when the caller will speak to anyone who answers) or person-to-person (when the caller wants to speak to a particular person or department). A person-to-person call, for which rates are higher, must be placed through an operator. A station-to-station call can be dialed directly without operator assistance. The caller dials an area code and the seven-digit telephone number.

Rates for long-distance calls vary, depending on the distance between telephones, the type of call (station-to-station or person-to-person), and the hour of the call. If you reach a wrong number, you can dial "Operator" immediately, explain the error, and avoid being charged for the call. Calls placed when one is away from the office can be handled by credit card (issued by the phone company upon request), and charged to the office telephone number.

*Mobile and overseas calls.* Telephone calls can be placed and received in a vehicle that contains a mobile unit. Mobile telephone service has the same features as regular telephone service, and numbers are listed in the regular telephone directory.

Overseas calls can be made by international direct-distance dialing to certain countries and by operator assistance to others. Give the long-distance operator the place, phone number, and other pertinent information.

Ship-to-shore calls are also placed through the long-distance operator who will connect you with the marine or high-seas operator. Then give her the name of the ship, the party you wish to reach, and the number.

*Messenger calls.* An operator at a point called may be authorized to send a messenger for someone who does not have a telephone. Charges for the call include the cost of the messenger service.

*Conference calls.* Several executives can talk simultaneously by means of a conference call. Ask the long-distance operator to connect you with the conference operator who will make the connections.

## 1.12. Special Business Services

The secretary should know how to select and use telephone services and equipment. A wide assortment of equipment and accessories is available to make your telephone service more convenient and useful. Your local telephone office can provide a list of convenience aids currently available. You can also contact a communications consultant from the telephone company to provide free advice on services and equipment and to recommend the combination most suitable for your office.

These are among the many services offered to subscribers:

*Wide-area telephone service (WATS).* WATS is designed for companies that place and receive numerous long-distance calls. Access lines to customers are connected to a nationwide dialing network.

*Switching systems: PBX, Centrex, and console.* Private Branch Exchange (PBX) is a switchboard system, which may be cord or cordless, dial or nondial, that channels calls throughout a firm. Centrex, popular in large organizations, permits direct dialing to office extensions, bypassing the switchboard. Console is a cordless, desk-top switchboard used by companies that do not need a full-time PBX operator.

*Teletypewriter service.* Teletypewriters transmit messages at high speed. The private line (TWPL) connects two or more machines. The central exchange (TWX) connects any registered office with another listed in the directory.

*Data-Phone service.* Two machines can transmit information at high speed in any form (e.g., photographs) over regular telephone lines.

*Tie lines.* A tie line makes direct contact between two offices locally or nationally.

*Answering service.* This arrangement will give you a line connection to an independent service of trained operators who will answer your phone when you are away. There are also automatic devices to attach to your telephone that can record and play messages.

### 1.13. Using Telephone Lists and Directories

*The telephone directory.* A telephone directory lists the names of persons and companies, personal and business telephone numbers, and street addresses. If you frequently make calls to other cities, directories for those cities can be obtained by calling your local telephone company office. Directories are useful not only for the alphabetical listing of names and numbers, but for the information provided in the Yellow Pages—an ideal source of places to call or visit to secure products, services, or just information.

*The desk telephone list.* There are some telephone numbers you call frequently in your work. The handiest and most efficient way to keep these numbers readily available is a desk telephone list.

Your list will include business numbers the manager frequently calls; emergency numbers, such as the fire and police departments; the manager's personal numbers, such as his family and his doctor; and, in large concerns, it may include the extensions of people in other offices.

If the list is very short, a straight alphabetical listing may be best. For longer lists, it may be more convenient to group numbers into business, personal, and emergency categories.

## PRINCIPAL TELEGRAPH SERVICES

When speed in transmitting a message and having a written record are important, a telegram or cable is the best means of communication. Thus, it is essential to keep abreast of the latest domestic and international services offered by telegraph, cable, and radio companies. To avoid needless expense and effort, it is also important to know how to type and count charges correctly for telegrams and cables.

### 1.14. Domestic Telegraph Service

Western Union domestic service includes messages sent to any location in the continental United States, Canada, Mexico, and Saint Pierre and Miquelon Islands.

*Fast telegram.* This service is quicker than that of any other class. The charge is based on a minimum of 15 words, with an additional charge for each word in excess of 15.

*Night letter.* The night letter is the least expensive service. Delivery is made the morning of the next day (or the next business day if it is a business message). The charge is based on a minimum of 100 words with an additional charge for each group of 5 words in excess of 100.

*Mailgram.* You can send a 100-word mailgram anywhere in the continental United States by telephone, Telex, TWX, computer, or tape. Messages go directly to the post office nearest the addressee and are delivered in the next regular mail.

*Sending a telegram to someone on a train.* Send your telegram in care of the conductor. Give the passenger's name, the name of the train and the direction it is traveling, the passenger's car and reservation number, the station he is arriving at, the arrival time, and the city and state. Send the telegram to any station where the train will stop.

*Sending a telegram to someone on a plane.* You can send a telegram to an airport for delivery to a passenger. In the address give the passenger's name, the airline and flight number, the direction of travel, the airport and arrival time, the city and state.

*Telegraphing money orders.* This is a service that provides the quickest way to send money to anyone within the United States and most countries in the world. Give the money to the telegraph office, which wires the destination office to pay that amount to the person you name. The recipient, of course, must be able to identify himself.

## 1.15. Typing the Telegram

You may either type your message on telegraph blanks available from Western Union or transmit it by telephone. If you type the message, you may need up to four copies: the original to go with the messenger, a copy for confirmation by mail, a copy for your files, and a copy for the accounting records.

Check the class of service (domestic or international) on the telegraph blank and type this two spaces above the address. Also type the date and hour in the upper right corner, two spaces above the address. (Use hyphens rather than slashes in the date as hyphens are nonchargeable.) If the telegram is to be charged, type the account name and number in the blank provided for this.

For the body of the telegram, double-space the message and use all caps only for code words. Do not divide words at the end of a line. Omit the salutation and complimentary close. Be conservative—omit articles (*a, an, the*), and nonessential words such as "Mr." and "please."

In the lower left corner type your reference initials, whether the message is "Charge," "Paid," or "Collect," and the address and telephone number of the sender.

### 1.16. Counting Charges for Telegrams

*Nonchargeable words.* Punctuation marks are free, except when used as *words,* such as "stop" and "comma."

Essential words in the address are free, except for alternate names or addresses. Accompanying instructions such as "personal" are also free.

The sender's name and address, including his company name and title, are free (but not his department).

*Chargeable words.* Within the body of the message, states, counties, and cities are counted according to the number of words they contain (New York City is three words).

Initials written without spaces (NYC) count as one word (but N Y C would be three words).

Mixed groups of letters, figures, and the characters $, /, &, %, #, '(feet or minutes), and "(inches or seconds) are charged at the rate of one word for each five characters.

Proper names count according to the number of separate words or initials (R. A. Jones is three words).

Compound words if hyphenated (e.g., father-in-law) count as one word.

Combinations of single dictionary words count according to the number of words of which they are composed (roundtrip is two words).

*How to economize.* Consider the wording of the message, the time differential, and the urgency of the message. Word the message as concisely as possible. Complete sentence structure is not necessary. Then analyze the time differential. Perhaps the less expensive night letter would get the message to your destination no later than a fast telegram. Finally, if the message is not urgent, you may be able to pick a less expensive alternative to the fast telegram.

### 1.17. Sending International Messages

Messages are sent to foreign countries by cable, radio, or satellite. The principal international carriers are ITT World Communications (ITT), RCA Communications (RCA), and Western Union International (WUI). If you want to send a message by Telex, file it directly with ITT, RACA, or WUI. Contact the Western Union telegraph office to send it by cablegram.

*Full-rate messages (FR).* This is a fast service used for regular or coded messages. The per-word rate varies according to the destination. There is a minimum charge of seven words.

*Letter telegrams (LT).* Letter telegrams (night letters) are used for longer messages that need not arrive until the next day. Registered code addresses may be used (see below). The charge is half that of the FR message. There is a minimum charge of 22 words.

*Shore-to-ship and ship-to-shore radio.* To transmit a message to or from a ship, give the name of the passenger, his stateroom number, the name of the ship, and the radio station. File the message with Western Union or directly with ITT or RCA.

*Radio photo service.* You can transmit a great variety of photographs by radio with this service, for example, a financial statement, an architectural design, or a legal paper. Contact Mackay Radio or RCA.

*Leased-channel service.* This is one of several direct international services. It offers an economical means of direct-wire communication for large-volume users, who may rent a channel for daily use.

*Overseas Telex service.* Several companies offer teletypewriter-to-teletypewriter service to a number of countries. The TWX system of Western Union is integrated with the Telex system by computer, thus permitting TWX subscribers to use Telex service. Charges for both Telex and TWX are on a time basis.

*Registered code address.* Addresses can be registered with a local carrier to obtain a code for use in cablegrams. Since there is a charge, otherwise, for full addresses and signatures in cablegrams, expenses can be reduced by use of a registered code.

### 1.18. Counting Charges for Cables

The means of counting charges for cablegrams differs from that for domestic telegrams. But economy is a similar consideration, and one should again evaluate the urgency and wording of the message and the time differentials (see chapter 14, Global Time Chart).

The name of the place of destination, including the country, is counted as one word. Names of persons or streets may be run together and counted as 15 letters to the word. For example, Middlestreet is one word, Middle Street, two.

Each word of the signature and address is counted. However, the cable may be signed with a code signature or not signed at all. Code words are counted at the rate of five characters, or fraction thereof, to the word.

In the body of the message each word of 15 or more letters is counted as one word. A word containing more than 15 letters is counted at the rate of 15 letters, and fraction thereof, per word.

Mixed groups of letters and figures are counted at the rate of five characters, or fraction thereof, to the word. However, characters such as the dollar and pound sterling signs must be spelled out and are charged as one word each. Fraction bars, commas, and decimals are counted as one character each, but punctuation marks, hyphens, and apostrophes are not transmitted unless requested, in which case each counts as a single word. Abbreviations such as COD are counted as one word per five characters.

---

## IMPORTANT POSTAL REGULATIONS

To handle outgoing mail in the best way, you must be well-informed about available services. Chapters 1 to 6 of the *Postal Manual* and the *Directory of International Mail,* which contain domestic and international regulations, are available from the U.S. Government Printing Office in Washington, D.C. Classes of mail and special services are described below. (See also 14.3, How to Dispatch Mail.)

### 1.19. Classes of Domestic Mail

*First-class mail.* All sealed matter is first class unless it qualifies as third or fourth class and is properly marked. When first-class matter is included with second, third, or fourth, postage at the first-class rate is required for the first-class matter. The rate for first-class mail is based on the ounce, or fraction thereof, up to 13 ounces. First-class mail weighing over 13 ounces is based on pound and zone rates (see *priority mail*).

*Second-class mail.* 1. Publishers. Only newspapers and periodicals published at least four times a year bearing a printed notice of second-class entry are admissible for mailing to established lists of paid subscribers. Publications produced by stencil or hectograph methods are not admissible as second-class matter. The rate basis varies with the weight, frequency of publication, percentage of advertising, and zone.

*2. Transient, copies mailed by the public.* Address an envelope and slit the ends. Wrap the entire newspaper or periodical inside but do not seal it. Write "Second-Class Matter" above the address, "To" in front of the address, and "From" in front of the return address. The rate is based on a set fee for the first two ounces and an additional amount for each additional ounce or fraction thereof, or at the fourth-class rate, whichever is lower.

*Third-class mail.* Writing, except something in the nature of an autograph or inscription, is not permitted on third-class mail. Third-class mail is subject to postal inspection, but may be sealed if clearly marked "Third Class." The rate is based on a minimum of 2 ounces with an increase for each 2 ounces or fraction thereof, without regard to zone. The weight may be up to 16 ounces; over 16 ounces it becomes fourth class or parcel post. (For bulk-rate mail, contact your local post office for information and instructions.)

*Fourth-class mail.* 1. Parcel post. Consult your local post office for size and weight limits of parcels sent by fourth-class mail. Rates are by the pound according to distance and zone. Do not seal the package unless it bears an inscription that it may be opened for postal inspection. A letter may be enclosed if postage is paid at the first-class rate for the letter. Write "First-Class Mail Enclosed" on the package. Special handling entitles fourth-class mail to receive the same handling as first class.

2. Special fourth-class mail. This category of mail applies to books of 24 pages or more of which at least 22 are printed, films of 16 mm or narrower width, printed music in bound or sheet form, printed objective test materials, sound recordings, playscripts and manuscripts for books, and loose-leaf pages and binders containing medical information. Each package should be marked "Special Fourth-Class Rate" and should include a description of the item.

*Priority mail.* Mail over 10 ounces, except that liable to damage by freezing or explosion, may be sent by air as priority mail. It may be registered, insured, or sent C.O.D. or special delivery. The rate for matter weighing over 10 ounces to 4½ pounds is based on the pound. Rates vary according to distance and zone.

### 1.20. Special Domestic Services

*Registered mail.* This service offers additional safeguards for valuable mail. Mail may be registered for any amount, but the fee is based on the declared *actual* value of the goods. The indemnity limit is $10,000. All registered mail, except second- and third-class mail valued at not more than $100 must be sealed. Mail without intrinsic value may be registered for the minimum fee or certified (see *certified mail*). A return receipt will be sent for an additional fee.

*Certified mail.* First-class mail without intrinsic value may be certified. The sender gets a receipt and a record of delivery is kept at the office of address. Return receipts are available for an extra fee.

*Certificate of mailing.* The sender may establish that he has mailed an item by purchasing a certificate showing that the item was mailed. No insurance is provided.

*Insured mail.* Third- and fourth-class mail may be insured. First- and second-class mail cannot be insured, but may be registered. The insurance fee depends on the declared value of the matter. The indemnity limit is $200. Do not seal, but wrap insured mail securely. Return receipts are available for an extra fee.

*Special delivery.* For the payment of a fee, any class of mail may be sent special delivery. This provides for immediate delivery by the office of destination. (See also, special handling of fourth-class mail.)

*C.O.D. mail.* Domestic third- and fourth-class mail and sealed matter of any class bearing postage at the first-class rate may be sent C.O.D. (collect on delivery). The sender must pay the postage and the C.O.D. fee. The maximum amount collectable on a single C.O.D. is $300. The post office sends collections to the sender by money order.

*Business-reply mail.* The sender who wants to encourage responses by paying the postage for them may apply for this service. The mailer guarantees he will pay the postage for all replies returned to him, and he must pay a fee for use of the service. Envelopes mailed must carry the words "Business Reply Mail," "No Postage Stamp Necessary if Mailed in the United States," and "Postage Will Be Paid by Addressess." The envelope must also bear the permit number and the name of the issuing post office.

*Stamps by mail.* This service makes it possible to buy limited amounts of postage stamps by mail. An order blank obtained at the post office provides a place to specify the stamps desired. The order must be mailed (postage free) along with a check to the post office. A nominal fee is charged for handling. Stamps will be sent by return mail.

*Self-service postal centers.* Self-service centers offer round-the-clock, seven-days-a-week mailing for letters and parcels. Automatic vending equipment enables customers to purchase individual stamps, books of stamps, post cards, stamped envelopes, and insurance. Units are located in post office lobbies, shopping centers, and other public places.

*Money orders.* Postal money orders provide for sending money through the mail safely. Fees depend on the amount of the money order, which may be purchased and redeemed at any post office. The amount of a single order is limited to $300.

*Mailgram.* A mailgram is a combination letter and telegram designed to provide overnight service to addresses in the continental United States. The customer presents his message to a Western Union office or toll free to a Western Union centralized telephone operator. The message is sent electronically to a teleprinter at a post office near its destination. From there it is delivered to the addressee by a regular postal service letter carrier.

*Express mail.* Express mail is a high-speed, inter-city delivery system geared to the special needs of business and industry for fast, reliable transfer of time-sensitive documents and products. The service is customized to a mailer's specific needs, using a network linking six major metropolitan areas of the United States plus several foreign countries.

*Controlpak.* Controlpak is intended to assure maximum safety to mailers of credit cards and other high-value items. Mail is prepared in the usual way. Pieces are then sorted, packaged, and heat-sealed in a special plastic bag. The bag is transported to the destination post office within the registered mail system, where it is opened under controlled conditions. Individual pieces are removed and delivered by regular letter carriers.

*Forwarding mail.* First-class mail will be forwarded for a period of one year from one post office to another without additional charge. Second- and third-class mail will be forwarded for a period of 90 days, without additional postage, to a known address in the local area. Fourth- and second-class mail (after 90 days) can be forwarded from one post office to another on a "postage-due" basis. Special delivery mail may be forwarded under the same rules that apply to mail sent by regular delivery, but will not be delivered as special at the second address.

*Return of mail.* First-class mail will be returned to the sender free of charge. Consult your local post office concerning the return of second-class mail. Third- and fourth-class mail will be returned to the sender and the return postage collected on delivery when the sender's address is in the upper left corner and when the words "Return Postage Guaranteed" appear immediately under the return card. Upon request, address corrections will be sent to the mailer for an additional fee.

### 1.21. International Mail Services

*Postal union mail.* This category of international mail is divided into LC mail and AO mail. LC mail (letters and cards) consists of letters, letter packages, aerogrammes, and post cards. AO mail (other articles) includes printed matter, matter for the blind, and small packets. Registration, return receipt, special delivery, special handling, and airmail are available for postal union mail to practically all countries. Insurance and certified mail are not available for postal union mail. Consult your local post office for details on special services.

1. *Letters and letter packages—LC mail.* All typewritten material must be sent under the classification of "letters" and cannot be sent at the lower rate applicable to printed matter. The rate is based on the ounce or fraction thereof, varying according to the country of destination and for surface or air transport. Write the words "Letter (lettre)" on the address side of letters or letter packages. Airmail should be clearly marked "Par Avion" in writing or by label. Consult your local post office for restrictions and requirements.

2. *Aerogrammes—LC mail.* Aerogrammes consist of sheets that can be folded in the form of an envelope and sealed. They can be sent to all foreign countries at a uniform rate. No enclosures are permitted.

3. *Post cards—LC mail.* Only single cards are acceptable in international mail. The maximum size is 6 by 4¼ inches and the minimum size is 5½ by 3½ inches. The rate varies according to country of destination, with surface or air rates applying.

4. *Printed matter—AO mail.* Printed matter may be sealed if postage is paid by permit imprint, postage meter stamps, precanceled stamps, second-class or controlled-circulation indicias. The rate is based on two ounces or fraction thereof, with surface and air rates applying. Write "Printed Matter" on the wrapper and specify the type, such as "Books," as special rates apply to these categories.

5. *Matter for the blind—AO mail.* Consult the post office regarding matter admissible in international mail as matter for the blind. The surface rate is free; air rates are by the ounce or fraction thereof according to AO rates. The weight limit is 15 pounds. Do not seal this matter.

6. *Small packets—AO mail.* This class is designed to permit the mailing of small items of merchandise and samples. The postage rates are lower than for letter packages or parcel post. The rate is based on four ounces or fraction

thereof, with surface rates applying. Packets may be sealed. The weight limit is one or two pounds, depending on the country to which it is sent. Mark the address side of the packet "Small Packets." Consult your local post office for restrictions and requirements.

*Parcel post.* Parcel post may be sent to almost every country in the world, either by direct or indirect service. The parcels are sent from the United States by surface vessel or by airplane to a port in the country of destination, or to a port in an intermediate country to be sent from there to the country of destination. In the latter case, the parcels are subject to transit charges in the intermediate country. Consult your local post office for customs and other restrictions and regulations. Registration, special delivery, insurance, and air service are available to some countries. Special handling entitles parcels to priority handling between the mailing point and the United States point of dispatch. Fees vary. C.O.D. and certified mail are not available for parcel post.

### 1.22. Using Zip Codes

To speed delivery of your mail, observe these practices:

1. Always use the two-letter abbreviations for a state plus the zip code (see 14.4, State and Postal Service Abbreviations).
2. Use only two spaces between the state abbreviation and the zip code.
3. Use abbreviations for long post-office names (available from the U.S. Postal Service, Washington, D.C. 20260) along with the zip code.

A zip code directory is available for reference in every post office. Copies also may be purchased from the U. S. Government Printing Office, Washington, D.C. 20402.

---

### HANDLING IN AND OUT MAIL

Processing incoming and outgoing mail is a daily function for most secretaries. Efficient procedures and a thorough knowledge of current postal regulations (see Sections 1.19-1.22) are therefore essential, not only to save valuable time for the secretary, but to free the manager from needless attention to details. This part of the secretary's job takes on added importance when the manager is away, as described in Section 1.27.

### 1.23. How to Sort Incoming Mail

Unless your company has a mailing department, you will have full responsibility for the incoming mail. Before opening the mail, sort it into piles of (1) correspondence, (2) bills and statements (if you can distinguish these from the correspondence at a glance), (3) advertisements and circulars, and (4) newspapers and periodicals. If the mail load is heavy, and there are more than three or four categories of mail, sorting devices may be helpful, for example, desk trays and racks. Most office supply stores have a variety of useful devices that will save you time and effort.

### 1.24. Opening the mail

When incoming mail is heavy, a letter-opening machine is frequently used. This machine cuts a very thin edge of paper from the envelope without cutting the letter inside. When not using a mechanical letter opener, adopt the following procedure:

1. Pile up the envelopes, face down. Open one at a time.
2. Use a paper cutter along the top of the envelope and down one side.
3. Take out the letter and any enclosures. If an enclosure should be there and is missing, write "Enclosure missing" somewhere on the face of the letter.
4. Mark down the day and time the letter was received.
5. Attach the envelope to the letter if there is no name or return address on the letter itself.
6. Never open letters marked "personal" or "confidential" unless the manager has specifically asked you to do so. Assume that a letter written in longhand is personal, even if not marked as such.

### 1.25. Sorting and Routing Letters

After you have opened those letters not marked "personal," sort them into three piles: (1) those that require the manager's attention, (2) those that require the attention of someone outside your office, and (3) those that require your own attention. This also applies to inter-office memoranda.

Get the manager's mail on his or her desk as quickly as possible. If there is previous correspondence that relates to the letter, attach it. Arrange the mail in the order of importance, with the most important on top.

If a letter should go to someone outside your office, attach a routing slip that indicates to whom it should go. If the letter is to go to more than one person, indicate the order in which these people should receive it.

Keep a daily mail record of all mail sent *out* of your office for action by someone else. Loose-leaf sheets can be used, with columns for the date, a description of the mail sent out, to whom it is sent, action to be taken, and follow-up information.

When sorting the mail, include in a separate pile the letters you will personally answer. Further segregate this into those letters that require the manager's signature, and those you will write over your own signature. (See sections 11.10-11.17.)

### 1.26. Handling Incoming Literature

If the manager leaves the handling of advertisements and circulars to your discretion, treat them in the manner you and he have worked out. You should never indiscriminately throw away circulars and advertisements. Some are of educational value and will keep you informed of new products, services, seminars, and so on. Others might be of interest to the manager or someone else in the company.

Select the newspapers and periodicals the manager likes to read. Unwrap, flatten out, and put them in a folder labeled "Newspapers and Periodicals." Place the folder on his or her desk.

If the manager happens to be paying for a periodical that he or she does not want and that is not needed elsewhere in the company, ask about canceling the subscription.

### 1.27. When the Manager Is Away

If the manager is going to be away from the office for a length of time, find out his or her preference regarding the opening, forwarding, answering, or acknowledgment of mail. In the absence of express instruction, however, the following procedure may be used:

Acknowledge every important letter. The correspondent should be informed that his letter has been received, and that it is being forwarded or will be held awaiting the return of the addressee.

Try to dispose of as much correspondence as possible by covering the subject in your acknowledgment to the writer or by referring correspondence to others in the company for reply.

If the manager phones the office every day, be ready to tell him the gist of all correspondence. If he does not call, you should contact him about any urgent matters.

If a letter requires the manager's immediate, personal attention, send him a copy and save the original for your files. Number consecutively the packets of mail you send as a means to check whether the manager has received all of them.

Sort out any mail that accumulates during the manager's absence into folders marked "Correspondence to be signed," "Correspondence requiring attention," "Correspondence that has been answered," "Reports," "Miscellaneous reading."

See also sections 10.9 and 11.10 on the handling of correspondence in the manager's absence.

## 1.28. Getting Signatures on Outgoing Letters

Before you give a letter to the manager for his or her signature, remove the carbon copy and insert the flap of the envelope over the original letter and any enclosures. Place the enclosures, such as checks, bills, and the like, face up on top of the letter, clipped even with the upper left-hand corner of the letter.

Some executives find it easier to sign letters when they are presented without their envelopes. If you do not submit addressed envelopes with letters, you can address the envelopes from the carbon copies or wait until the manager returns the letters to you.

When presenting letters to the manager for signature, separate those that he or she dictated from those that you or someone else wrote for his or her signature.

Never file the carbon copies until the letters are signed and you have made any necessary changes on the copies.

Before mailing, check to be certain each letter is signed and that enclosures and envelopes are still attached to the correct letters.

## 1.29. Folding Letters for Insertion

A letter should be inserted into its envelope so when the letter is removed and unfolded it will be in normal reading position, type side up.

A letter written on a standard letterhead to be inserted in a standard envelope should be folded as follows: fold one-third of the letter up from the bottom; make a second fold from the bottom to within one-sixteenth of an inch of the top. Insert into the envelope, top up.

A letter written on a full-sized letterhead for insertion into a short envelope should be folded as follows: one fold from the bottom to within one-quarter of an inch of the top; a second fold from right to left, about one-third of the way across; a third fold left to right within one-quarter of an inch of the right edge. Insert with the right edge up.

Letters written on half-size letterheads should be folded as follows: one fold from right to left, about a third of the way across; a second fold from left to right, leaving about one-sixteenth of an inch between the edges at the right. Insert in a small envelope with the right edge up.

### 1.30. How to Treat Enclosures

When it is necessary to fasten enclosures together or to a letter, use staples. The U.S. Postal Service objects to pins or metal clips because they might injure mail handlers and damage post office canceling machines.

1. *Enclosures the size of the letter.* Enclosures approximately the same size as letters include carbons of letters, typed outlines, mimeographed instruction sheets, price lists, and so forth. These are easily folded and inserted, with their accompanying letters, into commercial envelopes of the ordinary size. If the enclosure consists of two or more sheets, staple them together but do not fasten the enclosed material to the letter. Fold the enclosure, then fold the letter, and slip the enclosure inside the last fold of the letter. Thus, when the letter is removed from the envelope, the enclosure comes out with it.

2. *Enclosures larger than the letter.* These enclosures include booklets, pamphlets, prospectuses, circulars, catalogs, and other advertising material too large to fit into a commercial envelope of ordinary size. The accompanying letter may be sent in the envelope with the enclosure or as part of a combination envelope. If a letter is enclosed in the envelope, the entire package will require first-class postage.

A combination envelope permits both the enclosure and the letter to travel together but at different postage rates. This device consists of a large envelope for the enclosure with a flap that is fastened *but not sealed*. The large envelope is charged third-class rates. The large envelope comes with a letter-size envelope attached, in which the letter is sealed and charged at first-class postage rates. The package is handled as third-class mail, but the letter and the enclosure arrive together and the postage is much less than if both went as first-class mail.

3. *Enclosures smaller than the letter.* Such enclosures may be checks, drafts, notes, and other commercial paper, as well as small-sized bills and various memoranda.

When enclosures are considerably smaller than the letter, they should be folded inside the letter. If the enclosures are different sizes, place the smallest on top so that the largest will be next to the letter.

## 1.31. Preparing the Letter for Mailing

Before you place the letter in its envelope for mailing, you must carefully check the following:

1. Has the letter been signed?
2. Are all enclosures included?
3. Are the inside address and the envelope address the same?

Arrange the envelopes on the desk, face down with the flaps up, each envelope covering the one underneath it as far as the gummed edge of the flap. Apply a dampened sponge to the gummed edges. Turn down the topmost flap and rub it lightly against the lower part of the envelope with a clean cloth. Toss aside the envelope and do the same thing with all the other envelopes. Then turn the entire pack of envelopes over, so that the typed names and addresses are on top.

If you are using a sheet of postage stamps, tear off a strip horizontally. Rub your damp sponge along the gummed side of the stamps. Then, holding the strip of stamps in your right hand, press the first one against the first envelope in the upper right-hand corner. When the stamp sticks, place your left thumb against it, and with your right hand, tear off at the perforation. Toss the envelope aside with your left hand and repeat the procedure on the other envelopes.

Instead of a sponge, you can use a patented moistening device that consists of a roller dipped into a base filled with water. The roller revolves and always presents a moist surface.

Other procedures for stamping include the use of postage meters (see 4.8, *Postage meters and sealing machines* and 1.20, *Business-reply mail*), permit imprint matter, and precanceled stamps. Permits are issued by your local post office for mailing matter in envelopes bearing a preprinted imprint, thus eliminating the need to apply stamps to each individual piece. Use of precanceled stamps also requires a permit, issued by your local post office. All of these procedures reduce time and costs of mail handling.

### 1.32. How to Cut Mailing Expenses

One important way to cut office expenses is to guard against postage waste.

1.  *Group mailings* whenever possible. If you mail several letters separately to the same place, each wastes a stamp, an envelope, and the time it takes to address each envelope.
2.  *Use a postage scale.* If you guess at the weight, you may apply more postage than is necessary.
3.  *Eliminate unnecessary enclosures.* Such items often add weight and thus increase postage costs.
4.  *Use routing slips.* It takes more time to prepare numerous carbon copies and costs more in postage to mail them.
5.  *Keep letters brief.* Lengthy, long-winded letters take longer to prepare and can raise the postage costs.
6.  *Use the telephone if possible.* For local contacts it is often faster and less expensive to call than to write.
7.  *Use microfilm for bulky mailings.* Constant bulky mailings can be costly. If your office has access to microfilm equipment, you can greatly cut the weight of your packages—and cost of postage—by converting bulky material into light-weight strips of microfilm.

# 2

# A GUIDE TO
# OFFICE ETIQUETTE

## BASIC OFFICE CONDUCT

Rules of secretarial etiquette are designed to help you in your dealings with other people. They set a framework of accepted behavior for you to follow in the office, to help you avoid misunderstandings and resentments. Good manners are essential for the effective conduct of business in a cooperative and harmonious atmosphere. When genuine consideration for others is combined with an understanding of the basic rules of office etiquette, the secretary can contribute a great deal to successful working relationships both inside and outside the office.

### 2.1. Acting as a Company Representative

The secretary's role as a representative of the company and the manager is vital. Although common sense is always necessary in contacts with both co-workers and the public there are specific do's and don'ts that can help you act in a courteous, careful, and ethical manner. (See chapter 1.)

    1. You cannot have dealings with your own company for personal

profit, unless the company consents. For example, you cannot sell the manager's old office equipment to yourself.

2. You may not disclose your employer's trade secrets during or after your period of employment. Trade secrets have been interpreted by the courts as special processes, formulas, or plans known to your employer and not generally known by his competitors. A list of customers carefully accumulated through the years is an example of a trade secret.

3. You cannot, without your employer's consent, engage in a competitive business.

4. You must follow the manager's instructions to the letter in performing routine duties. In performing duties that involve discretion, you must act carefully and competently.

5. Find out the exact boundaries of your authority and do not exceed them. Always request complete, clear-cut instructions, which will greatly lessen the chances of entering into an unwanted, and yet binding, agreement with a third party. Just as important, let the party with whom you are dealing know the exact scope of your authority.

6. Always convey an attitude of sincerity and receptiveness to others within and outside the company, in spite of your personal feelings about any particular person.

7. Remember that your appearance creates the first impression to a visitor, even before you speak. To create a favorable impression, it is necessary to dress appropriately and pay special attention to neatness and cleanliness. Good posture and a pleasant expression will also go a long way toward presenting an appearance of assurance and capability.

## 2.2. The Secretary-Manager Relationship

The secretary-manager relationship is perhaps the most critical of all office relations to the secretary. A good working relationship, tempered with understanding and respect, is essential for both individuals to perform effectively.

The manager is expected to treat a secretary with respect and consideration for her position and responsibilities, and to maintain a regard for her personal welfare without intruding into her personal life. The secretary is expected to be cooperative, supportive, and courteous in communicating with the manager and carrying out his or her assignments. She should observe the same rules as the manager in keeping his or her confidences, but avoiding any intrusion into private matters. At all times she should remember that the manager is first of all her employer and that the purpose of their relationship is to conduct the business of the company. Thus, conversation should primarily focus on business matters. Small talk and personal subjects should be avoided.

Certain formalities, as indications of respect, must be maintained, particularly in the presence of customers and other employees. If the manager asks you to call him by his first name, do so only when you and he are alone in the office. In the presence of others, address him and refer to him by his last name. Avoid referring to the manager by surname only; always precede it with *Mr., Mrs., Miss, Ms.,* or by professional title such as *Dr.* or *Professor.* See also 1.4, *Making introductions.*

The manager might ask for permission to call you by your first name. If so, you should feel absolutely no offense. This is common practice in many offices.

See also section 3.1, Working with the Manager and 3.11, When the Manager Has a Problem.

## 2.3. Getting Along with Co-Workers

As a secretary needs the cooperation of co-workers in carrying out her daily tasks, she must exercise skill and tact in communicating and working with others.

When you enter an office for the first time, take your cue from how the workers address each other. But even if the atmosphere seems informal, do not assume you can call *everyone* by first name. Certain people, because of age, title, or position with the company, are entitled to special deference.

Good human relations require thoughtful consideration for everyone. No matter what your personal feelings are, it is essential for the sake of a harmonious atmosphere to treat all your co-workers with fairness and courtesy. Fair conduct means accepting one's share of the work load and responsibility and handling personal and business matters ethically and impartially. The careful secretary will avoid gossip, personal involvements, office cliques, friendships that waste time at the office, and other potential hazards. A friendly, cooperative, and responsible attitude will promote efficiency throughout the office; a negative, thoughtless manner can hinder everyone's performance.

See chapter 3, Handling Personnel Problems, for further details on avoiding common pitfalls in personnel relations.

## 2.4. Dealing with Personal Matters

In an ideal situation personal matters would not enter the office atmosphere, but that situation is rarely achieved. The alert secretary will be prepared to handle money problems, romance, gossip, and other personal matters that confront her. (See also chapter 3.)

*Gossip.* Information about personal or company matters passed around unofficially from one employee to another may well be inaccurate and should be received with caution. Gossip is dangerous and can unexpectedly involve participants in embarrassing situations. If someone passes a rumor along to you, make certain it stops with you. If the news casts someone in an unfavorable light, you could cause misfortune or harm to come to that person by spreading the rumor further. In addition, it is important to keep in mind the personal consequences: it does not take much to be considered a "gossip," a label that could do great harm to you and certainly no good.

*Borrowing and lending.* Personal money matters are often the principal ingredients in cases of ill-will. The best rule about borrowing and lending is not to do it. Borrowing large sums of money from co-workers and friends is frowned upon. If you must borrow smaller amounts, such as lunch money, be certain you return it promptly. If someone owes you money and is late in returning it, tactfully remind him. But it would be wisest not to lend money to co-workers in the first place. You can always politely refuse by saying you simply do not have that much available.

*Romance.* Although romance does not belong in an office, this does not mean two people may not form legitimate romantic attachments. But emotional displays are out of place at work, and it is improper to use company time for long, intimate conversations. If you are faced with unwanted romantic advances from a superior, simply tell the person you are sorry, but you already have a friend, or you definitely do not want to become involved with anyone at the office.

### 2.5. Etiquette at Your Desk

When you are at your desk, you probably are in full view of anyone who enters the office. The etiquette you practice at your desk is therefore especially important. There are two practices that require particular attention: grooming and taking refreshments.

*Grooming.* It is considered bad manners to attend to grooming at your desk. Even when you are alone, it is a mistake to comb your hair, file your nails, or apply makeup at your desk. Someone might walk in at any moment.

*Refreshments.* Whether you are at your desk or dining in someone's home, you should observe proper table manners. It is particularly important to keep your desk neat and free of cluttered ashtrays, unwashed coffee cups, and crumbs.

## 2.6. Rules for Gifts and Collections

*Collections.* If you are asked to contribute for a gift or company event, be guided by your own ability to give. It is perfectly acceptable for you to determine how much you will give or whether you will give at all. If collecting is your responsibility, do not pressure people to give or to give more than they want. Company policy must always be observed in handling collections.

If collections during working hours are permitted, there are various ways of going about it. One method is to list probable contributors and, as each person donates, write the amount beside his name. A far better way is to route a sealed envelope or box throughout the office, so no one need reveal how much he has given, if anything. Naturally, it shows poor taste to request from people or departments not connected with the event being planned or from an employee who has only been with the company for a week or two. Some offices agree that each employee will contribute a small amount from each paycheck into a fund from which presents and flowers are bought as needed.

*Gifts.* There is nothing compulsory or automatic about the manager giving his secretary a Christmas or holiday gift. But even if you receive one, it is not necessary for you to give one in return. It is never proper, under any circumstances, for a secretary to initiate the practice of exchanging gifts with an employer.

There might be some co-workers with whom you exchange gifts on various occasions. If so, avoid embarrassment with other workers by making the exchange outside the office (see 14.13 and 14.14 for gift ideas).

*Cards.* When it comes to Christmas or other holiday cards, you should be guided by what is customary in your office. If you receive a card from someone who was not on your own card list, thank him or her for the card, but do not apologize for not having sent one.

*Office parties.* Many offices have an employee party during the holiday season. Remember that you will be back at work the next day and must live with whatever you say and do. Do not use the relaxed atmosphere as an excuse to start calling everyone by his first name or to let out all of your office gripes. If the party becomes unruly or if any guest becomes troublesome, leave quietly—and alone.

## 2.7. Common Office Housekeeping Practices

A secretary can make the office a pleasanter place to work by making office housekeeping a regular part of her secretarial routine. *Office housekeeping* refers to those tasks that add neatness, efficiency, and beauty to the surroundings. Flowers, plants, wall pictures, and other decorations can transform a cold, impersonal room into one that is warm and inviting. If your decorating objectives are more ambitious, first consult the manager to determine company policy. If you are asked to make suggestions for redecorating, you can obtain numerous ideas and cost figures from interior decorators and furniture, floor and wall covering, and drapery stores. Extensive redecorating is an occasional or one-time project. There are also daily housekeeping duties you will tend to each morning before the manager arrives. Some or all of these tasks may be your responsibility:

1. Before you regulate the air conditioner or heater, get the mustiness out of the room by opening the windows and letting in the fresh morning air. If the manager has loose papers on his or her desk, make sure they will not be blown away.

2. Dust the room if this has not been done by cleaning personnel. Ask the person in charge of supplies to get you a soft flannel cloth. Keep it in the bottom drawer of your desk so it will be at hand for your morning dusting.

3. If cut flowers are in the manager's office, the water should be changed daily. If there are plants, they should be watered and the dead leaves trimmed.

4. Make sure the manager's pencil container is filled with sharpened pencils and that the pen on his or her desk is loaded and clean.

5. Replenish the manager's supply of scratch pads, paper clips, and all types of stationery he or she regularly uses; do not wait until an item completely runs out.

6. If the manager uses a water carafe, make sure it has fresh water in it and that both the thermos and the glass are gleaming.

7. Take care of any outgoing letters or memoranda left from the previous day.

8. Make sure your appointment calendar and the manager's agree in every detail.

---

## RULES OF GENERAL BUSINESS ETIQUETTE

Since the scope of business etiquette extends far beyond the immediate office, a secretary must be familiar with the rules that apply to the business world in general—whether inside or outside the office: how to act at a business-related social function; how to introduce people; how to behave in places outside the office, such as the lunch room; and what rules to observe when traveling with the manager.

### 2.8. Handling Introductions

Most secretaries face numerous occasions when introductions are required. Much of the time a secretary is concerned with introducing visitors to the manager, but she will also have occasion to introduce co-workers and other persons to each other.

The key is to learn one simple rule: except in cases of an older person, a dignitary, or a woman, always introduce a lower ranking person to a higher ranking person. This means you mention the name of the higher ranking person first. For example, if Mr. Warner is a senior executive and Joe Adams is a junior executive, you might say: "Mr. Warner, this is Joe Adams."

One common exception to the basic rule applies when introducing women—state the woman's name first, regardless of rank. For instance, if Mrs. Davis, the assistant director of research at a branch office, is calling on Mr. King, the director of research and development at the headquarters office, you might say: "Mrs. Davis, I'd like you to meet Mr. King."

Another exception to the basic rule involves a dignitary or older person. Again, you would mention the dignitary's name or the older person's name first. For example, if a retired employee, Mr. Lewis, stops to see the director, Mr. King, you might say: "Mr. Lewis . . . Mr. King."

A secretary also has many opportunities to introduce herself—sometimes daily if there are frequent visitors to the office. The procedure is very simple: "I'm Miss Jones, Ms. Hart's secretary. May I help you?"

Making introductions is half of the problem, perhaps the more important half. But an introduction must also be acknowledged. One simple response is always appropriate: "How do you do?" If you feel more is required, you might add: "It's nice meeting you." A secretary should wait for a visitor to make the first gesture toward shaking hands.

## 2.9. Common Courtesy Outside the Office

A secretary may spend most of her time in the office, but she must also call on others and make use of common areas such as elevators, reception rooms and lobbies, the parking lot, and the lunch room or cafeteria.

*Visiting other offices.* Arrive promptly for your appointment. If you know you will be late, call and arrange a later time. When you enter another office, introduce yourself (see 2.8) and state your business. Always smile and respond pleasantly to others. If you have to wait, try to avoid interrupting the work of others with idle conversation or appearing to be overly interested in the telephone calls or discussions of others.

*In the elevator.* Men usually let women enter and leave an elevator first, unless it is crowded, when all persons nearest the door exit first. Cigarettes must be put out before entering an elevator as a matter of safety as well as courtesy. If a self-service elevator is crowded, the person nearest the board should press the buttons called out by others.

*In the lobby or reception room.* A lobby or reception room should not be used as a racetrack when you are late for work or as a place to lounge informally when you are tired. Walk slowly and be careful not to brush others aside. As visitors may be lingering in the lobby or waiting in the reception room while waiting for appointments, it is important to present a good image for the company.

*In the parking lot.* In their haste to leave, employees often forget to observe the basic rules of etiquette in the parking lot. Not only does a frantic exit display bad manners, it can be dangerous. It is often wiser to work an extra ten minutes and avoid the rush of people and cars.

*In the lunch room or cafeteria.* The lunch room or cafeteria is another place where common courtesy is sometimes forgotten. It is rude to enter a line ahead of others or hover over a diner in hopes of pressuring him to leave. Always indicate a willingness to share your table. It is perfectly appropriate to join in polite conversation with another diner, whether or not you know the person. When you are finished, do not linger endlessly over a cup of coffee. There may be others waiting for a table.

## 2.10. Business-Related Social Occasions

*Attending company functions.* If you receive an informal invitation, reply on the enclosed card or, if there is none, by letter or telephone. If the invitation is formal, reply in longhand on good quality stationery. The invitation will tell you whether the dress will be formal. Dinners and luncheons should be treated the same as a meal in someone's home— common courtesy and table manners are basic requirements for everyone. Dinner or luncheon guests who attend a cocktail hour first should not delay going to their tables at the established time. If there is a guest speaker, do not talk during the address. Guests introduced by the master of ceremonies or the chair should stand briefly. For suggestions on conduct at office parties, see section 2.6.

*When there is illness.* If the person is a business acquaintance, the manager can send a note and possibly flowers or a plant. If the person is a personal friend of the manager, you may be asked to buy a gift, such as a book or something connected with the patient's hobby or other special interest.

If the patient is still in the hospital, call and find out if visiting is permitted, and what the visiting hours are. If the patient is home, contact the family to find out the most convenient time for a visit.

*When the manager is ill.* Others in the office might arrange collectively to send a card and flowers, but you will probably want to send your own get-well card or a gift. The gift should not be personal.

If it is important that you talk over work problems with the manager, first check with the doctor to see if it is appropriate to set up a visiting schedule. Do not overtax his strength or give him unnecessary details about problems at the office.

*When there is a death.* If the acquaintanceship with the manager was casual, a sympathy card is appropriate; where close friendship is involved, flowers and a letter of condolence are appropriate. If the deceased was a Catholic, a gift of Masses will be appreciated by the family. Mass cards can be obtained at any Catholic church. (A money offering is customary; you can inquire as to the usual amount.)

Letters of condolence should be written by the manager in his or her own hand. But you may be called upon to contact a florist.

If a death occurs in the manager's family, you may be asked to keep a record of incoming condolences. If expressions of sympathy are too numerous to permit the manager to send handwritten acknowledgments, you can arrange for engraved cards.

*If the manager dies.* If the family accepts your offer of assistance, you are in a position to take care of some of the funeral arrangements and attend to many necessary details. You can, for example, send out the death notice to the company and the newspapers. If you have records of insurance policies carried by the manager you may remind his or her family. You might remind the family later to check with the Social Security Administration for any benefits due. Clip articles and notices in newspapers and trade publications; the family might appreciate having them.

## 2.11. Traveling with the Manager

When you make room reservations for yourself and a male executive, specify that you will require two rooms, preferably on separate floors. Each individual should register separately.

The manager should have a studio bedroom or a parlor suite if dictation is to be taken in his room. The room should be made up and each person dressed in business clothing when work is conducted in the manager's room. Dictation can also be taken in the hotel lounge.

Meals, except for breakfast, may be taken in the manager's room, or the secretary and the manager may lunch or dine out. It is not necessary to take all meals together. Drinks with dinner are acceptable, but the secretary and the manager should not go out together just for cocktails. The secretary should plan her own entertainment for the evening.

The purpose of the trip is business, so the secretary should come prepared with shorthand notebook, pencils, stamps, and other supplies. A typewriter can be reserved for use through the hotel.

# 3

# *HANDLING PERSONNEL PROBLEMS*

## Principles of Office Supervision

The secretary plays an important role in seeing that the office functions smoothly at all times. This is possible only if she is able to work in harmony with the manager, with co-workers in her own department, and with employees in other departments. Because of illness, vacations, or an expanding work load, she also may have to find, train, and work with assistants and substitutes. An understanding of the basic principles of office supervision will make the secretary's job a lot easier and much more enjoyable.

### 3.1. Working with the Manager

The manager is a key person in the secretary's business life. Just as in any successful relationship, each person contributes something.

Your attitude can make the difference between a tiresome and formidable job and an exciting and rewarding position. This means you have to step beyond the level of "personal" bias. Whatever your likes and dislikes, you must view the manager first as your employer—someone who needs *all* your cooperation and assistance in carrying out managerial duties for the company. You may not always agree with the manager's decisions, but it is your responsibility to support his or her policies and, in fact, to interpret them to others in a positive manner.

Although it is your job to carry out the manager's instructions, this does not mean you should never offer ideas or information that might change the manager's mind about something. If you know a more efficient way to perform a task, describe it and ask the manager if it is practical. But respect his or her decision, even if your idea is rejected. Similarly, you should point out major errors or errors in figures—tactfully, of course. Minor errors you can correct without mentioning them.

If you take criticism from the manager personally, your working relationship will suffer, and so will you. Remember that it is the manager's job to point out legitimate mistakes or substandard work. If the criticism is justified, use it to your own advantage to improve your performance and become a more valuable employee to the company. If the mistake is not yours, tactfully explain this when you are alone with the manager, being careful not to make too much of it. In all instances, remain calm and poised and avoid any appearance of being negative, defensive, or unable to take constructive criticism.

If you are unlucky enough to have a difficult employer, learn another key to successful relationships—adaptability. It would be foolish to try to remake a person and even more foolish to harbor resentment over some trait that annoys you. If you are going to make the most of your job, accept the fact that you must be pleasant, cooperative, and supportive. You are both still on the same team.

### 3.2. Supervising Assistants

The supervision of an assistant involves planning the work, delegating it, and supervising the assistant's performance.

*Prepare a job plan.* A complete job plan would include the following items:

1. A schedule of daily routines plus a brief description of how each duty is performed
2. A list of all other duties, when they will have to be done, and an explanation of how they are to be done
3. A list of all department heads in the company

4. A list of all executives and companies with whom the manager frequently has correspondence

5. Samples of all forms, letters and memos that are used

To prepare a job plan, you will have to jot down every task that you do, just as you do it, for a period of about two weeks and segregate tasks into daily duties, Monday duties, monthly duties, and so forth. Include samples of the work process wherever possible and sample letters you write for your own signature and sample letters of any correspondence you write for the manager's signature. If you have an office manual covering all routine and nonroutine jobs, it will greatly simplify your training and supervising duties.

*Delegating duties to your assistant.* The assignment of duties to a new full-time secretary depends entirely on whether she is a second secretary or your assistant.

The manager may give a second secretary all his or her dictation directly and assign other duties for her as well. Many executives, however, prefer to work only through one secretary and leave it to her to delegate all duties she does not handle herself. If this is the case, assign the simplest duties to your assistant first. Such tasks might include:

Opening, date stamping, and partial routing of mail

Transcribing mechanically recorded dictation

Handling copy work

Filing marked material

Taking dictation from you

Doing routine, follow-up correspondence, without dictation

Assembling factual material from reference books or files

Running miscellaneous time-consuming errands

When your assistant becomes proficient in these simpler duties, gradually assign her more complicated ones that require further responsibilities and skills. These responsibilities might include:

Marking material for filing (material she can later file herself)

Writing letters that are not routine follow-ups

Handling telephone calls

Keeping the appointments calendar

For further details on training an assistant, refer to sections 3.5 and 3.6, Training Substitutes and Assistants.

*How to teach effectively.* Consider the following nine pointers when you are presenting new work to a new girl in the office:

1.  First tell why the job is done so that she understands how the work fits into the total company picture.
2.  Show her how the job is done and explain the operation of a new machine or any other process that requires physical movement.
3.  Let her practice and note how much she has absorbed.
4.  Praise her when her work is done well. Appreciation and recognition are essential to motivate a beginner to work harder and do better.
5.  Make sure she understands you.
6.  Be patient if she is slow, and encourage her to ask questions.
7.  Practice the art of constructive criticism and give the impression you are trying to help, not simply watching for mistakes.
8.  Have consideration for your assistant's feelings and dignity. Do not tell her to do something, ask. Corrections should be given in private.
9.  Be modest about your own knowledge when you explain work to be done.

## 3.3. Working with Other Departments

It is not enough to have a good working relationship with co-workers in your own department. There are times when you will need assistance from other departments to complete your tasks, for example, in getting a stencil run off. If you are on good terms with employees outside your department, you will have a distinct advantage.

Always contact the appropriate person in another department—the person in charge of assigning work. Even if you have a "rush" job, do not bypass this person and contact his or her superior, thinking this will ensure quick action. Some people have a tendency to wait until the last minute and then place a request for rush service. Employees in other departments will soon resent it if all of your work is rush work. Even worse, they may fail to take the rush status seriously after a while.

If you encounter a delay, try to find out the cause. If another executive's work has priority, you could contact the higher ranking executive's secretary and arrange a switch, assuming your work is truly urgent. However, if the delay is based on a personality conflict (perhaps someone dislikes your employer), a solution may take longer. You will have to create a stronger relationship on your own, so employees in the other department will eventually cooperate with you *in spite of* their feelings about your employer.

Your attitude toward others will largely determine your success in working with others. People are inclined to treat others the same way they are treated. If you are considerate and helpful, there is a good chance your reception in other departments will be similar.

### 3.4. Finding and Interviewing New Employees

*Where to look.* If the extra help you need is not available from your own company, you will have to consider an outside source. The most frequently used outside sources for temporary help are:

1. Temporary office help services
2. State employment agencies
3. Employment bureaus in schools and charitable organizations

Suppliers of temporary office help are listed in the Yellow Pages of your telephone directory. You can give them your requirements over the phone, and they take care of the rest. If necessary, they can manage on short notice, but it is wise to give them time whenever you can.

If the manager asks for your help in hiring a permanent assistant, there are several personnel sources you can investigate:

1. Commercial employment agencies
2. State employment agencies
3. Newspaper advertisements placed by the manager
4. Employment bureaus in schools and colleges
5. Employment bureaus in charitable and social organizations
6. Calls from casual applicants
7. Applications on file
8. Applicants recommended by employees and friends
9. Newspaper advertisements placed by applicants

An agency can be very helpful in screening applicants and sending over only personnel who are qualified. Let the agency know about the following qualifications you seek in an applicant:

1. Technical skills
2. Education
3. Experience
4. Personality

The manager may ask you to place an ad for a secretary in the "Help Wanted" columns of your local newspaper. You can place the ad by phone, by letter, or in person. The advertisement should be effective enough to attract only the qualified and keep away the unqualified. Start with the job title and phrase your ad in a way that will sell your company to the prospect. Try to arrange to have your advertisement run on a daily basis.

*Interviewing applicants.* If you conduct an interview, be thorough and efficient.

1. Know the precise requirements of the job.
2. Know the exact qualifications you seek in an applicant, for example, technical skills, education, experience, appearance, physical requirements, personality, and age.
3. Prepare a list of the major points you want to discuss with the applicant—points concerning the company and points concerning the applicant.
4. Conduct the interview in a private room. Also, see to it that there are no telephone interruptions.
5. Set the applicant at ease in the first few moments of the interview with a few friendly, general questions.
6. Let the applicant do the talking. Guide the interview with your questions and then show an interest in the answers she gives by paying close attention.
7. Try to keep personal prejudices out of your judgment.
8. Be accurate when you describe the job, the company, the benefits, and the salary.
9. Be as courteous as you are with any visitor to the firm.
10. To test the skills of a secretarial prospect, dictate samples of work done in your office. In addition to speed and accuracy, you can test skill in grammar by including a few apparently careless grammati-

cal errors in your dictation along with some words that are frequently misspelled.

*Checking references.* A personal phone call will encourage more complete and confidential information than a letter, but some companies are reluctant to give out information about former employees over the phone. If this is the case, you will have to write. Your letter should include a brief explanation of the purpose of your inquiry and a list of pertinent questions that can be answered simply and briefly. If your company has a standard form for checking references, you may have to include a covering letter with the form. Such a letter may be patterned after the following:

Dear Mr. Clemens:

Miss Barbara Nelson, one of your former employees, has applied for the position of stenographer and assistant secretary at Siegfried Steel. As she has given us your name as a reference, we would very much appreciate having your opinion of her character and qualifications.

I'm enclosing a form for your convenience in replying. We would also welcome any additional comments you have. I'm certain your information will be most helpful to us in considering her application. Thank you.

                         Sincerely yours,

## TRAINING SUBSTITUTES AND ASSISTANTS

One of the most challenging responsibilities of a secretary is the training of substitutes and assistants. The training process requires a thorough knowledge of company policy and office procedures and a strong sensitivity to human relations. In addition to bringing these basic ingredients into play, the secretary can develop a work-description blueprint that will greatly facilitate the orientation and training period.

### 3.5. Making the Newcomer Welcome

A new girl hired on a permanent basis will require a more thorough orientation than a short-term replacement. If you are orienting the new girl, do everything you can to make her feel a part of the company as soon as possible.

1. *Show her around the office.* Point out places of interest such as the building entrances, the coat racks, the supply cabinets, the first-aid room, the rest room, and the way to various department with which she will have contact.

2. *Introduce her to co-workers.* When you are showing the new employee around the office, introduce her to the people working there. (See 2.8, Handling Introductions.) Explain briefly what each person does and how it ties in with his or her job. In addition to making personal introductions, give her a list of company names she will have to know such as officers and department heads and persons with whom she will be corresponding.

3. *Tell her about the coffee break.* If your company provides coffee breaks, try to accompany the new girl on her first coffee break. It will give you a chance to become better acquainted with her in a relaxed atmosphere. If your company does not provide coffee breaks, explain the procedure for taking refreshments at her desk.

4. *Tell her when and where she can eat.* The new girl will have to know how long her lunch period is and also the location and price range of several restaurants in the vicinity if there is no company cafeteria. See that she has someone to eat with for the first couple of days, or until she is able to get around on her own.

5. *Give her a company manual.* Give the new girl a company manual if one is available and direct her attention to the most important rules and regulations. If no manual is available, be sure that you personally discuss the following points with her:

A short history of the company

A brief explanation of company services or products

Working hours

Time clocks

Absence and tardiness

Holidays and vacations

Method and time of pay

House sales and employee discounts

Recreation rooms and library

Petty-cash regulations

Lost and found department

Suggestion system

Special safety rules

Hospital and insurance plans

Retirement and profit-sharing plans

Promotion and training programs

6. *Explain how the whole organization works.* Give the new girl a basic idea of how your department fits into the workings of the entire company. If you have time to prepare a flow chart visually outlining this organizational pattern, make one and show it to her.

7. *Be friendly and be responsive to her questions.* Make the new girl feel she has come to a friendly place. Let her know also that she is free to ask questions and that you are trying to be friendly and cooperative.

8. *Be sure that she has work to do the first day.* An eager beginner who has to sit around with nothing to do will quickly become bored and frustrated. Assign her something to do as soon as the orientation is over.

## 3.6. Basic Training Checklist

Although methods of training vary (e.g., individual instruction and observation, group sessions, self-instruction through manuals and conventional texts), the subject areas of instruction will be the same. These are the major topics you will cover:

1. *General policy and procedures.* A general review of the company, its policies, and your office or departmental activities should be covered during the orientation period (see 3.5).

2. *Stationery, forms, and other supplies.* Show the new employee where they are kept, how and when they are used, and procedures for reordering.

3. *Files.* Point out the location, types, and arrangement of files and explain filing procedures.

4. *Equipment.* Demonstrate the use and care of each piece of equipment.

5. *Telephone and telegraph.* Explain the type of telephone service in your office, use of the equipment, and how to handle incoming and outgoing calls. Discuss the method for sending telegrams and cables.

6. *Mail.* Show the new employee how to process incoming and outgo-

ing mail, including interoffice memoranda. Review current postal regulations.

7. *Typing and dictation.* Describe the layout styles for various items (e.g., reports, letters), and the typing and dictation procedures used in your office. Provide samples of typed material. Cover points of grammar and good letter-writing techniques.

8. *Appointments and meetings.* Show the new employee proper procedures for making appointments, receiving visitors, and handling special duties (e.g., taking minutes) at meetings.

9. *Travel.* Outline the procedures for making travel arrangements and cover additional duties when the manager is away. Explain company policy pertaining to travel expenses.

---

## DEALING WITH PERSONNEL PROBLEMS

To the extent that the secretary works closely with others, she runs the risk of encountering a variety of problems among office personnel. Although no one should play psychiatrist and seek out problems, there are certain difficulties that cannot be avoided or ignored. The following sections offer tips on handling the more common personnel problems.

### 3.7. How to Resolve Personality Conflicts

Sometimes disputes among co-workers can be traced to a specific source of disagreement, such as who takes a vacation first or which task has priority when the work load is heavy. Such difficulties can often be cleared away simply by asking the manager to settle the matter according to his or her needs. But when the clash between two persons develops from an unexplained dislike they seem to have for each other, the problem becomes more difficult to deal with. Unfortunately, such conflicts can do just as much or more damage to office morale as more specific disputes based upon procedural matters.

If a co-worker openly displays an unfriendly attitude, make an effort to overcome it by responding in a thoughtful, friendly manner. If the conflict develops between you and your assistant, try discussing it candidly—but calmly. If that fails, and your work is being affected adversely by the conflict, you will have to advise the manager of the situation and let him or her take whatever action is appropriate.

### 3.8. Working with Difficult Employees

If an employee's performance is inadequate, and you are responsible for the work, act as soon as possible. Always discuss such problems privately with the other person and be as pleasant and considerate as possible. Avoid direct accusations. Instead of telling an employee her work is sloppy or that she is slow or irresponsible, make your point seem less like a *personal* attack. Tell her you noticed some errors or that the work has been piling up and you wonder if the job is too difficult. If the employee responds positively by working harder and being more careful, be certain to praise her for the improvement.

Some employees are difficult to handle not because of poor quality work or a low rate of production, but simply because they resent being supervised. Occasionally a new employee will resent the direction of someone who has been with the company a long time. The resentment may be justified if the supervising employee is impatient or inconsiderate or condescending. To avoid any problems of that nature, it is especially important to be thoughtful and helpful in instructing others and never to show any sign of impatience, irritability, or snobbish superiority.

Older employees in particular require special supervisory skill. The danger is even greater that resentment will flare when a younger person has to direct an older employee. If the older employee shows any signs that she is ashamed to ask a younger person questions or advice, be prepared to anticipate doubts and volunteer information without being asked. Try to make your instruction seem more like a discussion or conversation and encourage the older employee to participate. Ask questions of *her* now and then to bolster her ego. Just as you would with any employee, create an incentive for good work by praising the older person when a job has been well done.

### 3.9. What to Do About Personal Problems

As a supervisor, you may be asked by other employees for advice about their personal problems. Although you should not assume the role of company counselor, it is important to listen and be sympathetic and to help others evaluate their problems. However, do not give direct advice, instruct them, or make decisions for them in emotional matters concerning their private lives. Remember, too, that information given to you about personal matters should be treated confidentially.

Some of the common problems employees will bring to you are marital difficulties, financial troubles, drinking or drug problems, romantic involvements, and general problems of stress in coping with life at home or at the office. The most helpful suggestion you can make to a seriously disturbed employee is for him or her to seek professional assistance. Thus, you should check the Yellow Pages of the telephone directory and become familiar with nearby professional persons and agencies, such as physicians, ministers, welfare organizations, legal-aid societies, and marriage counselors as well.

### 3.10. How to Criticize Constructively

Unless your assistants never make mistakes, you will have to criticize their work when they produce errors or poor quality work. There is no need to hurt anyone's feelings if you exercise care in your approach.

First, always discuss mistakes in private. Second, introduce your criticism with praise if possible, for example: "Jean, this letter is positioned beautifully and would be perfect, except for two misspelled words. It's a shame—because it looks so nice—but I'm afraid it can't go out like this." Third, in addition to *what* you say, consider the *way* you say it—your tone of voice. The object of constructive criticism is to help a person improve his or her performance, not to ridicule or destroy someone's confidence. If your tone of voice is not thoughtful and friendly, the employee may feel you are treating her like a child or just giving her "a bad time."

### 3.11. When the Manager Has a Problem

It is unrealistic to assume the manager is immune from personal problems. Therefore, you should be prepared to cope with situations that may directly affect your own position.

If the manager wants to confide in you about a personal matter (see, for example, section 3.9), be sympathetic and listen just as you would with another employee or assistant. But do not assume the role of professional counselor; rather, refer him or her to an appropriate agency or qualified professional person. You should keep the problem confidential unless of course it threatens the welfare of the company. If you are positive such danger exists, you have no choice but to consult the manager's immediate superior.

If the problem does not threaten the company, but does disturb you (such as heavy drinking or an overly romantic interest in you), there are two things you can do: You can try to ignore it, or you can discourage it in the case of romantic advances. Simply tell the manager you are firmly opposed to getting involved with company personnel, particularly someone in your own office. If that solution is unsatisfactory, you probably should ask for a transfer to another office.

# 4

# MASTERING OFFICE EFFICIENCY

## LEARNING AND APPLYING TIME-SAVING TECHNIQUES

Almost every day the secretary faces an endless succession of both routine and nonroutine tasks. The only way to control such a work load—and not let it control you—is to streamline basic office procedures. Plan your workday and organize your work load; learn the simple shortcuts in typing and filing; use prepared forms to save time; make your office layout as efficient and convenient as possible; and get rid of any step in your office procedure—or even the whole procedure—if it is no longer necessary.

### 4.1. Planning Your Work Load

Planning your work load simply means organizing the work and scheduling it. Before you can do either, it may be necessary to make a list of each task for a day or even an entire week. Number each job in order of importance, or according to which must be completed first. Then estimate the time for each and write that next to each item. Now all you have to do is schedule each item (e.g., open and sort mail: 9:30-10:00 a.m., daily). Be sure to allow time for phone calls and other interruptions and be prepared to revise the schedule if the manager comes up with a rush job.

One reason for inefficiency in some offices is the inability to distribute the work load over what are normally slack and peak work periods. Most fluctuations in the volume of work are predictable because they are part of a routine or the result of some outside influence under your control, for example, an unusual amount of orders that have come in as a result of an advertising campaign.

Keep track of the work done in your department over a specific period and determine the pattern of variation in the work. Then find out why your work load is heaviest on Monday, or during January, or in the Autumn, and decide what you can do about it. If, for example, your problem is sending out bills or other material at the start of a month, perhaps a system can be devised of staggering the mailing of bills throughout the month. You can also schedule for the slack periods all possible routine work, such as cleaning out files, bringing catalogs up to date, and retyping card files. You can prepare for your peak period by doing all the routine work in advance.

You may want to plan your work load to accommodate periodic assignments as well as regular duties. Suppose, for example, that each year the manager is responsible for arranging the company's annual convention. Why not start working on next year's conference while you are helping the manager plan the current one? Keep a file of all pertinent information, such as the people you contact, comparative prices of different items (such as food and flowers), the schedule of events, and travel arrangements. Next year, thanks to your file, convention preparations will be a breeze.

Job rotation is one way of getting the most out of office personnel. This means having several people who are capable of handling more than one job. A major advantage of job rotation is that if a worker is sick or on vacation, someone else is ready to step in and carry out his or her routine. There is also room for flexibility when assigning work; there would be no need to give an assignment to someone already overloaded with work, because no one else knows how to do it.

There are also disadvantages to job rotation. For example, it is time-consuming to train several people to do one job. Also, a person who is constantly changing jobs is in danger of not becoming proficient in any of them. The possibility of error is also increased when several people do the same work, and it is difficult to fix responsibility when errors do crop up.

### 4.2. Typing and Dictation Shortcuts

One of the best places to apply time-saving techniques is at the typewriter. Not only can you save a surprising amount of time by using shortcuts, you can make your typing chores much more enjoyable. Here are some examples of ways to cut your typing time:

*Centering material on a page.* Type a numerical scale, single-spaced, along the right margin of a sheet of typing paper. Insert it back of each page you type, letting the scale protrude to the right. Simply stop at the same number on the scale each time you type a new page.

*Typing addresses on form letters.* When you prepare the stencil or master, make a pin-point indention where the address should begin. This slight impression will appear on all the duplicated copies.

*Typing superior and inferior letters.* Use the ratchet detent lever, not the variable line spacer, to release the roller in typing footnotes or formulas above or below a line. Then engage the lever and you can return the platen to the same line on which you were typing.

*Typing envelopes.* Drop the envelope between the letter and the platen before you remove the letter. By inserting it to the left of the paper guide, you may be able to use your left margin stop, already set.

*Inserting rush jobs with other work.* Release the roller with the ratchet detent lever; backfeed the correspondence already in the machine until you see a top margin of two inches. Then insert the rush work behind the correspondence so it will come out on top.

Shortcuts in handling dictation can also avoid needless waste. Although it is always important to streamline routine steps, a few special time-savers can boost your efficiency even more. For example:

*Flipping pages.* Put a rubber finger on your left thumb and place it on the middle of the page with the other fingers under your notebook. After you have passed the center of the page, move your thumb upward until the paper arches at the top. Slip your index finger under the page and grip the sheet between your thumb and index finger. In addition to moving the paper, rather than your hand clutching the pencil as you write, you can now flip the page more rapidly when you reach the last line.

*Locating telegrams.* Fold the pages in your notebook that have telegram notes diagonally until they extend outside the book. Or take your notes directly on a telegram that needs a reply.

*Dating letters.* Place all dates at the *bottom* of each page, so each can be seen easily when searching for a letter.

Chapter 5 gives further tips on time-saving typing and dictation techniques.

### 4.3. Filing and Finding Time Savers

An amazing amount of time can be lost searching for lost files and misfiles. Poor filing procedures can actually double the time spent in filing and finding. But even when the system is sound, there are always special tricks that can be used to save further time. For instance:

*Loose-leaf back filing.* If you want the most current information to be readily accessible, always file backward, with the latest material at the front. This also means less wear and tear on other sheets since there will be less need to page through all of them.

*Finding oversized papers.* Fold the papers so the written material is on the outside and easily read without having to remove the paper and open it.

*Keeping current material.* Unfiled material can be located just as easily as filed material if you sort it daily into categories and place it in temporary folders in a special cabinet right next to your desk.

*Follow-up files.* Set up folders for each day of every month and one for each month, plus one for future years. Place the correspondence or item requiring follow-up on a certain date in the folder set up for that date. Although you will consult the file daily, there will be no need to waste time each day searching for items needing follow-up—simply look in the current day's folder.

Chapter 6 discusses more rapid filing and finding practices for the busy secretary.

### 4.4. Working with Forms

Reports typed in the same manner each week can probably be more economically and quickly presented on a form. If you work in a large office, there may be a department that prepares these forms. When you have a new form in mind or think an old form should be revised, let this department study the situation. Your streamlining of ideas can be of invaluable assistance, as you are closer to your particular problems than they are.

In a small office, you may be asked to design the form. Here are some basic points you should keep in mind:

1. *The form must be clearly worded.* The form by title and arrangement must clearly indicate its purpose. The reader should understand at a glance exactly what is being called for. If you are revising an old form, clearly distinguish the new one from the previous one.

2. *The form must have an efficient size and layout.* The dimensions of the form must be right for filing. Space must be provided for the date and signature. If the form is to be routed from one person to another, there must be space for "to" and "from." Perhaps routing instructions should be printed on the form. The most important items on the form should be placed near the top. There must be adequate space for the reader to write his answers.

If you need ideas, consult printers, typesetters, and other companies that manufacture forms. They may have samples to show you from which you can borrow ideas. Ask them about cost-saving and time-saving ideas, such as the pros and cons of carbonless sets and which colors to avoid if the forms must be photocopied later.

Set up a file of the master copies of all forms you use. These should be indexed by number. Any numerical sequence can be used, the easiest starting at one and working on up. A master sheet is then compiled with the name and corresponding number of each form. No one should be allowed to take a master copy from the file; they are for reference only. New forms are ordered by number from the master sheet.

The forms you use should be checked periodically. Perhaps it is possible to consolidate two or three into one multipurpose form. But once it takes you more than 15 minutes to fill out a form, it is time for an overhaul.

## 4.5. Streamlining the Office

When it comes to streamlining your office, you will need the approval of the manager. When suggesting changes in office layout, stress the point that saved steps mean saved money for the firm. With this approach, you are likely to get approval. Not only does an inefficient furniture arrangement increase the time spent on completing routines, it can also be a cause of accidents.

In a large company, a particular department or person will probably be responsible for such changes. Be certain to explain carefully to those responsible your reasoning in requesting a different arrangement. A thorough understanding of your work and your movements around the office will be necessary to prepare an improved layout.

Before you consider suggesting changes in the layout of your office, visualize how the present layout affects the flow of work. First, make a rough sketch of your office showing windows, doors, columns, and other immovable features. Then draw in rectangles to represent the desk, files, and other furniture. Next trace one of your regular office routines and place the number of each step on the rectangle representing the piece of furniture where that step is carried out. Then connect the numbers consecutively, drawing a line from 1 to 2, from 2 to 3, and so on. Unless the work moves smoothly from one place to another with little backtracking or wasted motion, your office layout can probably be improved.

Naturally, you want your work area to be as attractive as you can possibly make it. But don't sacrifice efficiency for the sake of appearance. Here are some ideas to help you get the best use from your desk space —ideas about what should be on and inside your desk.

1. Keep your desk top as clear as possible. A cluttered desk is *not* a sign of how busy you are; it shows a lack of organization.

2. Be sure that important items such as a dictionary are within easy reach.

3. At the end of each day, put everything away in its proper place. The few minutes you spend doing it will make things easier the next day.

4. Keep a package of chemically treated paper towels in your desk. It will save you trips to the washroom because of such hazards as carbon smudges and dirty hands from changing typewriter ribbons.

5. Keep a memo pad on your desk. Don't put too much trust in your memory; instead, use the pad to jot down assignments, such as phone calls to be made, errands to run, and file folders to be found.

---

## SELECTING THE RIGHT OFFICE MACHINES AND SYSTEMS

Each year there are more and more time-saving machines designed and manufactured to lighten your work load. Some are simply improved versions of old standbys (e.g., the typewriter), and others are more recent additions to the modern office (e.g., miniature electronic calculators). Salesmen, manufacturer showrooms, and local office and stationery supply stores are all good sources for up-to-date literature, advice, and display models available for inspection. Before selecting a new piece of equipment, however, it is essential to weigh all the pertinent factors: economy, speed, quality of output, operator training, maintenance service, and, of course, applicability to your particular functions.

## 4.6. Typewriters

The electric typewriter has replaced the manual model in most offices where the amount of typing is substantial or when a high-quality product is important. The three basic types of electric typewriter are the standard (most common), the selectric (using a small type element instead of a carriage), and the proportional spacer (such as the IBM executive, which can be used to justify right margins). Many models can be leased or purchased, and the manufacturer or dealer often provides annual service contracts.

Typewriter manufacturers put special features in their machines to help typists with special problems. For example, there is a ten-key decimal tabulator, which will greatly cut down your typing time if you do any statistical work. When certain keys are depressed, the machine carriage automatically moves to the proper decimal position for typing in the tens, hundreds, or thousands column. Another model has a correcting key that lifts an error from the paper so the correction is barely noticeable. Machines with an automatic paper injector enable the typist to feed paper automatically into the typewriter so each page will have the same top margin. Some models have interchangeable carriages, platens, and type bars. The majority of these versatile features will help you perform your typing duties in much less time, more easily, and even more enjoyably.

Automatic typewriters can prepare identical copies of material that is prerecorded on a perforated tape or roll. Each letter appears hand typed, even though large quantities (e.g., 100 or 200) have been produced automatically at high speed. Some automatic typewriters have paragraph selectors, which permit the operator to change paragraphs in the basic letter.

## 4.7. Dictation-Transcription Machines

A dictating machine can be a great time-saver in the office. While the manager is dictating into the machine, you are free to complete other work and no longer have the double task of taking dictation and then going over your notes to type the finished product. The manager can even use a portable model on the road and mail the transcriptions to you.

Dictating machines and transcriber units both differ according to size, function, and recording medium. Some units, for example, can be used for both dictation and transcription. Recording media vary, too, with a choice of plastic discs and belts and magnetic tapes and belts. Accessories include microphones and foot-operated activating devices.

## 4.8. Assembly and Mailing Equipment

Assembling literature and preparing pieces for mailing can be a slow and tiresome process if done by hand. Collating, folding and inserting, addressing, and mailing machines can save you time and reduce fatigue.

*Collating machines.* Collating machines, or collators, gather papers together into sets. Some collators will count, align, and staple pages, in addition to arranging them. They come in all sizes, some high-speed, fully automated models.

If your office regularly prepares reports or other papers that must be assembled, consider how much time and salary expense can be saved by one of these machines. For example, it eliminates the job of going around and around a conference table, picking up pages one at a time, and assembling them into sets.

*Addressing, folding, and inserting machines.* If your office sends out a large amount of mail to the same people, an addressing machine will eliminate the need to type labels or envelopes.

Folding machines fold papers for mailing. As they are used for bulk mailings, such as direct-mail advertising, they usually do not come into the secretary's province.

Inserting machines carry the mailing operation further by gathering the folded letters or papers and inserting them into an envelope. Some machines will even collect enclosures, fold and insert them, seal the envelopes, and stamp and address them.

*Postage meters and sealing machines.* If you are in charge of getting a lot of correspondence out of the office, suggest that the manager rent a postage meter. With a postage meter that automatically seals envelopes you can get out the evening mail in about a quarter of the time it ordinarily takes. The postage meter is taken to the post office periodically and set for the amount of postage you purchase.

## 4.9. Copying and Duplicating Equipment

A copying machine can save a secretary a great deal of typing time. Have you ever typed a letter and found to your dismay that you were one copy short? Copiers produce a photocopy directly from the original. They are commonly separated into wet (using chemical solutions) and dry (no solutions needed) machines. Like so many office machines, they vary in size and features, such as the number of copies produced per minute or the type of copy paper used. But all are intended primarily for limited reproduction, for example, a few copies at a time.

Duplicators are used when larger quantities, such as 500 or 1,000, are needed. These machines require a specially prepared stencil or master: the spirit master for the spirit duplicator and the stencil for the stencil duplicator (mimeograph). Offset duplicators can produce more copies than either spirit or stencil machines, beyond 5,000 copies from one master or offset plate. The quality of the offset material is also better than that of spirit or stencil products.

These machines are all time-savers, but the choice of method should depend on the type of copying or duplicating that is done, the number of copies needed at one time, and the cost of the machine.

## 4.10. Accounting and Calculating Machines

*Adding machines.* Adding machines are relatively inexpensive and should be used in any operation that calls for the addition of columns of figures. In standard models, the figures are printed on a paper tape. A full keyboard type is best for employees who use an adding machine only occasionally. The ten-key type is considered best for employees who use an adding machine frequently, because those employees will have the time and experience to develop high skill in operation. The ten-key machine is also considered best when numbers to be added are of five or more figures. Both are available in manual and electric models.

*Calculating machines.* Calculating machines are actually highly de-veloped adding machines that also subtract, multiply, and divide. The four basic types of calculators are printing, rotary, key-driven, and electronic. The printing calculator resembles a ten-key adding machine; results appear on a paper tape. Touching the keys activates the full-bank, key-driven type; results appear in dials. The full-bank, rotary type, which is speedy and versatile, has keys that remain depressed until the amount is registered; results also appear in dials. Electronic calculators, known for speed, quiet operation, and ability to perform complex operations, have either ten-key or full-bank keyboards; results appear in a small screen or on a paper tape. Some models can store programs for later use. The electronic calculator is available in a variety of models, including the small, pocket version and battery-operated units.

Any office that prepares numerous invoices, prepares its own payroll, computes percentages, or does any other mathematical work on a regular basis needs a calculating machine.

*Automatic checkwriters.* A checkwriter rapidly prepares and signs many checks, giving protection against alteration and safeguarding against forgery. Basically, all types of checkwriters operate in the same manner; they fill in figures, state the amount of the check in words, and add the signature of the executive in charge of salary distribution.

Some checkwriters perforate the amount as an added safeguard against alteration. Others punch holes that stand for the amount. Still another variety counts the number of signatures affixed, and correlates this with the number of checks processed, for bookkeeping purposes.

## 4.11. Information Storage and Retrieval Equipment

Massive amounts of file material sometimes require sophisticated storage and retrieval systems. Some systems, such as microfilming, reduce data for storage on film. Other systems retain data in file folders, but store them in special containers that can be moved in and out of a storage area automatically. Although both types of systems are gaining in popularity, they require particularly careful consideration of cost and other factors before purchase.

Microfilm not only conserves space, but can save time through its use of index signals, which make possible the rapid retrieval of information. Once located, the film can be magnified and read on a machine called a reader. Some models will produce a photocopy of the material.

Large, sophisticated information storage and retrieval equipment is not only a time-saver but a necessity if huge amounts of file material must be brought out and returned to storage frequently. The more complex machines can provide this rapid conveyance of material simply by the push of a button.

## 4.12. Miscellaneous Office Machines and Devices

If you spend a lot of time every day doing little things such as slitting open envelopes, sharpening pencils, and writing dates on incoming mail, you may be getting bogged down in miscellaneous office chores that eat into the time you need for your major duties—typing, filing, and so on. There are so many machines and devices available for these small, miscellaneous chores that there simply is no need to sacrifice time needed for more important work.

If you have to make a notation on every piece of correspondence, showing its time of arrival and date, it would be convenient to have a time stamp available in your office. It acts as a safeguard when date and time of arrival are important, and cuts down your work load. With one of these small, inexpensive machines you can stamp the date and time of arrival of a letter in about two seconds.

If you have a large mail volume, consider a high-speed, electric opener. Envelopes are automatically opened and stacked with this machine. Another model will open an envelope on three sides. If the mail volume is light, a hand-operated, mechanical opener may be sufficient.

The electric pencil sharpener is helpful if you are constantly taking care of pencils for meetings, in addition to those for the manager and others in the office. An electric machine will help you clear away this chore in a fraction of the time you would spend sharpening pencils manually.

Compile a list of all miscellaneous chores that you perform manually and estimate how much time you spend on each during a work day. Take your list to a local office supply store and find out what new devices and machines could save you time.

# 5

# *SUCCESSFUL TYPING AND DICTATION TECHNIQUES*

## Getting Organized and Planning Ahead

Most secretaries spend a substantial portion of their time at the typewriter. Familiarity with successful typing techniques can save time and effort each day. (See also 4.2, Typing and Dictation Shortcuts.) But good typing skills require more than a knowledge of *how* to type something. The quantity and quality of output are dependent upon the machine itself. Thus, becoming familiar with the equipment and learning how to care for it properly are the first order of business (see 4.6, Typewriters).

### 5.1. Getting Organized and Planning Ahead

Plan your typing steps before you do any actual writing. At the outset, make sure you have the right ribbon for your machine and for the work. For instance, nylon or silk will produce better carbon copies than cotton; carbon ribbons are preferred for important correspondence because they produce sharp, clean copies.

Also see to it that you have enough paper, and that it is properly arranged in your desk drawer so you can easily pick up a letterhead, carbon, and copy sheet in their proper sequence. Know in advance how many carbon copies are needed. Typing too many copies wastes money and work, and not typing enough means you will have to repeat the job.

Learn to estimate the length of the finished copy from the length of your shorthand notes. (Most transcribers get approximately 300 words for each two-column page of shorthand notes.) This will indicate whether a letter can fit on one page, if a short or long piece of paper is needed, and whether margins should be wide or narrow. When you are estimating length, be certain to allow for inserts.

Divide letters into five groups: under 50 words, 50-100, 100-150, 150-250, and over 250. Then make a table showing left and right margin settings and number of spaces down from the top of the sheet for each group of letters. A letter under 50 words looks better if the body is double-spaced with triple spacing between paragraphs. A full-page letter with minimum margins is preferable to a two-page letter. If you do use a second page, make the left and right margins the same as on the first page.

### 5.2. Typing Special Characters Not on the Keyboard

Certain characters not on the keyboard can be typed with some improvisation.

1. *Paragraph sign.* (¶) Type a capital "P"; backspace; type a "1."

2. *Division sign.* (÷) Strike the colon; backspace; strike the hyphen.

3. *Degree symbol.* (°) Turn the cylinder knob toward you very slightly; type the small letter "o" without a space between the figure and the symbol; then return the cylinder to the line-writing position.

4. *Exclamation point.* (!) Strike the period; backspace; strike the apostrophe.

5. *Section sign.* (§) Type the small letter "s"; turn the cylinder knob slightly forward, away from you; backspace; strike the lowercase "s" again.

6. *Cedilla sign.* (ç) Type a lower case "c"; turn the cylinder knob slightly forward; backspace; strike the comma. (A cedilla sign under a letter "c" shows that the letter is pronounced like an "s".)

7. *Caret.* (^) Type an underscore under the last letter of the word before the omission; type the diagonal, or slant, in the space between this word and the following one.

8. *Brackets.* ([]) Type the diagonal, or slant; backspace and type the underscore; roll the cylinder toward you one full click; type the underscore

to complete the top of the bracket. The second bracket is made by typing the underscore immediately after the last letter or character; you then type the diagonal, or slant; roll the cylinder toward you one full space; backspace once; type the underscore to complete the top of the bracket.

9. *Equal sign.* (=) Strike the hyphen; backspace; depress the shift key very slightly; strike the hyphen again. Do not depress the shift key too much or the space between the hyphens will be too great.

10. *Pound Sterling sign.* (£) Strike the capital letter "L"; backspace; strike the small letter "f". Or strike a hyphen through a capital "L".

11. *Roman numerals.* (I, V, X) Roman numerals are expressed by capital letters.

## 5.3. Rules for Spacing After Punctuation Marks

Observe the following rules for spacing *after* marks of punctuation:

| | |
|---|---|
| Colon | 2 spaces |
| Comma | 1 space |
| Dash (before and after) | no space |
| Exclamation points | 2 spaces |
| within a sentence | 1 space |
| Hyphen (before and after) | no space |
| Right parenthesis | 1 space |
| Period as final mark of punctuation | 2 spaces |
| which follows abbreviations and initials | 1 space |
| which represents a decimal point | no space |
| Period within an abbreviation | no space |
| Question mark | 2 spaces |
| within a sentence | 1 space |
| Closing quotation marks | 1 space |
| Semicolon | 1 space |
| X, meaning "by" (before and after) | 1 space |

## 5.4. Drawing Lines on Work in the Typewriter

To draw *horizontal lines,* lock the shift key and shift the ribbon to stencil position. Then insert your pencil, or pen, in the fork of the ribbon guide. Now move the carriage across the page for the ruled line by pressing down on the pencil or pen and using the carriage-release lever. On an electric typewriter you can use the automatic underscore key to make horizontal lines.

To draw *vertical lines,* release the platen as for variable spacing. Then roll the platen up while holding a pencil, or pen, point firmly at the desired spot—not, of course, through the ribbon.

### 5.5. Adding an Extra Line on a Page

If your work calls for typing on the very bottom of a page (last half inch or so), place a sheet of legal-size paper behind your 8½ by 11 original. Allow the longer sheet to protrude at the bottom, and clip the sheets together. The "tail" of the longer sheet will prevent the usual slipping that results from the carriage return.

### 5.6. How to Type on Forms and Ruled Lines

When you are ready to type on printed forms that have ruled lines, there are a few things you should do *before* you begin typing.

1. Place the form in your machine and check the vertical line spacing to determine if it corresponds to single or double spacing on your typewriter. If it does not match either, you will have to use the ratchet release lever and position each line by hand.
2. If you must type several copies, hold them up to the light and select the ones where the copy and rules are in close alignment.
3. Place the copies in your machine without the carbon sheets. After they are secure, slip in the carbons and roll the pack into position.
4. Use the variable line spacer to position the form so the tails of letters such as $y$ and $p$ will fall on the ruled lines.

### 5.7. Typing Numbers and Fractions

It is common business practice to spell out numbers ten and under. Some companies, however, are observing the modern trend to spell out numbers one hundred and under in nonscientific matter.

Fractions that are one word, such as two-fifths, should always have a hyphen between the numerator and denominator. But when either the numerator or denominator already contains a hyphen, do not add another hyphen between the two (e.g., two thirty-sevenths, not two-thirty-sevenths).

Numbers in columns should be aligned at the right. You can use the tabulator and then backspace to the first digit. For instance:

| | |
|---|---|
| 24 | XX |
| 135 | I |
| 2 | VIX |

### 5.8. How to Type Cards, Labels, and Envelopes

Some items, such as narrow labels, small cards, and envelopes, are odd sized or bulky and require special typing techniques.

*Cards*, for example, can best be chain-fed into the machine from the front of the platen. First type one card and feed it backwards until there is a top margin of three-quarters of an inch. Then, when you insert the next card, the bottom of it will be held in place by the first card. Continue this process with each new card.

*Narrow labels* present a special problem. The trick is to avoid having to hold them with one hand while typing with the other. First make an inch-deep horizontal pleat in a sheet of typing paper and feed the sheet into your typewriter as if you were going to type on it. The folded edge will form a shallow pocket. When you see this pocket at the front of the platen, insert the labels into it. Then feed everything back so you can type on the first label.

*Envelopes* require another technique. Fold a heavy sheet of paper through the center and insert the folded end into the typewriter. Roll it through until about an inch shows above the front scale. Next insert the envelope at the front of the roller *behind* the folded paper. Position the envelope so the flap is at the top turned away from you. Then backfeed the envelope to the proper position for typing.

Envelopes can also be chain-fed in the same way as small cards (described above). If the flaps are too thick or wide, feed from the back of the platen. Insert a second envelope, with the flap open, between the first one and the paper. When you rotate the platen knob, the first envelope can be removed and the second positioned for typing.

### 5.9. Making Carbon Copies

Adjust your carbons so they stick out slightly from the bottom of the writing paper. Use carbons with one corner cut off at the top or snip them off yourself with scissors. This makes it easier to separate the sheets.

If you want red lettering on your carbons, simply insert a small piece of red carbon behind the black carbon in the desired position, type the red copy, remove the red carbon, and proceed with the work. This process does away with the necessity of removing the report from the typewriter.

Suppose you want to write words on carbon copies *only*, such as notations of extra copies being sent out. Insert a small scrap of paper over the original letter and an additional scrap over each of the carbons on which you do not want the notation to appear.

Use the best carbon paper for the job—thin paper if you must make a large number of copies, heavy paper if you need only a few copies. Light-weight carbon paper will yield one to ten copies; medium weight, one to five; heavy weight, one to two; film (plastic), one to ten. When speed and convenience, not quality, are the primary considerations, there are two popular products available: treated carbonless paper in multiple sets and carbon sets that have a light-weight sheet of carbon paper already attached to a sheet of tissue.

## 5.10. Correcting Mistakes

When you erase, move the carriage to the right or left so the eraser bits do not fall into the typewriter's mechanism. To erase neatly, use two erasers—a hard one and a soft one. Start with the soft one to remove surface ink and then change to the hard eraser to remove the imbedded ink. Finally, use the soft eraser again to smooth off the surface. Rub with short, light strokes. You can use a sharp razor blade on a good grade of paper to remove punctuation marks and the tails of letters.

When you are erasing carbon copies it is best to use a metal guard or celluloid eraser shield. The guard or shield is thick enough to protect the under carbons and eliminates the danger of leaving scraps of paper behind carbons after you erase.

*New products.* Keep abreast of new methods of erasing, such as the following:

1. Correction papers and tapes and correction fluids are often used when appearance is less critical, such as on a rough draft. Both coat the error so you can type over it.
2. An electric typewriter is available with a built-in correcting key that "lifts" the error from the paper.
3. A glass-fiber eraser can be used to erase an original without the impression going through to the carbon.
4. An electric eraser will save some effort and can make it easier to control the eraser strokes on the paper.

*Erasures at the bottom of a page and on bound pages.* If an error is located near the bottom of a page, do not remove the paper. Simply feed the sheet back until the bottom edge comes out of the platen. Make the erasure and turn the page back into position for typing.

To make corrections on a page when it is stapled or bound *at the top* to other sheets of paper, do not remove the staples or binding. Make the erasure and then insert a blank sheet of paper in the typewriter, just as for typing. When the sheet protrudes about an inch above the platen, insert between it and the platen the unbound edge of the sheet to be corrected. Turn the platen back until the typewriter grips the sheet to be corrected. You can now adjust the bound sheet to the proper position for making the correction.

*Inserting an omitted letter.* If the carriage on your manual machine moves a half space when the space bar is depressed and held, you will be able to insert effectively an omitted letter in the following manner:

First erase the incorrect word. Then position the printing point directly over the last letter in the preceding word and space forward once. Press the space bar down and hold it; this will move the carriage one-half space. Now strike the first letter in the word to be corrected. Release the space bar after correcting the letter. Again hold the space bar down and strike the second letter. Release again after the stroke. Continue holding the space bar for each subsequent letter of the word, rele ing after each stroke until your correction has been made and the substituted longer word fits snugly into the short word space.

The same result will come about when you use a *backspacer,* if the backspacer pushes the carriage back a space and a half when it is depressed. When using the backspace method, though, the corrected word must be retyped backwards. If you use an electric model that has a half-space key, of course, you can insert a letter with little difficulty.

*Dropping an extra letter.* When an extra letter has been erroneously added, you can easily correct your mistake without having to retype. The steps to take are similar to the space-bar and backspace methods, except that you allow two full spaces instead of one for your starting point.

## 5.11. Typing Stencils and Masters

There are three general types of duplication used in a business office: spirit, stencil, and offset. Each has a special master or stencil that can be prepared on an ordinary office typewriter.

*Spirit master.* A master set consists of a master sheet attached to a carbon sheet. To type on a spirit master, leave the ribbon lever in the ribbon position. Use a typewriter with a medium-hard platen, if possible. A backing sheet will also be helpful. Type with a slow-to-moderate staccato stroke. Errors can be corrected by scraping off the carbon with a sharp blade and inserting a fresh piece of carbon behind the cleaned spot; by cutting the error out of the master and taping a clean piece of master in its place, along with a fresh piece of carbon behind it; by brushing correction fluid over the error and inserting a fresh piece of carbon behind it; or by covering the error with self-adhesive correction tape and again inserting a fresh piece of carbon behind it.

*Stencil.* Several types of stencils are available, some designed for different quantities of output, some intended primarily for typing or drawing, and so on. The use of cushion sheets produces sharper copy; pliofilm covers will keep the typewriter clean and reduce the tendency for letters such as "o" to punch out. Before typing, clean the typewriter keys and shift the ribbon lever to the stencil position. Use a steady, staccato touch at slightly less than your normal speed of typing. Errors can be corrected by applying a thin coat of correction fluid over the error and, after it is dry, by retyping. Stencils can also be cut and patched, just as a spirit master.

*Offset master.* Offset duplicating machines can use either plastic, metal, or paper masters. A paper master, called a *duplimat*, can be prepared on an ordinary office typewriter. Before typing, clean your type and insert one of these ribbons: carbon, offset carbon, or offset typewriter ribbon. An offset carbon ribbon will produce sharper letters; an offset fabric ribbon will produce more copies. Use the same touch you normally do, but reduce your typing speed slightly. To correct an offset master, use a special offset eraser and then type over the corrected area.

---

## POINTERS ON HANDLING DICTATION AND TRANSCRIPTION

Taking and transcribing dictation is a daily task for many secretaries. A number of personal qualities will aid in the process: having a good memory, being a good listener, knowing how to concentrate on the task at hand, learning more in advance about the company's business, and so on. Dictation material may consist of letters, reports, minutes, telegrams, memos, and a variety of other items. You may be expected to take and transcribe shorthand notes or transcribe by machine from dictation belts, discs, or tapes. Regardless of the method, the alert secretary will seek ways to perform the task carefully and efficiently. (See also 4.2, Typing and Dictation Shortcuts.)

### 5.12. Suggestions for Taking Dictation

Dictation should pose few problems to the efficient secretary. The following rules and cautions will help you take more accurate notes with less wasted motion:

1. *Be prepared.* The first thing each day, check your supply of dictation tools: pencils, pen, notebook, rubber bands, paper clips. Have a place on your desk where you always keep these items. For taking notes, you can use a No. 2 pencil, a fountain pen with a fine point, or a smooth-flowing ball-point pen. Use a colored pencil for writing instructions in your notebook.

2. *Date your notebook every day.* Put the date at the head of each day's entry in case you must refer to your original notes. For example, the manager might want to check on the accuracy of the carbon or you might want to refer to a name or address.

3. *Face the speaker, if possible.* Since it will be easier to hear when facing the manager, try to place your chair directly opposite his or hers. Rest your notebook in a good position for flipping over pages rapidly.

4. *Keep a rubber band around the used pages of your notebook.* You will be able to open your notebook to a clean page without any trouble or fumbling.

5. *Use only the left-hand column if the dictator often makes additions and changes.* If the manager often changes words and sentences, you will find it helpful to leave the right-hand column blank so you will have adequate space for corrections.

6. *Look over your notes if the dictator pauses or is interrupted.* It will help you to transcribe your notes properly if you can look for weaknesses and correct them when the dictation is fresh in your mind.

7. *Indicate who dictated the letter by putting the dictator's initials at the close.* This is particularly important when you take dictation from someone other than the manager. It avoids confusion when it is time to write a signature on the finished letter. Have a separate notebook for each dictator with different colored labels for quick identification.

8. *Wait until the end of the letter to ask for clarification.* Do not break the dictator's train of thought by interrupting. Let him or her finish a letter before you check on something that does not seem right.

9. *Correct grammatical errors when transcribing.* Do not correct the grammar while taking dictation. If the dictator questions your changes, comply with his or her wishes.

10. *Make a notation if extra copies are to be made.* Put this reminder at the beginning of your notes.

11. *Make a note of all special instructions.* These instructions may be put in your notebook or on an extra pad of paper.

12. *Do not throw away old notebooks.* Keep them for at least a year. You never know when you might have to refer to them again.

## 5.13. Transcribing Your Notes

A few simple rules will guide you to more efficient transcription of your shorthand notes:

1. *Organize your materials in advance.* Before you start typing, clear your desk. Be certain all materials you may need are close at hand, including files you may need for reference.

2. *Start transcribing as soon as possible.* The longer you wait, the harder it will be to clarify any rough spots in your notes. If you do not have a chance to transcribe your notes immediately, at least try to read through them; this will "set" them in your mind while they are fresh.

3. *Make sure your notes are accurate and thorough.* Reread your notes and do all your editing and correcting before you start to type. If there are gaps, or passages you are unsure of, check these with the dictator at once.

4. *See that all points are covered.* If the manager is answering incoming correspondence, see if he or she has answered all questions and has given all the information called for. This safety check can save you from typing unnecessary follow-up letters later.

5. *Estimate the length.* To be certain the copy will be centered properly on the paper, estimate the length in advance (see 5.1).

6. *Make sure of names, addresses, and dates.* Double-check the correct spelling of names and the accuracy of addresses from past correspondence or a telephone book. Also, take particular care when quoting prices and noting numbers and dates.

7. *Read the letter before submitting it for a signature.* Look for typographical mistakes and errors in grammar and spelling. Never hand in a sloppy letter. Draw a diagonal line through the notes of any completed letter.

## 5.14. Transcribing from a Dictating Machine

If you transcribe your letters and other material from a dictating machine, you have certain advantages. First, you are not constantly interrupted by being called into the manager's office to take shorthand notes. In addition, shorthand notes can become difficult to interpret with the passage of time but the recorded voice preserves the exact words. It is therefore not as urgent for you to stop everything and immediately transcribe dictation.

However, many of the same principles apply to machine transcription as transcription from notes. You should clear your desk and organize your materials in advance. Listen ahead to the dictation while you are inserting stationery into your typewriter so you can get the feel of the letter and also catch details to help you arrange the letter and plan editorial improvements and corrections. Listen for any instructions from the dictator. Also note the rate of speech of your dictator; a rapid speaker will dictate more words (and pages) in less time than a slower, more deliberate speaker.

When a letter is finished, proofread it carefully before submitting it for a signature. Finally, draw a diagonal line through the identification strip that accompanies a completed belt or tape.

# 6

# THE KEY TO RAPID FILING
# AND FINDING

## TYPES OF FILING SYSTEMS

Your office's important papers and correspondence must be conveniently located and so arranged that they can be produced quickly when needed. An efficient, consistent filing system is a must in any office.

The four basic filing systems are alphabetical, geographical, numerical, and decimal. The system, or combination of systems, that you use depends on the nature of your organization's business activity.

### 6.1. Alphabetical Files

Ninety percent of all filing is done alphabetically. Alphabetical breakdowns are usually by name or subject.

*The name file.* The name file is the simplest and most widely used method for classifying papers. You file the papers in alphabetical order according to individual or company name. Divide your file drawers into alphabetical divisions (A, B, C, etc.). Put a miscellaneous folder in each division for names with less than three papers. As soon as you have collected three or more papers for a particular company or person, take them out of the miscellaneous folder and assign a regular folder for that name. Place the new folder in alphabetical order within its proper division.

*The subject file.* Subject filing is used when the material to be filed lends itself to classification by subject and not by name. For example, a company that offers a large variety of items and services might use a subject file. All available material on a particular subject or item would then be readily on file.

Your files will be efficient only if subject headings are specific, significant, and technically correct. The choice of headings is all-important, therefore, and must be made by someone who is thoroughly familiar with the company and its business. As you become more familiar with your particular files, you will notice key phrases and words in correspondence that help you file and categorize correctly. If you cannot relate a paper to any existing classification, discuss it with the manager and you may both determine that a new subject heading is required.

*Arranging and indexing your subject file.* All subject folders are arranged alphabetically, with subheadings filed alphabetically within each main heading. To make it easier for you to locate material, prepare an alphabetical list or a card index of every main and subheading. Type the main headings in capital letters. Next to each subheading, type in parentheses the main heading under which that subheading is classified. The list or index should be kept up to date. Here is an example of how the list or index would be arranged:

Pan-American (see Transportation)
PERSONNEL
Plumber (see Repairs)
REPAIRS
Roofer (see Repairs)
Sick Pay (see Personnel)
TRANSPORTATION
United States Lines (see Transportation)
Vacations (see Personnel)

When material can logically be placed in more than one folder, insert a tinted cross-reference sheet in the folder you decide not to use.

*A combined name and subject file.* Even though you maintain a name file it is possible to come across material that can only be classified according to subject. On the other hand, if you have a subject file you will occasionally have correspondence that should be filed by name. Whenever there is a necessary inconsistency in your filing, make a cross-reference to avoid any possible confusion.

## INDEXING AND FILING ALPHABETICALLY

1. *Individual names.* When indexing, the surname comes first, then the first given name or initial, and then other names or initials.

Alston, Thomas A.
Brandt, Alvin
Brown, H. W.

2. *Company names.* When organization names are composed of names of individuals, follow the order that applies to individual names (see preceding rule); otherwise, each word comprising the name is considered in the order in which it appears.

Hogan, G. T., & Sons
Jackson, Allen & Spinelli Co.
Karry-On Trucking, Inc.

3. *Names with personal titles.* Titles, whether preceding or following names, are disregarded in alphabetizing. Place the title in parentheses at the end of the indexed name. An exception is made if the name of an individual contains a title and a given name, but no surname. You consider the title as the first word.

Adams, Veronica (Sr.)
Baxter, John (Dr.)
Madame Helene
Parrish, Joan (Miss)
Stanislav, Igor (Count)

4. *Lineal designations that follow names.* Retain the designations and alphabetize in the following order: 2nd (Second), III (Third), Jr., Sr.

Black, Gregory, 2nd
Black, Gregory, III
Black, Gregory, Jr.
Black, Gregory, Sr.

5. *Married women.* The name of a married woman should be indexed and filed according to her husband's surname, followed by her first name. Place the husband's given name and middle name or initial in parentheses

below the wife's name when it is convenient or important to have this information.

Moss, Susan Jackson
(Mrs. Kenneth A. Moss)

6. *Surnames with prefixes.* If a name begins with a prefix such as *D',
Da, De, Mac,* or *Mc,* alphabetize the name as if the prefix were part of an unbroken word.

D' Angelo, L.
Davis, W.
Da Vito, G.
De Marco, P.
Develin, R.
Mac Intosh, W.
Macready, G.
McCarthy, J.
Vargas, D.
Von Gronicka, R.

7. *Abbreviations.* Treat abbreviations as if they were spelled out.

Fort Wayne (not Ft. Wayne)
Mount Carmel Cemetery (not Mt. Carmel Cemetery)
Saint Luke's Infirmary (not St. Luke's Infirmary)

8. *Names that are hyphenated.* If the letters, words, or syllables of a name are joined by one or more hyphens, treat the name as one word. However, if the hyphen is used instead of a comma in a firm name, treat the individual parts of the name as separate words. A hyphen is sometimes used in place of a comma when the firm name is made up of individual names.

White-Pauling & Co. (hyphen used instead of comma)
White, Vincent, W.
White-Brite Soap Products (treat as one word)

9. *Names with numbers.* Alphabetize as if all numbers were spelled out. An exception is made, however, for numbered streets and branches of organizations; they should be filed by numerical sequence. Thus, Branch Number 7 precedes Branch Number 8, even though spelled out and alphabetized, Eight would precede Seven.

Note that in the examples below, Thirty-Eight and Thirty-Five are hyphenated and therefore treated as one word for purposes of alphabetizing. Since "thirty-eight" is indexed as "thirtyeight," it is natural that it should follow "thirty."

Thirty Fifty-Five Lexington Ave. Corp.
Thirty-Eight Cooper Square, Inc.
Thirty-Five Club, The

10. *Articles, prepositions, and conjunctions.* Disregard these parts of speech when alphabetizing. When "The" occurs before a name, place it after the name when you index.

Netherlands Bank, The
Society *of* Christians
Society *for the* Needy

11. *Similar names of unequal length.* Similar names can be unequal in length (because of the use of initials or the presence or absence of middle names, for example). In this case, so long as the key name is identical, file the shorter name first.

Craig, W.
Craig, William
Craig, William A.

12. *Letters as symbols of company names.* When a letter or letters are used as a word in a name, treat the letter or letters as if they were words by themselves. The ampersand symbol (&) is not considered a letter and should be disregarded in determining alphabetical order.

AAA Insurance Co.
ABC Stores
A B & D Tobacco Co.
AFTRA
Andrews Shoe Corp.

## 6.2. Geographical Files

When geographical filing is used, the papers are first grouped according to the name of the state, then by city, then by name of the correspondent. If the company does an international business, such as exporting, the largest heading in the file would be a country.

The geographical filing system requires the use of a cross-index. A 3- by 5-inch name card is made out for every correspondent. The geographical location and any other pertinent information relating to the individual or company is written on this index card. After you find out the location of a company from the name index, it is an easy step to locate the material you want in the geographical file itself. Keep in mind, however, that the maintenance of this cross-index involves an extra step and thus additional time.

A geographical file is used principally by sales organizations where a review of the activity in any given territory is of more importance than a review of individual accounts.

## 6.3. Numerical Files

Numerical filing, like geographical filing, is an indirect method that requires a cross-index. When preparing a numerical file, arrange your index in alphabetical order and assign each folder a number in numerical order. As new names are filed give them a number and record them in the index.

Once your system is set up you should have no trouble in making it work efficiently. Assume, for example, that the manager has received a letter from Hamilton Company. You do not know Hamilton's code number, so you consult the cross-index under *H*. If there is a Hamilton file, find the number it is filed under. Write this number on the upper right-hand corner of the letter for easy reference when you are ready to file it.

The advantages of the numerical filing system are the rapidity and accuracy of refiling and the opportunity for indefinite expansion. The principal disadvantage is the extra step involved in keeping a cross-index file.

## 6.4. Decimal System

A decimal system of filing provides a code number for each subject matter to be filed. Assigning code numbers is a time-consuming procedure, but once the file is coded properly, it is comparatively easy and quick to file or find your material.

With a decimal system, there are main divisions ranging from 000 to 900. Each division is subdivided decimally so great expansion of subjects is possible. A manufacturing company, for example, might have divisions for raw materials. Let us say wood is in the 500's; mahogany can be 512; African mahogany, 512.5.

The most widely used classification system of this type is the Dewey Decimal System, maintained by some public libraries and highly specialized businesses.

---

### SOUND FILING PRINCIPLES AND PRACTICES

Certain principles and guides, when followed, will help you maintain an orderly, efficient filing system. These principles are valid no matter what type of filing system your office uses.

The only way to have an efficient filing system is to file every day. If the volume of papers is great, you may have to file more than once a day. Ideally, a secretary should have a specific time set aside for filing; in practice, the busy secretary files whenever she has a spare moment.

## 6.5. How to Prepare Material for Filing

After you are certain that material has been released for filing, follow these steps:

1. Segregate papers according to the files in which they belong—personal correspondence, business correspondence, documents, and the like. Also, separate material that must be kept for a long or indefinite time, for example, a lease, from material that will be retained for only a short time. These infrequently used papers should be placed in your *inactive files; inactive files* do not have to be situated in as accessible a spot as the *active files.*

2. Check through all papers that are stapled to see whether they should be filed together.

3. Remove all paper clips; use staples to keep papers together.

4. Mend torn papers with cellophane tape.

5. Mark filing instructions on each paper. For a name file, underline the name in colored pencil; for a subject file, write the main heading and subheading in the upper right-hand corner. Place guide or file number, if used, in the upper right-hand corner.

6. Circle important words in colored pencil to facilitate location of a particular paper when it is wanted. For example, if a paper is to be filed by name, circle the name in which it is filed.

7. Make necessary cross-reference sheets as each letter or paper is handled.

## 6.6 Typing Index Tabs and Labels

Index tabs and guide and folder labels have limited space for typing; therefore, brief designations and abbreviations should be used, with little or no punctuation. Initial caps and lowercase letters are easier to read than all caps. Avoid underlining.

*Folder labels.* Position your copy in the visible area of the label, beginning with the first typing space below the score or fold. Start two typing spaces from the left edge and indent second and third lines of copy an extra space or two.

*Guide labels.* Type as high as possible on guide labels, centering one- and two-character designations. Begin other copy two spaces from the left edge, as you would with a folder label. Large type is recommended.

*File-drawer labels.* These labels must be read from a distance, which means very large type or hand printing is preferable. Center your copy on the label, with a double space above and below detailed descriptions.

### 6.7. Make Cross-References for Easier Filing and Finding

Whenever material might be looked for under more than one entry, make a cross-reference for your files. Write the cross-reference on a colored sheet.

Moss, Kenneth A. (Mrs.)
    *See* Moss, Susan Jackson (Mrs.)

ABC
    *See* American Broadcasting Company

Railway Express Agency
    *See* REA Express

Gentlemen's Quarterly Magazine
    *See* Esquire, Inc. (*publisher*)

Do not forget to make a three by five-inch cross-reference card for your cross-index.

Sometimes, if information must be secured frequently, it becomes time-consuming to have to check in two places because of cross-referencing. A good solution in that situation is to make a photocopy of the original to file in place of the cross-reference sheet. Write the cross-reference to the original in the upper right-hand corner of the photocopy.

### 6.8. Keep a Record of Material Removed from the Files

You must keep track of all papers removed from the files no matter who takes them out and how long he wants them. Whenever material is removed, a *substitution card* or *OUT guide* must be put in its place. Use a guide the same height as the file folders in a different color. Print the word OUT on the tab. The guide should provide space to designate who has taken the material, the date of removal, the anticipated date of return, and a brief description of the material. The person who fills out the guide should insert it in the place of the folder that was removed from the file. Although other employees may remove material, only you should replace it.

## 6.9. Eliminate Unnecessary Material

Infrequently used magazines and periodicals are too bulky to keep tucked away in your active files. Reading matter of this type should be handy when it is current. After everyone has had a chance to see it, and there is a chance that it might be referred to in the future, store it in your less-accessible, inactive files. Other objects such as tape reels are also too bulky for the regular files and should be stored elsewhere. Although items such as photographs may be retained in the active files, cardboard backings should be removed.

Unnecessary duplications are often the cause of overcrowded files. Perhaps you are making too many carbons of memos and routine letters. Multiple sets of galleys and page proofs are also unnecessary. Similarly, identical copies of brochures, reports, and so on do not belong in the active files. If you must retain a number of such items, place them in storage areas along with other printed material such as stationery and form letters.

You can save an enormous amount of office space by transferring your records onto microfilm. To protect especially valuable records, you can make two copies at the same time, one for reference and the other for storage in a fireproof vault. Microfilming equipment can be purchased or rented. (See 4.11, Information Storage and Retrieval Equipment.)

## 6.10. Know When to Dispose of Filed Material

Your company may have a definite procedure for the destruction of papers; if so, follow it. If no such policy exists, ask the manager about the period for retention. The policy for disposition is based on the availability of duplicates, the likelihood of future reference, and legal considerations, such as statutes of limitations. Some companies transfer material to microfilm before destroying originals (see sections 6.9 and 4.11).

Mark the disposition date on all papers with a colored pencil. Be sure that the date is in accord with company policy or has the express approval of the manager.

## 6.11. Physical Setup of Filing Systems

*File cabinets.* The size of your filing cabinet should be related to the size of the papers you want to file. Legal papers, for example, are larger than ordinary business letters and require wider drawer space. Architectural blueprints would require a drawer with still larger dimensions. Filing cabinets come not only in all sizes, but also in many colors.

To save unnecessary stooping and reaching, file most current material in two upper drawers of a four-drawer cabinet or the middle two or three drawers of a five-drawer cabinet. When it is necessary to file in the lower drawers, sit on a low stool. You will also find it easier to work from the side of the file drawer rather than from the front.

Your file cabinets must be properly illuminated. Have lights in the area immediately in front of the filing cabinet for maximum visual advantage when the drawers are open.

Open-shelf cabinets are sometimes preferred because the files (and their tabs) are easily visible and more accessible. In addition, open-shelf cabinets use up less floor space than drawer cabinets and are manufactured with doors so your files can have the same dust, dirt, and fire protection as drawer files.

Still other alternatives include rotary files, which rotate folders back and forth or around in a circular motion—designed to move the material to you and save you the effort and time of walking around to it. Visible files, which hold material in metal trays in clear plastic or other transparent pockets, make it easy to spot items at a glance. Some automated equipment will move large quantities of material in and out of storage areas (see 4.11, Information Storage and Retrieval Equipment).

*Folders and guides.* File folders are available in a variety of sizes, weights, and cuts (types of tabs). Some are designed for special purposes, such as hanging folders and pockets. Metal frames can be purchased to convert regular files into suspension files. Hanging *pockets*, which hold a number of individual folders, are particularly desirable as space-saving dividers.

Guides, also, are available in a variety of sizes and styles, with a variety of tabs. If preprinted captions are not used, inserts can be typed and positioned in the metal or plastic tab holder. (See 6.6, Typing Index Tabs and Labels.)

Color coding can be applied to almost any filing system to aid in the location of material. Labels of different colors are often used to segregate subjects visibly. Consult your local supplier for a description of the many products available and the features applicable to your office needs.

*Index-card files.* The most commonly used index card is 3 by 5 inches. Index guides are helpful in directing you to the desired index card, just as folder guides will help direct you to the desired folder. In a small alphabetical card file arranged by name, a guide for each letter of the alphabet is sufficient. If the file is larger, you might find it convenient to have a guide for each letter and, in addition, guides for commonly used names.

If your file is arranged according to geographical location, you can set up your index-card file with guides that indicate the territory or state as the first division, the town in the first subdivision, and the individual correspondent next in order.

If you are maintaining a subject file, group your index into main headings and then subdivide into specific classifications.

---

## PURCHASING AND STORING OFFICE SUPPLIES

It is the secretary's responsibility to order and store the supplies used in her office. In a large company, items may be obtained from a central supply room or through a purchasing department; in a small office, the secretary will likely order directly from a local supplier. When supplies must be ordered, received, and stored, a number of factors should be considered to control inventory, costs, daily accessibility, and general efficiency.

### 6.12. Ordering and Requisitioning

Generally, an *order* is a request for supplies submitted directly to a manufacturer or supplier; a *requisition* is a request submitted to a department within your company.

When you have to order or requisition supplies, try to foresee any special need. For example, under ordinary conditions you might safely maintain 1,000 sheets of letterhead stationery in your supply cabinet. If, however, your company is about to initiate a sales letter campaign, you would have to place a special order for additional letterheads.

Check your supply cabinet at regular intervals; once a week should be enough in most offices. Check thoroughly each time, but avoid ordering small quantities of items that are only slowly depleted. It is expensive to process small orders.

*Submitting requisitions.* You can save time and effort in making up requisitions by using a preprinted requisition sheet on which are listed the supplies you use regularly. All you need do is check the item needed and enter the amount. Unusual items can be written in. If your company does not furnish such a sheet, you can easily type one up and have it reproduced.

You probably are required to submit any *special order* to office management for approval. A special order would be any out-of-the-ordinary request for supplies—a request for an unusually large quantity of an item or a request for an item that is permanent by nature.

In most companies, requisitions are considered *standard* unless clearly marked *rush*. Hold your "rush" requisitions to a minimum; you are expected to anticipate the demand for most of the supplies in the office and place your order for them well in advance. If you stamp *every* requisition RUSH, the supply department may soon doubt the urgency of *any* item you ask for.

*Placing direct orders.* When you place an order for supplies, make sure you have ordered the quality and quantity you need at the best price being offered. If you have the authority to order supplies, you have the responsibility of using good judgment when doing so.

*Learn about new products.* Most companies are happy to provide free samples that enable prospective purchasers to try out a product at no expense. When it is time to choose between competing products, you may have to weigh lower cost against higher quality and perhaps sacrifice one for the other. Always keep a written record of exactly what you ordered.

### 6.13. Receiving and Distributing Supplies

*When you receive stock.* When your supplies arrive, there are certain procedures to follow. If the delivered goods have been ordered from a manufacturer or supplier, you may have to sign invoices, initial bills of lading, and also verify these forms by a quick inspection of the shipment. You may have to check the invoice against copies of the original order so any errors in filing the request may be detected.

If you receive supplies that have been requisitioned, verify the contents of the delivery by checking them against your requisition form. Even the smallest mistake by the person who fills a requisition should be brought to his attention; otherwise, the internal records of your company will be inaccurate.

*Distributing supplies.* Although many companies adopt a "help yourself" policy with regard to the use of supplies, other companies put supplies under lock and key, with a supervisor in charge of the key.

In a controlled-distribution system, only certain people are given access to storerooms and cabinets, and these people are responsible for close supervision of the supplies on hand. They are in charge of issuing supplies as they are needed, recording depletions, returning unused items to cabinets, checking the index (see 6.14), preventing surpluses, and ordering or requisitioning when necessary. In large companies, such supply supervision is a full-time occupation

Under an unsupervised system, employees are permitted to take as many supplies as they need, and the main deterrent to abuse is the consideration for the needs of co-workers.

### 6.14. Storing Supplies

The prerequisites of an effective storage arrangement are *orderliness* and *accessibility*. If you permit supply cabinets to become overstuffed or sloppily arranged, you will find yourself losing precious time sifting through a lot of material for the items you need. You will also waste supplies, since some items will be impossible to find and others will be useless because of dust, dampness, and manhandling.

Here are some tested ways to store supplies efficiently:

1. Place wooden dividers on shelves to separate various grades and types of paper.
2. Install plastic boxes, similar to refrigerator dishes, to hold small items, such as erasers, paper clips, binder rings, and staples.
3. Store manuals, bound reports and pamphlets vertically with the titles printed on the bindings for easy reference.
4. Label compartments in each cabinet.
5. Place new supplies on the shelf back of the older supplies. Each time supplies are added or removed, mark the current quantity on the front package.
6. Keep frequently used supplies on the easily reached shelves, with other items on the top or bottom shelves or toward the back.
7. To avoid running out of supplies and to be able to take advantage of quantity discounts in ordering, some form of inventory control is necessary. One method is to prepare an index or inventory-control sheet so you have a record of what is stored and also a reference that indicates what items have to be reordered. In the index, list the maximum quantity of each item on hand, the allowable minimum, the date of the last ordering or requisitioning of each item, plus a statement of the time that normally elapses between requests for individual supplies. You can use a company ledger book for the index, but it is preferable to maintain a book with detachable pages so the information can be typed rather than handwritten. This index should be kept near the supply cabinet and, depending on how rapidly supplies are depleted, updated weekly or monthly.

# 7

# *PROCESSING BUSINESS INFORMATION*

## Data-Processing Principles and Practices

Without the aid of machines and automated work processes, offices would be overloaded. The amount of information that must be handled in an office each day would be staggering without labor-saving and time-saving devices and equipment.

Data-processing systems are commonly classified as automated, electronic, or integrated. An *automated data-processing (ADP)* system uses primarily automated equipment; an *electronic data-processing (EDP)* system employs electronic computers; and an *integrated data-processing (IDP)* system converts data into a form (e.g., punched tape) that can be used by mechanical or automated equipment.

### 7.1. Basic Data-Processing Procedures

When data is processed in an office, it must be (1) classified and sorted, (2) computed and recorded, and (3) summarized and communicated. These steps are followed whether the information is handled manually or automatically.

1. *Classifying and sorting information.* Information can be *classified* in many ways. Incoming mail, for instance, might be classified as interoffice, personal, and so on. More specifically, data can be classified or coded in one of three ways: alphabetically, numerically, or alphanumerically. But sometimes the volume of information is so great that data must be further *sorted* within each classification.

2. *Computing and recording information.* Certain data, for example, receipts, must be *computed,* that is, added, subtracted, multiplied, or divided. After information has been computed, it must be *recorded* somewhere, such as in a ledger, for retention for further use.

3. *Summarizing and communicating information.* Before information can be used or transmitted, it must be *summarized* and put into a form for interpretation according to the amount of detail or emphasis desired. Although some data are obviously processed and immediately stored, the purpose of the preceding steps is also to make it available for someone's use; thus processed information may be *communicated* orally or in writing or it may be transmitted in some other form by machine.

## 7.2. Punched-Card and Punched-Tape Processing

Machines require a common language to process information and transmit it from one machine to another. Punched cards and tapes are frequently used for this purpose.

Punched cards are processed by a variety of machines, the most common being the keypunch, sorter, reproducer, and tabulator. A *keypunch* is similar to an ordinary typewriter and will punch both alphabetic and numeric data into a card. *Reproducers* repeat certain information (e.g., identification number) on successive cards. *Sorters* put the cards into a desired sequence. A *tabulator* "reads" the data on a card, makes any necessary computations, and punches the new information on the card.

Paper tape can be processed by *tape-controlled typewriters* that will (1) punch the tape, (2) read it, and (3) automatically type the information taken from the tape as a letter or in some other form. A *document writer* will read and punch paper tape or edge-punched cards. Like a document writer used exclusively for punched cards, a tape-controlled document writer can also make further computations and punch the results on the tape.

### 7.3. Electronic Data Processing

Electronic computers vary in size, complexity, and cost. But they all process data by means of electrical impulses that permit operations at extremely high speeds. A "program" must first be designed for the kind of processing desired. Computer programs may be tailored to suit almost any need, from analyzing a set of building specifications to processing the weekly payroll data.

Data and instructions are recorded in machine language, for example, on punched cards (*input*). A *central processing unit,* which actually consists of three units, provides (1) a *memory* where the data are translated and the electrical impulses are stored; (2) a *central unit* that interprets instructions and directs other units; and (3) an *arithmetic unit* that reads the data and makes computations and summaries. Finally, the results are read out in some form such as punched tape (*output*).

### 7.4. The Automated Office

To the secretary, automation is a labor-saving advance and the automated office is a place where he or she can perform more efficiently and more effectively. By now, machines have either eliminated or reduced the drudgery and time spent in many clerical tasks.

A wide assortment of machines and systems is used to speed and simplify the processing of information: electric typewriters, copiers, calculators, postal machines, duplicating equipment, electronic computers, information storage and retrieval systems, dictating equipment—to name just a few. (See also 4.6-4.12, Selecting the Right Office Machines and Systems.) Although these machines and systems have reduced the repetitive routine in secretarial work, they have also created the need for greater skills in other areas such as communications. The constant need for the secretary to process more and more information—and to do it faster —underscores the increasing importance of the secretarial role in the modern business office.

---

## EFFECTIVE RESEARCH PROCEDURES

Not all information flows automatically into a business office, ready for processing. When the desired facts are not readily available, the secretary must know how to conduct the necessary research. If you are asked to find some facts, you should have an idea of where these facts are compiled and how you can get your hands on them. If your fact finding leads you to a particular reference book with any regularity, have a copy of it ordered for your office. If you have to go to a library, have an idea of the scope of the books in its reference department. Business and professional people also seek information within the pages of books, magazines, and newspapers.

## 7.5. Using the Telephone for Rapid Fact Finding

Depending on the information you need, it may not be necessary to leave the office to find it. The telephone is one of the most effective tools available for quick and easy fact finding. Many businesses always keep a number of current directories in the office covering local and out-of-town areas where calls are frequently placed. (Directories can be ordered through the business office of your local telephone company.) If you do not have the desired directories in your office, however, you can visit your local telephone company or the local library, copy the numbers you need, and take them back to the office. Or you can simply call Information and request the numbers, assuming you have the correct names and addresses.

Often information is needed about products, services, costs, and so on. Although you may want a manufacturer or dealer to send literature for the manager, it can save time to call, explain what you want, and ask to have details sent immediately. Sometimes you can find out everything you need to know just by asking a few questions over the telephone. Local businesses are good sources of information and their personnel are usually happy to answer questions. The Yellow Pages of telephone directories are invaluable in conducting telephone research—for both local and out-of-town sources. (See also sections 1.8-1.13, Using the Telephone.)

## 7.6. What Associations and Schools Can Offer

Two of the best sources for information—schools and associations—are often overlooked. Yet in both places there are qualified professionals —authorities in various fields—able to supply reliable information and make sound recommendations. Most people will be eager to help in any way they can. Of course, there is a fine line between requesting information and expecting free consulting services, and one should never confuse the two.

Nearby schools and colleges will be listed in your telephone directory, although there is no reason to restrict yourself geographically. In fact, it might be wise to call a larger university so you can ask to be connected with a department or division in the area of your concern (for example, architecture, law, economics). Keep in mind also the specialties you will find in technical and vocational schools (for example, electricity, cosmetology, aviation). In addition to answering questions, the instructors and department personnel you contact will be able to suggest further sources of information, including published reports and other literature.

Trade associations, professional societies, and other nonprofit institutions can be found in the Yellow Pages. But you may prefer to consult a directory of associations (see section 7.12) to determine how many organizations are available—and where—related to your area of concern. Often these organizations publish magazines, reports, books, and so on in their field. If office personnel cannot answer your questions, they can always refer you to certain members of the association. Because the membership of these organizations is comprised of professionals in various fields, there is almost an endless list of authorities to contact.

### 7.7. How to Use an Outside Library

Even the best office library cannot have every book on every subject. The manager might, therefore, send you to an outside library. This should present no problem if you have an idea of the workings of libraries in general.

Every library has a card catalog in which its books are listed. Cards are usually indexed by author, book title, and subject. If you do not have a particular book or author in mind, simply look at the cards under the appropriate subject (e.g., real estate). Each card will contain an index number that will correspond to one of the numbers marked on the library shelves where the book is located. You can also check the vertical file index for pamphlets and literature other than books. (See also section 7.13, Guides to Periodicals and Newspapers.)

Find out where the reference section of the library is located. This section, often a separate room(s), contains all the directories, encyclopedias, and other reference works. If you are unable to locate the information you need here, in the card catalog, or in the vertical file, ask the reference librarian or one of the other librarians for assistance before you give up. If the information you need is not in a book that can be checked out, or if it is too detailed for note taking, ask if the library has copying or microfilming services.

### 7.8. Maintaining an Office Library

*What to have in your library.* You should include in your library reference material relating to the particular operations of your company with an emphasis on books concerning new methods in business, new machines, or laws affecting the business. You should also stock the shelves with handbooks, directories, statistical books, and trade magazines. Trade magazines, besides having pertinent articles, often review or carry advertisements for the latest books in your field—books you might want to order for your library.

*Setting up a card catalog.* If your library contains many books you will have to set up a card catalog. The card catalog is an index to every book in the library. It tells an employee whether you have a particular book and (if you do) where it is located on the shelves.

Every book should have three cards in the catalog—one filed by title, another by author, and the third by subject. In addition to title and author, include on each card the names of any co-authors, the publisher of the book, copyright date, and additional information such as the number of pages and perhaps a brief description of the contents. All cards are then filed alphabetically, regardless of whether they are author, title, or subject cards.

You may also find it useful to set up a separate index covering company files, books, and other records. These items will not be on the shelves of your library, and each card will have to specify the location, for example, file folder XYZ, Research Department.

*Arranging the library books.* Books must be arranged on the shelves in some kind of logical order. The particular arrangement you choose depends on your office, the number and kinds of books it has, and whether the people in the office are more likely to ask for the book by title, author, or subject. The three basic methods of book arrangement are:

1. Division by subject and then alphabetically either by title or author within each subject. (Arrangement of books by subject is most practical in an office that uses books on varied topics for reference purposes.)
2. Alphabetically by title without regard to subject.
3. Alphabetically by author without regard to subject.

*When an employee borrows a book.* The most efficient way to keep track of borrowed books is to have a supply of 3- by 5-inch cards with space on them for the title, author, publisher, name of borrower, date books are borrowed, and borrower's telephone extension. Each person who borrows a book must fill out one of these cards, which is then filed alphabetically by title in a box. When the book is returned, take its card from the box and destroy it. Keep available a small table for employees to put returned books after they have used them.

*Clip articles of interest.* Clip items carefully and mount them on 8-½- by 11-inch paper. Indicate on the paper the source, date, and page number of the item. When the item is too long to clip, or is in a magazine that you do not want to mutilate, just mark the article. Place the mounted clippings and the marked magazines in a folder and ask the manager to mark those items he or she wants you to file. Mark the file folders according to broad categories pertinent to your particular company or division and then file them alphabetically. Make sure an item is of no value before you throw it away, no matter how dated it is.

---

## SOURCES OF INFORMATION

This section describes some of the reference books that you are likely to encounter in your secretarial duties. If the information you seek is not in the works described in these pages, a librarian can usually suggest the reference book that will help you out.

### 7.9. Dictionaries

A dictionary gives you the spelling, pronunciation, and definition of a word, and, in some cases, synonyms and antonyms. You will also find the correct spelling of the plural forms of many nouns and the spelling of unusual variant forms of verbs.

Dictionaries tell you the accepted way of pronouncing words, with the words phonetically spelled out in parentheses. A phonetic key is at the front of the dictionary and (in some dictionaries) at the bottom of each page.

Different definitions are grouped under separate headings as to the part of speech. Specialized meanings (such as those related to law, architecture, chemistry) are labeled as such.

Paperback "pocket" dictionaries are available, but are not advisable for office use. Even if you have an unabridged dictionary in your office, you should have an abridged desk version on your desk for quick reference, as *Webster's New Collegiate Dictionary* (G. & C. Merriam Company).

### 7.10. Encyclopedias

Encyclopedias were conceived to set into print a complete coverage of knowledge. Today's encyclopedias, in addition to giving broad scholarly discussions of major subjects, present all sorts of practical data, for example, population figures and mileage charts.

The *Encyclopaedia Britannica* is perhaps the best-known work of its kind. It is generally acknowledged to be the most scholarly general encyclopedia, with the articles written by experts in their respective fields. The *Britannica* is multivolumed and necessarily has to take up a lot of office book space.

## 7.11. Almanacs

Either the *World Almanac and Book of Facts,* published by the Newspaper Enterprise Association (Doubleday), or the *Information Please Almanac Atlas and Yearbook,* published by Simon and Schuster, can be very useful as a one-volume source of general facts of all kinds. These books, updated and published annually in paperback, are crammed with statistics on government (state, national, and international), history, geography, science, religion, sports, famous people, and so on.

## 7.12. Directories

Most libraries have a great number of directories in their reference section, for example, directories of manufacturers, newspapers, lawyers, executives, banks, hotels, associations, and so on.

*Industry information.* One of the best-known directories giving names, addresses, and products of manufacturers is *Thomas' Register of American Manufacturers* (Thomas Publishing Company). Standard and Poor's Corporation publishes a three-volume set of data on corporations, executives, and directors. The *Encyclopedia of Associations* (Gale Research Co.) lists and describes national organizations such as technical societies and labor organizations.

*Biographical data.* Directories about people are plentiful. For example, there might be reference to an individual in an encyclopedia; you might find a complete synopsis of his or her life in an obituary column of *The New York Times* (getting the date the obituary appeared from the *New York Times Index*); you might try looking into *Webster's Biographical Dictionary;* if the person is alive you can probably find biographical information in the various *Who's Who's* (remembering that the information is gathered from questionnaires filled out by the persons themselves, and perhaps is not entirely objective).

*Government information.* The *Official Register of the U. S. Government* is a publication that appears annually, listing, by agency, all persons holding administrative or supervisory positions in the legislative, executive, and judicial branches of the federal government and the District of Columbia. The *Official Congressional Directory* lists the names and addresses of officials associated with the federal government, including members of the press. The *Congressional Record* is a daily record of the proceedings of Congress, including a complete history of all legislation.

## 7.13. Guides to Periodicals and Newspapers

*N.W. Ayer and Son's Directory of Newspapers and Periodicals* has a complete compilation of published newspapers and periodicals, including the frequency of publication, special features, circulation, size of page and column width, subscription price, policies and character, and names of editor and publisher.

*Reader's Guide to Periodical Literature*, published by H. W. Wilson Company, covers over 100 periodicals of general nature. Each article in these periodicals is referred to by author and subject; titles are given only for works of fiction.

The *Business Periodicals Index*, published monthly by H. W. Wilson Company, is an index, by subject matter, to various business periodicals. The fields covered include accounting, advertising, banking and finance, general business, insurance, labor and management, marketing and purchasing, public administration, taxation, specific businesses, and specific industries and trades.

*Applied Science & Technology Index*, published monthly by H. W. Wilson Company, is an index, by subject matter, to various scientific and technological periodicals. Some of the fields covered are aeronautics, automation, chemistry, construction, electricity and electrical communication, engineering, geology and metallurgy, industrial and mechanical arts, machinery, physics, and transportation.

The *New York Times Index*, published by The New York Times, is an index to the contents of that newspaper.

*Periodicals: Price List 36*, published by the U. S. Government Printing Office, provides information on all periodicals published by the U. S. Government.

## 7.14. Financial and Industry Information

*Value Line* (Arnold Bernard and Co.) is a loose-leaf service that gives detailed investment information on companies and industries.

Moody's Investors Service publishes a number of manuals. *Moody's Dividend Record* is a semiweekly, cumulative record of dividends and dates of payments and corporate meetings. *Moody's Bond Record* is a pocket guide to bond information. *Moody's Manual of Investments, American and Foreign* are annual volumes of information about the issuers of securities. *Moody's Industrial Manual*, an annual with weekly supplements, gives detailed information on firms listed on the major stock exchanges. *Moody's Handbook of Common Stocks* is a quarterly that provides detailed investment information on common stocks.

Standard and Poor's Corporation also has a number of guides and services. *Standard Corporation Records*, issued daily, provides information on major American and Canadian corporations and their securities. *Standard and Poor's Trade and Securities Service* offers a weekly outlook for securities markets, a monthly earnings and ratings guide, and a monthly statistical section. *Standard and Poor's Bond Guide*, issued monthly, gives information on each security.

*Industry Surveys* is a quarterly publication that provides detailed information on industries. Dun & Bradstreet has a special service that provides credit information about persons and firms in all lines of trade.

---

## REPORT PREPARATION

The processing of business information is varied and complex. Some data are best handled by machine, as described in Sections 7.1-7.4. But there are also many aspects of information processing that require other procedures. The preparation of reports is one of the more important of these areas. Here the manager may rely heavily on his or her secretary to collect much of the data (sections 7.5-7.14), organize it, and type the final report in acceptable form.

### 7.15. Organizing the Report

Information that has been collected for a report is usually meaningless in its original state. Before the manger can begin writing the report, the raw data must be sifted, classified, and arranged in some meaningful order.

One of the simpler groupings or divisions of information is according to the key parts of the report, for example, (1) background or introduction, (2) discussion of data, and (3) conclusions and recommendations. However, the manager may want you to prepare a more detailed outline of the information you have collected. Thus, you would divide the introductory material into subdivisions. For example, the introduction to a report in which the time span is significant might be subdivided into early history, middle history, and recent history. The material to be used for the body —the discussion of data—might be subdivided into numerous categories, for example, theoretical or analytical information, models or case histories, pro and con discussions, illustrations such as tables and graphs, and so on.

An outline can be simply a rough grouping of information that will help the manager find what he or she needs more easily; or it can be a well-planned blueprint, so logically arranged that the manager can use the outline as a precise guide in writing, and with topics so well-chosen that they are suitable for use as subheads in the report. The extent to which you organize the information will depend upon your manager's instructions.

### 7.16. Writing the Report

If you are preparing an informal report, it may be written in letter form. Thus, it would use most or all of the traditional parts of a letter: heading, date, address, salutation, body, complimentary close, and signature. The address and salutation might begin with the word "To," and the signature might consist of the company's name rather than that of an individual.

A formal report would have a cover page, table of contents, and the body, which would consist of the introduction, discussion, and conclusion. Within the text, there might be quotations (extracts), footnotes, bibliographies, and illustrations (see section 7.17 and sections 13.1-13.3).

The formal report takes a more impersonal tone and style of writing (we propose . . .). The informal report, on the other hand, is sometimes conversational in tone and more often employs the first person (I propose . . .). Objectivity is essential in either type of report. Opinions may be expressed but should be supported by facts.

The language in a report may be nontechnical or technical, depending on the reader's familiarity with the subject matter. Regardless of reader-comprehension levels, a well-written report never uses a long, complex word or phrase in place of a short, simple one. Similarly, titles and heads should be short and concise, and paragraphs and sentences should be short and easy to read. No one has time to linger over long, confusing sentences and paragraphs, trying to decide precisely what the writer means. Strong verbs will help make a point more forcefully (e.g., "decreased," instead of "showed a decrease"). Sentence beginnings should vary—avoid a succession of "it is" and "there are" openings. (See also chapter 12, Using Correct English.)

## 7.17. Typing the Report

Formal reports are usually double spaced, unless it is necessary to condense material, perhaps to keep duplicating costs as low as possible. Informal reports are usually single spaced. In either case, double-space between paragraphs. Margins should be at least one inch, with two or more inches at the top of chapter-opening pages. Indent paragraphs five to ten spaces. Preliminary pages are numbered with small Roman numerals (i, ii, etc.). The rest of the report should have Arabic numerals, beginning with 1. Center numbers a half-inch from the bottom of a page or position them in the upper right corner. Indent and single-space quoted or extracted material. For guidelines on typing tabular material, see 13.2, Setting up Tables.

*Title page.* The title page of a formal report (which is usually the front cover in a report that is bound) should state (1) the report title, (2) who is submitting it, and (3) the date. It might also indicate to whom the report is being sent. Items should be centered on the space left after any edge taken up by a binder. There should be at least four line spaces between each item, but only two spaces between second and third lines of a single item.

*Table of contents.* The table of contents can be single or double spaced, depending on its length. The chapter or topic numbers and titles are listed at the left and the page numbers at the right. Center the table on the page, again allowing for a binder edge. Periods may be used as *leaders* to guide the reader from a title to the appropriate page number. Be certain to align each row and space once between each period.

*Subheads.* Subheads should be consistent throughout the report. If there are several levels of importance, you can differentiate by using all caps, underscoring, and so on. (A numbering scheme is common, but may be omitted.) For example:

I.  FIRST TOPIC HEADING

A.  SUBDIVISION HEADING

1.  Minor Subdivision Heading

a.  Minor Heading

To further differentiate, you can center the upper level heads and position the lower level heads flush left. If the report is double spaced, leave four line spaces above heads and two or three below.

*Footnotes.* Footnotes are usually numbered from 1 on; if there are only a few, asterisks or other symbols may be used. In the text, they appear as *superior* figures, slightly raised from the line (for example[1]), or typed on the line between diagonals (for example /1/). The note itself is usually typed single spaced at the bottom of the page. For example:

*Donald W. Moffat, *Concise Desk Book of Business Finance* (Englewood Cliffs, N.J.: Prentice-Hall, Inc., 1975).

**Georges Carousso, "In Praise of Public Relations Writing," *Writer's Digest,* November 1976, p. 17.

*Bibliographies.* A bibliography, typed at the end of the report, is usually alphabetized. Thus, the form differs slightly from that of a footnote. For example:

Moffat, Donald W. *Concise Desk Book of Business Finance.* Englewood Cliffs, N.J.: Prentice-Hall, Inc., 1975.

Carousso, Georges. "In Praise of Public Relations Writing." *Writer's Digest,* November 1976, p. 17.

*Reference list.* Some reports use a numbered reference list placed at the end of the report, instead of footnotes typed at the foot of text pages. Such a list would be typed in a form similar to the footnote. For example:

1. Donald W. Moffat, *Concise Desk Book of Business Finance* (Englewood Cliffs, N.J.: Prentice-Hall, Inc., 1975).

2. Georges Carousso, "In Praise of Public Relations Writing," *Writer's Digest,* November 1976, p. 17.

# 8

# KEEPING COMPANY BOOKS AND PERSONAL RECORDS

## How to Maintain Personal Records

The secretary is frequently in charge of the manager's personal business records. These records may include some or all of the following:

1. Insurance policies (e.g., premiums, due dates)
2. Investments (e.g., transactions of stocks, bonds, mutual funds)
3. Income tax (e.g., income, medical expenses, contributions)
4. Nondeductible living expenses (e.g., recreation, clothes)
5. Travel and entertainment (e.g., expenses pertaining to dates, places of entertaining)
6. Bank account (e.g., checkbook, bank statement reconciliation)

Great care must be taken to see that these records are complete, accurate, and up-to-date at all times.

## 8.1. Keeping Insurance Records

The manager probably has many types of insurance policies. You will therefore find it easier and more efficient to keep a separate folder for each policy. File the folders by the month in which the premium is due or the policy expires. In this way you simply pull the appropriate folder at the beginning of each month and check the policies to see that the premiums are paid on time and that the policies are kept up-to-date. With most types of insurance, a new policy is sent periodically, and a bill accompanies it, so you are automatically reminded of premium due dates by the insurance company or the agent.

You could also keep a tickler card file, using 3- by 5-inch cards filed by month, as a reminder of expiration dates. Information on each card should include the policy number and insurer, name of the agent, names of insured, property covered, type of coverage, expiration date, and amount of premium. For life insurance, since a new policy is not issued periodically, you should also include premium due dates, to whom payable, and information concerning dividends.

An insurance portfolio will generally include policies covering automobiles, property, health, and life. You might suggust that the manager check each policy each year before you mail in the premium, so he or she can consider whether coverage is still adequate.

In case of cancellation, notify the insurance company that the manager no longer wants the coverage afforded by the present policy. If he or she does not plan on taking another policy, ask for a return on the unused portion of the premium.

Keep a record of all claims. If the manager has had trouble on more than one occasion with any one company, it may be time to find another insurance company.

## 8.2. Keeping Investment Records

Records of the manager's stock and bond investments will have to be kept for federal tax purposes. In addition to filing the papers on each transaction, you should keep a ledger with an account of every purchase and sale. Some secretaries prefer to keep a record of securities information on file cards or loose-leaf sheets in a binder. You may also keep a file of annual reports and other investment literature that can be cleaned out and kept up-to-date every six months or so.

As soon as an order is completed by the manager's broker, the broker will send a confirmation of the purchase or sale. Sometimes the purchase slip is printed in black and the sales slip in red. Both documents contain essentially the same information.

A confirmation slip carries the name of the company whose securities were bought or sold, the number of shares or bonds involved, the unit price, the broker's commission, and the total price of the transaction. Enter this information in your ledger and file the slip in the folder for the month in which the transaction was completed.

When the stock certificates arrive, take out the purchase slips and compare with the delivery slip. Make a note of the certificate numbers in your ledger. Then place the purchase slip and delivery slip back in the file until the broker's statement arrives at the end of the month.

The monthly broker's statement lists all transactions made within the month. Take out your folder of purchase and delivery slips and compare them, one by one, with the statement. After everything has been checked out, you may file the purchase and delivery slips with the broker's statement in a permanent file. Any further reference to the transaction can usually be satisfied with a glance at the ledger.

Some states have a tax on stock transfers. Usually the seller pays this tax, unless an odd lot (less than 100 shares) is involved, in which case the buyer pays it. If your state has such a tax, be careful to make a note of it on each transaction, and see that the tax gets paid when it is the manager's responsibility.

Records of bond transactions can be kept in generally the same manner as stock records. In the case of corporate bonds, you should note the dates on which the interest payments are due. With savings bonds, you can note the maturity dates.

## 8.3. Keeping Tax Records

You will have to keep a record of the income the manager has as well as a record of the deductions he or she may claim.

A simple *daily record* of taxable income and deductions is adequate for the person with a regular or consistent form of income. The daily record can be kept in a simple journal you can purchase in any stationery store. Each day record any entries that affect income tax, such as salary and dividends received or local taxes paid. In addition to the amount received or paid, enter the date and description.

A *classified record book* is necessary for the executive with various and irregular sources of income, and numerous items of various kinds of deductible expenditures. A classified record book can be made from an ordinary journal, or a columnar journal, just large enough to take care of one year's records. The book for each year is filed with the other tax records of that year. Divide the book or sheets into parts for:

1. Income
2. Contributions
3. Expenses of business trips
4. Investment expenses
5. Medical expenses
6. Miscellaneous deductions

The income portion of the classified record book should show the date received for each item of income, from whom and for what paid, and the amount. Use a columnar page with a column for each type of recurring income and a miscellaneous column for nonrecurring items. (See below for an example.) Include a total column; this can be used as a check against the accuracy of the addition of the other columns when you get to the bottom of the page. Adapt the form of the income record to the manager's needs. For example, he or she might need a column for rent income in addition to the more usual ones of salary, dividends and interest, and miscellaneous.

Income 19____

| Date | From whom rec'd and for what | Total | Salary & Commiss. | Dividends & Int. | Trust Income | Misc. |
|------|------------------------------|-------|-------------------|------------------|--------------|-------|

Divide the deductions section of the record book in much the same way; that is, use enough columns to take care of all recurring items for income-tax purposes and have a miscellaneous column for unusual items. Show the date paid, to whom and for what, and the amount.

## 8.4. Keeping Records of Nondeductible Living Expenses

The manager may want to know what it cost him or her over a definite period for any particular class of expenses, even though the expenses are not deductible for income-tax purposes. Keep a separate column in your journal for each class of expenses in which the manager is interested. For example, he or she may want a record of one or more of the following nondeductible expenses:

1. House expenses, if the manager owns his or her home. This includes expenditures for repairs, replacements, decoration, out-

side painting, grounds maintenance, and the like. (Taxes and mortgage interest are deductible expenses.)

2. Wages paid to servants. These records must be kept for Social Security tax purposes and for filing an information return required by the government.

3. Life insurance and other premiums.

4. Education of children.

5. Clothes.

6. Recreation, including expenses incurred at country clubs and other social clubs.

7. Money spent in support of a dependent.

8. Travel, other than in connection with business. (A record of business travel expenditures must be kept for income-tax purposes.)

9. Automobile expenses, other than in connection with business. (A record of business automobile expenses must be kept for income-tax purposes.)

10. Membership dues, other than those that are deductible.

11. Hobbies, such as expenditures on greenhouses, raising chickens, keeping stables, and the like.

12. Gifts.

13. Federal income tax.

## 8.5. Travel and Entertainment Records

The Internal Revenue Service requires records in detail to support deductions for travel and entertainment expenses. You will have to help the manager keep an accurate and detailed account of all his or her business expenses so he or she or the company can get a deduction.

The current federal requirements on "proof" are extremely strict. In effect, everyone who incurs travel and entertainment (T&E) expenses—from the company president to the newest salesman—will have to be a bookkeeper. The manager will have to keep a complete and accurate diary, listing expenses as they are incurred. On expenditures of $25 or more, the manager has to back up his or her diary entries with receipts or itemized bills. The same proof is generally required for all lodging expenses while on business travel, regardless of amount. Although the manager must prove transportation and lodging costs (e.g., with receipts), daily meals, cab fares, and gasoline and oil can simply be totaled. Records must also show dates of departure and return, number of days away overnight, destination of travel, and business reason for it.

In goodwill entertaining—following or preceding a substantial and bona fide business discussion—the manager will have to have a record of the following items:

Amount of entertainment expenses

Date of entertaining

Place and type of entertaining

Names and titles of persons being entertained

Business relationship of person being entertained

Business reason for the entertainment

Date of business discussion that preceded or followed the entertaining

Nature of business discussion

Duration of business discussion

Place of business discussion

The manager, however, can keep certain matters confidential. He or she will not be required to list the names or the subject matter in his or her diary. Neither does the manager have to turn this information over to whoever handles expense accounts in the company. *However, he or she must keep a complete record of it privately.* Then, if and when the Internal Revenue Service wants the information, he or she will have to turn it over to the agent. You should keep your desk appointment book complete, including names and reasons for all appointments, so the manager can use it as a cross-check on his or her diary entries if necessary.

When the manager makes a business trip, set up an itinerary of his or her travels and file it with the expense records. When you order plane or train and hotel or motel reservations, ask that the costs be stated on the confirmations. Put these figures on the itinerary sheet. The manager should, however, get receipts when he or she pays, no matter how small the amount.

### 8.6. The Manager's Checkbook

If you keep the manager's personal checkbook, be sure to fill out the check stubs accurately and with complete information. Any additional records you may keep are based on the information on these stubs.

1. Fill out the stub with the number and amount of the check, the date, the name of the payee, and the purpose for which the check is drawn, before you write the check itself.

2. Be sure the explanation on the stub is specific enough to enable you to post the payment to the proper records.

3. Usually, space is provided on each stub for entering the balance brought forward and also any deposit that is made. When a deposit is made, enter the amount on the stub and add it to the last balance brought forward to show the amount in the bank account at that point. Subtract the amount of the check drawn to find the balance that is carried forward to the next stub.

4. Many checkbooks bound with three checks to a page provide for the entering of a balance only after the third check is drawn. If you write many checks, you will find that this type of checkbook is time saving.

5. After all the checks in a checkbook have been used, paste a label on the outside cover giving the name of the bank, title of the account, and dates on which the first and last checks were drawn. Number the books. This procedure will help you find any particular stub later without trouble.

### 8.7. Bank Statement Reconciliation

Each month, as soon as the bank statement is received, reconcile the balance shown on the statement with the balance shown in your checkbook. The statement may provide a place to work this out, or you can use the back of a check stub or a separate sheet of paper. The usual method of reconciliation involves the following steps.

1. The bank statement shows all withdrawals against, and deposits to the credit of, an account. When a statement is sent to you, the canceled checks are arranged in the order in which the items appear on the statement. Compare the amount of each check with the amount entered on the statement for it. If there is discrepancy, notify the bank immediately.

2. Now arrange the canceled checks in numerical order. Beginning with the first check, compare the amount of each canceled check with that shown on its stub in the checkbook. If the amounts are in agreement, put a check mark by the amount on the check stub; if they are not in agreement, there is an error and you will have to adjust your balance accordingly. Once you have adjusted the stub entry, check it off. You should also compare the name of the payee on the check with the name on the stub.

3. As you compare checks and check stubs, make a list of the outstanding checks (the stubs that do not have check marks on them) at the place where you'll do the final reconciliation. Show just the number and the amount of each check.

4. Enter in the checkbook any service charges or other charges the bank has made against the account, and subtract them from the balance. This is your actual balance and it is the amount with which the balance shown by the bank's statement must agree.

5. Check the deposits shown on the bank statement against those marked on your stubs. Make a list of any late deposits not shown on the bank statement. If deposits that the bank has received are not entered on the statement, get in touch with the bank immediately.

6. The actual reconciliation can be done more than one way, but the following example shows a common method:

Reconciliation, May 31, 19___

| | | | |
|---|---|---|---|
| Bank statement balance | | | $1,385.45 |
| Add late deposit | | | 865.80 |
| Subtotal | | | $2,251.25 |
| Subtract checks outstanding: | | | |
| | #734 | 200.00 | |
| | #742 | 16.50 | |
| | | 216.50 | 216.50 |
| Balance | | | $2,034.75 |

This balance should agree with the balance in your checkbook after you subtracted service or other fees. If the balances do not agree, there is an error somewhere. Check carefully the addition and subtraction on each stub, and the balance carried forward from stub to stub. This should reveal any error that you may have made. Once you locate an error, do not forget to adjust the final stub to correct the balance.

---

## TIPS ON KEEPING OFFICE AND COMPANY RECORDS

Maintaining an efficient set of records is the only way to keep track of the dealings and operations of a business. The record-keeping responsibilities of secretaries vary. In some offices the secretary may be responsible for keeping the books for all operations of the business. Whatever your actual duties are, it is important that you be aware of the importance of keeping complete and accurate records, and that you know all of the fundamentals of accounting and bookkeeping procedure.

### 8.8. Taking Care of Petty Cash

As a general rule, all disbursements of money in the office should be by check. There are many small expenses, however, for which it is inconvenient to draw a check. No one would think, for example, of writing a check to pay cab fare, pay a restaurant bill, or tip a delivery man. An employee is entitled to be reimbursed for any such out-of-pocket expenses and his or her company is entitled to have records on file as to how the money was spent. To meet this problem of controlling petty cash expenses, secretaries are often asked to manage a petty-cash fund.

To meet petty-cash expenses, a fixed-balance fund is first set up. The manager might decide that a fund of $50 is appropriate for your office's need, and he or she would have a check for that amount issued to you, which you would then cash.

Once you have the money for the fund, keep it in a strongbox in your desk. After an expense is incurred, the spender of the money fills out a *petty-cash voucher*, which explains the expense and gives the amount. If you have a receipt or paid invoice for the expenditure, attach it to the voucher. The typical petty-cash voucher is a printed 5½- by 4-inch slip of paper with space indicated for the date, amount, reason for expense, and signature of executive who approves the reimbursement.

No one should use the fund as a source of small loans unless company policy definitely permits such use. If borrowing is allowed, be certain that anyone who withdraws funds completes a voucher.

### 8.9. Keeping Office Payroll Accounts

A secretary with bookkeeping responsibilities in the office will more than likely have duties connected with making out her company's payroll. Payroll work may include such duties as recording the time put in by each employee, computing gross pay and deductions from the gross pay, and writing the actual paychecks.

*Payroll records.* There are records that almost every employer keeps for each employee, some of them required by federal and state law.

1. An employer must keep for each employee an Employees Withholding Exemption Certificate (Form W-4). This is the employee's statement of income-tax exemptions. The number of listed exemptions determines the withholding tax for the employee.

2. The time an employee works is recorded—often mechanically on a time-clock card. At the end of the week you can compute the regular and overtime hours the employee spent. Companies vary in their treatment of fractional parts of an hour; most firms compute to the nearest quarter of an hour.

3. A payroll record must be kept containing a summary of the wage data for a pay period. The record is kept on a sheet with columns provided for recording names of the employees, the regular and overtime hours worked, the hourly rates, the total earnings for the period, the deductions taken, and the net wages to be paid the employee. The deductions are broken down into such items as Federal Withholding Tax, State Withholding Tax, Federal Insurance Contributions Act (F.I.C.A.) taxes, State Unemployment Insurance taxes, hospital and accident insurance, pension fund, and others that depend on the particular fringe benefits given by your company. Quarterly and annual payroll tax and Social Security reports are compiled from these records.

4. The Withholding Tax Statement (Form W-2) should be prepared in quadruplicate at the end of the year, with two copies given to the employee by January 31. The statement contains the employee's name, his earnings subject to federal income tax, the amount of income tax withheld by the employer, earnings subject to F.I.C.A. tax, and the amount of F.I.C.A. tax withheld. Send one copy of this statement to the Internal Revenue Service and keep the other copy for your files.

## 8.10. Keeping Company Books

If you are involved in keeping records for your company, you must understand how a bookkeeping system works.

Almost all companies, even the very small ones, organize their financial records in the form of accounts, so they can keep track of where money goes and where it comes from. For example, a separate account is usually kept for each kind of asset in a business, for each kind of liability, and for each element of owners' equity. Bookkeeping is essentially the process of getting information about financial transactions entered into the proper accounts.

An account is just a piece of ruled paper set up with a left side and a right side. Any amount entered on the *left* side of an account is called a *debit*; any amount entered on the *right* side is called a *credit*. Every financial transaction affects at least two accounts (hence, the name "double-entry bookkeeping"). One account will be affected on the left, or debit side, and the other on the right, or credit side. How this works will be clearer shortly.

A company's accounts are kept in a ledger, one of the two major kinds of bookkeeping books. The other kind is called a journal, which is also known as a book of original entry because you enter information there first. In the journal you collect and record the information that is scattered in the form of sales slips, invoices, checkbook stubs, and so on—the everyday paperwork that is common to every office. Depending on your business and on the system of books you keep, you might make journal entries as often as every day or as seldom as once a month.

Each entry in the journal shows both sides of the transaction; that is, it shows which account is debited and which is credited, and by how much. The basic rules for deciding whether you should debit or credit an account are these:

*Debits* increase:
Expense accounts (rent, salaries, etc.)
Asset accounts (cash, buildings, machinery, accounts receivable, etc.)

*Credits* increase:
Income accounts (sales, dividends received, etc.)
Liability accounts (accounts payable, accrued taxes, etc.)
Owners' equity accounts (common stock, retained earnings, etc.)

Naturally, if an account is increased by a debit, then it is decreased by a credit, and vice versa.

If you were recording in the journal the fact that you paid the rent for the office (information you would be getting from a check stub), you would make an entry something like this:

Rent [an expense, so a debit increases it]     200
Cash [an asset, so a credit decreases it]                200

Keep in mind that the dollar amount of debit entries must always equal the amount of credit entries. In other words, the books must balance. Sometimes a debit entry is balanced by two or more smaller credit entries (or vice versa) if two or more accounts are affected on the credit side. The basic rule, however, is always the same: the amount of debit entries must equal that of credit entries.

At the end of each month you transfer the information in the journal into the individual accounts in the ledger. This transfer is called *posting*. The entries in the ledger for the transaction above would look like this, in the two accounts affected:

| Rent | Cash |
|------|------|
| 200 | 200 |

Many bookkeeping systems use special journals in addition to a general journal, and some offices maintain only a file of papers, for example, invoices, instead of a journal. Some keep subsidiary ledgers in addition to a general ledger. It is also possible to automate the ledger-posting process, using a magnetic-tape record instead, which can be read by machine.

### 8.11. The Balance Sheet

A balance sheet is a financial statement showing at a specified time and in a systematic manner the balance in the accounts representing the assets, liabilities, and capital of a business organization.

The arrangement of the conventional balance sheet follows the elementary concept of the fundamental equation in accounting—*assets equal liabilities plus capital.* The assets are listed on the left (debit) side of a columnar page, the liabilities and capital are listed on the right (credit) side. The left and right side totals are equal, or in balance.

The assets and liabilities shown on a balance sheet are arranged in a definite order. The arrangement of assets is in the order of liquidity, usually with current assets listed first and fixed assets shown last. Liquidity in assets refers to the ease with which they may be converted into cash in the ordinary course of business. Current assets are cash and other assets that will be converted into cash during the normal operations of the business, as well as those assets that can be quickly converted into cash without interfering with the regular operations of the business. Fixed assets include all property of a permanent nature that is used in the operation of the business and that is not intended for sale. With respect to liabilities, those that mature first are generally listed first, while those that mature last are listed last.

On the assets side, the order might be:

> Current assets
> Investments
> Fixed assets
> Deferred charges and other assets

On the liabilities side, the order might be:

> Current liabilities
> Long-term liabilities
> Capital accounts

The balance-sheet amounts are based on the assumption that the company will continue in business indefinitely, and therefore the net worth shown in the statement is in no sense an indication of the amount that might be realized if the company were to be liquidated immediately.

### 8.12. The Profit and Loss (Income) Statement

A profit and loss (income) statement is a summary of the income and expenses of a business, in classified form, showing the net income or loss for a specified period.

Many progressive corporations make every effort to simplify the profit and loss statement that is included in annual reports to stockholders, employees, and the public. A typical short and uncomplicated form of income statement will have three captions: (1) what the company received, (2) what the company spent, and (3) what the company earned. This is sometimes referred to as a single-step statement because all of the deductions from income are taken in one step rather than in groups. The three-caption form has found ready acceptance because (a) it eliminates possible misunderstanding of profits by using the word "profit" or "income" only once in the statement, and then with the meaning of net income; (b) it suggests there is no ranking of costs or priority of expenses deduction; (c) it educates the reader to know that all costs must be recovered before there is a profit; (d) it is easily understood by the casual reader.

Here is an example of a single-step profit and loss statement:

ABC CORPORATION
Profit and Loss Statement
For the Year Ended December 31, 19____

| Income: | | |
|---|---|---|
| Net Sales | | $180,000 |
| Dividend Income | | 1,000 |
| Total Income | | 181,000 |
| Expenses: | | |
| Cost of Goods Sold | $130,000 | |
| Selling Expenses | 10,000 | |
| Administrative Expenses | 9,000 | |
| Interest Expense | 200 | |
| Federal Income Taxes | 11,000 | |
| Total Expenses | | 160,200 |
| Net Income | | $ 20,800 |

The profit and loss statement is the basic operating statement of the business and is the most eagerly awaited report. It should be issued to management, along with other operating reports, as early as practicable.

# 9

# *PREPARING FOR*
# *BUSINESS MEETINGS*

## Making Preliminary Arrangements

As it becomes increasingly difficult for executives to arrive at decisions without consulting others, it becomes necessary to arrange meetings for discussion. These business meetings may consist of small groups that meet around a conference table or large groups that meet in an auditorium or conference hall. Many of these meetings, whether with colleagues or with people outside the office, involve special preparations and duties that can be handled by the secretary.

### 9.1. Selecting a Room or Auditorium

Unless the meeting will be in the manager's own office, you will have to arrange for a meeting place. If your company has a conference room and the manager wants to use it, make sure it is available. Reserve it, if possible, with the appropriate person. If it is more convenient to hold the conference outside the office, you will have to reserve a hotel conference room, arrange for a luncheon room, or reserve other accommodations. You must make reservations as soon as the time and date are decided.

It may be necessary to make reservations in another city. The selection of a site must take into consideration the travel and business requirements of the participants. Not only should the city be one that will appeal to attendees, the hotel should be appropriate, with adequate meeting rooms, dining facilities, and sleeping accommodations. Many busy executives are more inclined to attend conferences if the hotel is in a convenient location, for example, near a major airport.

## 9.2. Making Travel Arrangements

You may be expected to assist in making travel arrangements for participants. Usually this is limited to sleeping accommodations and car or limousine service to and from the airport and train station. However, if the meeting is at your company or in your city, other secretaries may call you for general information. It is a good idea to have certain facts at your finger tips, such as the distance and travel time from the airport or train station to the meeting location and whether arrangements have been made in advance for limousines, taxis, or rental cars.

If the manager asks you to handle sleeping accommodations for attendees, you will need to know approximately how many overnight guests there will be, whether spouses will accompany participants, and the probable arrival and departure times. It is common procedure to relay this information to the hotel representative and ask that a block of rooms be set aside especially for persons attending the conference or meeting. Participants should be told that rooms are being held for them so they can indicate this when they check in.

The manager also will likely have to attend some meetings out of town. Chapter 10 describes the secretary's duties in making his or her travel arrangements.

## 9.3. Preparing the Meeting Room

How much preparation is necessary depends on where the conference is being held. When the meeting takes place at your company's building, preparing the room is often a matter of simple housekeeping.

1. Make sure there are enough chairs. Be certain they are positioned to avoid glaring and distracting light.
2. Place several ash trays at different points along the conference table.
3. Place a pad and sharpened pencils at each place.

4. Check the temperature and air out the room before the conference begins. (It is usually best to have it on the cool side; it will warm up.)

5. Set up a small table for refreshments, if they are to be served.

6. See to it that any confidential reports or papers the manager will use are out of sight.

7. Provide a place for coats and hats.

8. Have all necessary visual aids (blackboards, display boards, etc.) moved into the room and set up, ready for immediate use.

9. If projection equipment is needed, be certain the correct type has been reserved and delivered, and that it is functioning properly.

### 9.4. Helping the Manager Organize Meeting Material

Be sure the manager has all the papers he or she will need at the conference, arranged in a folder in the order in which the various items will be discussed. Prepare the folder as soon as you know the meeting has been called, and place in it all pertinent material that comes across your desk. If there is too much material for one small folder or if the manager may have trouble finding information rapidly, organize it in separate folders by agenda item or by committee. Use different colored tabs if necessary to further categorize material and make it easier for the manager to find something in a hurry. Be sure to retrieve this folder as soon as the meeting is over. File it with any reports or other relevant data submitted at the meeting. The folder will then be available when another meeting is called on the same subject.

Get whatever data is available on items that other participants have suggested for discussion. The manager will probably want this material several days before the meeting so he or she can study the background of problems.

You should also prepare the manager for any problems that might evolve from the listed topics, that is, know what supporting material will be necessary should the conference continue beyond the planned schedule. When the conference is held in your office building it will be enough to know where such additional material can be obtained, or, at most, to have it close at hand at your desk. When the conference is out of town, pack the additional material in the manager's briefcase, marking each folder or envelope clearly so he or she will know at a glance exactly what material is enclosed.

## 9.5. Preparing the Meeting Agenda

At a meeting, particularly a large one, matters to be brought up are usually known in advance. By preparing a list of topics as an outline for the meeting, you will avoid confusion and wasted time, and insure that everything important is covered. It will probably be your responsibility to draw up the agenda of meetings and type them or get them reproduced. Specifically, and especially if a meeting will be a formal one, you may have to:

1. Obtain from the manager a list of the topics he or she wants discussed and the order in which they are to be discussed. Do this well in advance of the conference.

2. Distribute copies of this list of topics, also well in advance, to each person who will attend the meeting, asking for additional items and suggestions for the order in which the topics should be discussed. (See also section 9.6.)

3. Type a rough draft of the proposed final schedule, incorporating all the suggestions you have received.

4. Show this rough draft to the manager. He or she will decide the final order of items and may decide to omit some of the suggested topics or to make other revisions.

5. Type and distribute the final list to all those who will attend, and do it well in advance of the meeting. (See also Section 9.6.) Participants must be given enough time to assemble papers, prepare figures, and perhaps write arguments to support different points of view.

## 9.6. Notifying Participants

Notice of an informal meeting can be given by telephone or by letter (or by interoffice memorandum for people in the company). This notice should include a copy of the preliminary agenda (see section 9.5).

Printed invitations are sent to special guests and speakers for a formal meeting planned well in advance. If the meeting is a stockholders' or directors' meeting, consult the bylaws to see if there is a prescribed method of notification; if there is, be very careful to follow it.

If the same people may be called to future meetings, organize a mailing list on 3- by 5-inch cards, making appropriate additions, deletions, and changes throughout the year, as you learn about them. If you have an up-to-date list available at all times, it will simplify the process of mailing notices for future meetings, particularly those unexpected, last-minute affairs.

---

## PROCEDURES AT THE MEETING

Once the meeting has started, the secretary's responsibilities vary, depending on the size of the meeting or conference. At a smaller meeting you may be required to read the previous minutes, handle telephone calls and messages, serve refreshments, and take the minutes (see section 9.11).

### 9.7. Reading Previous Minutes

If you are the recording secretary at a formal meeting—such as of the board of directors—you may be asked to read the minutes of the previous meeting. Read them clearly and unhurriedly. The reading of the minutes is not a meaningless formality; the decisions of the present meeting probably hinge on the decisions made at the previous one, and those listening to your reading want to know exactly what happened so they can take appropriate action. If instead of reading the minutes you are responsible for presenting them to someone else to read, double-check to be certain they are typed properly (see section 9.12) and that all pertinent documents are attached.

### 9.8. Handling Telephone Calls and Messages

Unless the manager has asked you to put through important calls to the conference room, handle the calls as if he or she were out of town. In other words, handle those calls that you can, pass on to some available executive those that you cannot, and take any messages on calls that the manager can return later in the day.

If it is necessary to give someone a message while a meeting is in progress, type the message and, without saying anything, hand it to the person for whom it is intended. Wait to see if he or she is going to leave the room, or just write a reply on the message slip for you to relay to the caller.

When you are asked to take minutes of the meeting, arrange to have all calls handled by someone else, or have them stopped at the switchboard.

## 9.9. Providing Refreshments

Refreshments during a meeting usually consist of coffee and rolls. Depending upon the layout of the meeting room, the table should be set up at one side of the room or in an adjacent room or lobby. Although 10:30 a. m. and 3:00 p. m. are usual times to take a coffee break, the participants will not likely halt important proceedings until a logical pause occurs.

Order the coffee, rolls, cups, napkins, and so on in advance from an appropriate source, such as the company cafeteria or local delicatessen. If everything on the table is prearranged, the participants can break whenever they like and serve themselves.

## 9.10. Parliamentary Procedure

If you know something about parliamentary procedure, you will find it easier to take the minutes at a meeting. Also, you will be able to answer questions if there is any doubt among participants about proper procedure.

*Parliamentary law* means the rules and precedents governing the proceedings of organizations. The basic principles in parliamentary procedure are:

1. The majority vote prevails.
2. Only one topic at a time may be considered.
3. Participants have equal rights and obligations.
4. The chairman must be impartial and see that everyone's right to speak and to understand motions is preserved.

A complete table of motions is presented in chapter 14 (see section 14.16).

## TAKING AND TYPING MINUTES

Organizations must keep a careful record of the proceedings of their meetings. The secretary's role in recording the minutes is of critical importance both to the participants and to the sponsoring organization(s). To handle the preparation of the minutes with ease, the secretary should know the proper procedures for taking minutes, typing and correcting them, and indexing the minute book. (See also, typing and dictation techniques in chapter 5.)


## 9.11. Taking Minutes

The notes you take at a meeting must be accurate, but not necessarily verbatim. If the meeting were to be very formal and complicated your company would more than likely want a record of every word and hire an expert stenotypist or use a tape recorder.

If you are not accustomed to taking minutes, prepare yourself before the meeting by consulting the minutes of previous meetings. This will give you an idea of the style and format to be followed, and some idea of what is expected of you. The following suggestions will be helpful to you, though, no matter what your previous experience is with taking minutes.

1. Try to remain constantly alert so each time a new topic is introduced you will be prepared to record the name of the person who introduced it, the main points covered, and general comments.

2. Make a seating chart before you begin, to help in identifying speakers during the meeting.

3. Keep a copy of the agenda and other pertinent material handy for reference. Various facts and figures to be recorded can be taken from these previously prepared documents.

4. Take verbatim notes on resolutions, amendments, decisions, and conclusions. If the resolution has been prepared before hand you need only refer to it by number in your notes; but if it is framed at the meeting you will have to take it down word for word. Use preprinted forms to aid in recording details of motions (e.g., proposed by, seconded by, etc.).

5. Take down verbatim the words of anyone who asks that his views be made part of the record.

6. Take down verbatim all important statements along with the name of the person who made the statement.

7. Record the name of each person who proposes any action, opinion, or plan.

8. Know something about parliamentary procedure to help you respond to questions about motions and amendments. (See sections 9.10 and 14.16.)

9. Use a large, easily seen symbol—such as an asterisk or capital letter—to mark in your notes any items on which action is to be taken immediately after the meeting, or on which the manager is responsible for future action. This marking will help you pick out these important sections if you must refer to them before the minutes are formally typed.

10. Arrange some signal with the chairman by which you can alert him or her to the fact that you do not have complete notes on some action. He or she will then stop the proceedings and clarify the matter for you or have the statement or motion repeated.

## 9.12. Typing the Minutes

Write a draft of the minutes immediately after the meeting while the events are still fresh in your mind. Submit the draft to the manager for his or her approval before typing it in final form into the minute book.

The following is a suggested list of rules relating to the form to be followed in typing the minutes into the minute book. Check, however, with the manager before changing to this method if it does not conform to the style your company is currently using.

1. Capitalize and center the heading (name of the group and the kind of meeting) in two lines. Type the date directly below in upper and lowercase letters. In the left margin, as a caption, specify if the meeting is regular, special, annual, or other.

2. Give the day, date, and hour, the place, the name of the presiding officer, and the type of meeting in the first paragraph.

3. Double-space the text.

4. Double-space between each paragraph, and triple-space between each item in the order of business.

5. Indent paragraphs 10 spaces.

6. Indent names of those present or absent 15 spaces.

7. Indent resolutions 15 spaces and single-space them.

8. Put captions in the margin in capitals or red type.

9. Make references to specific officers of the corporation either in capitals or lowercase, but be consistent. Always capitalize the words "Board of Directors" and the word "Corporation" when reference is made to the corporation whose minutes are being written.

10. Capitalize all letters in the words "Whereas" and "Resolved," and follow with a comma. The next word, usually the word "that," begins with a capital.

11. Write a sum of money mentioned in a resolution in words and then follow it with the numerical figures in parentheses.

12. Leave margins of an inch and a half.

13. Give the time of adjournment and the date for the next meeting (if any) in the last paragraph.

14. Make signature lines at the bottom for the secretary and the chairman.

15. Attach pertinent documents, for example, budgets and committee reports.

### 9.13. Correcting the Minutes

The minutes of a meeting are usually approved at the following meeting. Sometimes, however, they are approved only after certain corrections are made. To make a correction, draw a red pencil mark through each line of the incorrect material. Write the correct minutes over the red lines. In the margin of the corrected minutes make a reference to the minutes of the following meeting so the reader can see where the correction was ordered.

If there is too much to cross out and too much new material to insert, draw a line through the incorrect text and indicate in the margin that you are inserting the corrected material (to be signed by the secretary and the chairman) at the end of the original minutes.

Do not throw away the incorrectly written minutes. Keep them in the minute book for possible reference.

### 9.14. Indexing the Minute Book

The minute book contains the minutes of all meetings and is arranged chronologically. If the manager asks for the minutes of the meeting of June 21, for example, it is not difficult for you to turn to the June 21 minutes. You may be asked, however, to look for information on a particular *topic*, and that is when you need an index, and why you should maintain one.

Your index should be a file of 3- by 5-inch cards arranged alphabetically by topic. After you type the minutes of each meeting, read them carefully and see to it that each major topic discussed is entered in the index. Type the heading, *Hopkins Real Estate Contact,* for example, in the upper left-hand corner of the card. Now enter the date and location of the minutes pertaining to this topic on the card—*8/16/55—Book 5—p. 19.* Use the same card to indicate the date and location of the minutes every time that particular topic is discussed.

# 10

## PREPARING FOR BUSINESS TRIPS

### Pʟᴀɴɴɪɴɢ ᴛʜᴇ ᴛʀɪᴘ

If business trips are part of the manager's job, he or she probably relies on you to arrange many or all of the details of each trip. Thoughtful and careful planning will help make the trips a success and will save the manager time and worry. To avoid errors and confusion, you must be aware of the company's travel policies (e.g., regarding expenses, funds, credit cards, etc.) before making any arrangements.

### 10.1. Find Out the Manager's Plans

Before you can be of help to the manager you have to find out *why, where, how,* and *when* he or she is going. You cannot be of assistance unless you know:

1. Whether he is traveling alone
2. The cities to which he is going
3. The people he will see
4. The day and hour he would like to arrive at each city

5. The day and hour he would like to leave each city

6. How he wants to travel—plane, ship, train, automobile—and whether he travels first class

7. The hotels he prefers and the accommodations desired

## 10.2. How and When to Use a Travel Agency

If the manager travels a lot, it might be best to handle his or her trips through a travel agency. All you have to do is give an agency the basic facts—where, how, and when—and the agency makes all travel arrangements for you. It will map out an itinerary, obtain the necessary tickets, arrange hotel accommodations, have rented cars waiting where they are needed, even supply information about places in which the traveler will be spending time.

When you go through an agency, therefore, the arrangements are made by experts, and you are saved time and trouble.

If you have had no previous contact with an agency, you might want to obtain a list of qualified agents from The American Society of Travel Agents, Inc., 711 Fifth Avenue, New York, New York 10022.

## 10.3. Material and Supplies to Take Along

*Material the manager must take.* Start collecting and labeling the papers and material the manager will have to take along as soon as you can. Prepare a folder for each firm he or she will visit. Each folder should contain:

1. Carbons of past correspondence between the manager and the company he or she will visit

2. A list of the people he or she will visit

3. Any other pertinent material relating to the firm and the business at hand—contracts, a list of the board of directors, names of subsidiaries, and so on

*Supplies the manager must take.* What supplies the manager takes will depend on the business he or she will transact and the length of time he or she will be away. Preparing in advance a list of the supplies the manager might need will save a lot of last-minute fumbling. A typical list would include items such as:

1. Stationery (all sizes)

2. Envelopes—manila and plain

3. Memo paper
4. Carbon paper
5. Address book
6. Business cards
7. Cash
8. Credit cards
9. Checkbook
10. Expense-account forms
11. Mail schedules
12. Timetables
13. Stamps
14. Fountain pen and pencils
15. Paper clips and rubber bands

See section 8.5, Travel and Entertainment Records, for further details on expense-account records.

## 10.4. Preparing the Itinerary and Appointment Schedule

*Prepare a written itinerary.* After the travel and hotel arrangements have been made, type an itinerary that lists places the manager will be on any given day of the trip. The schedule should include dates and times of departure and arrival, flight number or train, the airport or railway station of arrival and departure (this is important; some cities have more than one), and the hotel at which the manager will be staying.

Type an itinerary for the manager, a copy for the office, and if he or she requests, a copy for the manager's family.

*Prepare an appointment schedule.* The manager should have an appointment schedule with him or her on the trip. Prepare a schedule and keep a copy for yourself so you will know where to contact the manager on any given day. Your schedule of appointments should include the following headings:

1. Name and address of firm to be visited
2. Person to see and his title in the company
3. Date and time of appointment
4. Phone number of party to be seen
5. Remarks and reminders—such as if it is a luncheon appointment

---

## DOMESTIC TRAVEL

Most business and professional persons travel frequently. The secretary is usually involved more with their domestic than with their foreign travel arrangements. Since trips vary in duration and distance, it is important to be familiar with all types of domestic travel and the procedures for making reservations.

### 10.5. Traveling by Air

Information on air travel can be secured from timetables, from the *Official Airline Guide* (Reuben H. Donnelley, 2000 Clearwater Drive, Oak Brook, Illinois 60521), from travel agents, and by telephone from the airlines themselves. After adequate information is available for the manager to indicate his or her preferences, the next step is to make the reservations.

Reservations can be made by telephone, and tickets can be paid for either by check or credit card. The reservations clerk will need to know (1) points of departure and destination, (2) preferred date and time of departure, (3) flight number, and (4) the class of travel (e.g., first, standard, coach, thrift) desired.

The airline reservations clerk will work out the most favorable schedule for the manager, taking into account all stopovers and other forms of travel. Be sure to ask the name of the reservations clerk in case you must make modifications in the schedule.

### 10.6. Traveling by Train

Information on train travel can be secured from timetables, from *The Official Guide of the Railways* (National Railway Publications Company, 424 West 33rd Street, New York, New York 10001), from travel agents, and by telephone from the railroads themselves. Procedures for making arrangements for train travel are similar to those for air travel.

Tickets can be purchased by check (in advance), and some railways honor credit cards. The Amtrak or other railroad agent will need full details on (1) points of departure and destination, (2) preferred date and time of departure, (3) train number or name, and (4) the accommodation (e.g., compartment, bedroom, roomette) desired.

Railways will *not* work out a complete schedule if portions of the trip involve air travel. They will, however, make arrangements for the passenger to have his car put on the train and delivered at his destination. In case of modification in plans, it is a good idea to take the name of the reservations clerk.

### 10.7. Traveling by Automobile

Information on trips by auto is available from the American Automobile Association—AAA (8111 Gatehouse Road, Falls Church, Virginia 22042). Members of AAA are entitled to detailed route maps and information, and assistance in securing motel and hotel accommodations. Information on car rental facilities is available from the major car rental agencies.

A car can be reserved and waiting at the manager's destination or at any stopover point. Reservations can be made by telephone with a local representative and paid for by credit card at time of pickup. The car may be returned or left in another specified location with a representative of the car rental agency.

### 10.8. Hotel Accommodations

Information on hotels is available from local hotel associations, some credit card organizations, certain hotel and motel chains, the American Automobile Association, *Hotel and Motel Red Book* (American Hotel Association Directory Corporation, 221 West 57 Street, New York 10019), and *Hotel Guide and Travel Index* (Ziff-Davis Publishing Company, 1 Park Avenue, New York, New York 10016). The manager may have a preference of hotels and motels; if not, you may have to gather information on a number of them from the above sources.

Reservations can be made by telephone, telegraph, or letter, and paid for by check or credit card at checkout time. The reservations clerk will need to know (1) the name of the person(s) who will be staying at the hotel, (2) expected time of arrival and departure and if the arrival is guaranteed, and (3) type of accommodation desired. Ask the clerk to confirm the reservation by mail. You will also need to know the time for checkout.

### 10.9. While the Manager Is Away

The manager will want to be in contact with the office during his or her absence, particularly when urgent matters come up. You should have a copy of the itinerary handy and know where he or she will be on any given day. If there is any doubt as to which hotel in a particular city the manager is to stay at, arrange beforehand to send written communications in care of American Express in that city. American Express maintains this service in all major cities at no cost to the user.

Check the manager's calendar for appointments scheduled during his or her absence. These appointments will have to be changed, postponed, or canceled. Discuss any pending business so you can handle it properly while he or she is away. The manager will have to let you decide what mail should be forwarded. Do not bother him or her with details that you or someone else in the office can handle. You should, though, acknowledge at once all mail received in his or her absence.

It is a good idea to number consecutively all envelopes you mail to the manager so he or she will know whether he or she received them all. You should keep a record of the contents of each mailing, too. Keep the originals of letters you mail in the office and send photocopies to the manager. It will also be helpful to write a memo about anything of interest and importance that has happened around the office during his or her absence. Make sure the memo is not unnecessarily long.

## 10.10. When You Travel with the Manager

Business and professional persons depend greatly on their secretaries when they conduct business and consequently may take them along when they go on certain business trips. Most of the problems you will confront when traveling with the manager involve the intricacies of etiquette.

*Hotel accommodations.* Advise the reservations clerk of your secretarial status when you travel with a male employer. Be certain the rooms are on different floors or at least that they are not adjoining.

*Tipping.* When you arrive at a hotel the same time as the manager he or she takes care of the tipping. This is also true when you dine together. Of course, when you travel or lunch alone, you must tip the required amounts. Keep a record of the gratuities you hand out so you may be reimbursed later.

*Doing work at the hotel.* The hotel lounge or sitting room may be used for taking dictation. Dictation should be taken in the room of a male employer only if he has a separate sitting room or if his room is completely made up, the door remains unlocked, and both parties are wearing business clothing.

*Clothing to take.* Avoid the temptation to take too many outfits. As you are a reflection of the manager and the company, it is preferable to dress conservatively at all times on a business trip.

—————————————◆•◄◆►•◆—————————————

## TRAVELING ABROAD

When the manager travels overseas, there are many details to be arranged beforehand. A travel agent is especially useful in taking care of most of the arrangements for foreign travel, but some things, such as obtaining a passport, must be handled personally. You can help by seeing that the manager does not overlook any important details.

### 10.11. Obtaining Passports and Visas

*Getting a passport.* The manager must appear in person to obtain a passport. He or she should apply to the nearest agent of the Passport Office, Department of State. You can remind the manager that he or she must take along:

1. Proof of United States citizenship—such as a previous passport, birth certificate, baptismal certificate, or certificate of naturalization.
2. Any previous passport.
3. Two duplicate photographs, 3 by 3 inches.
4. Proof of identify—such as a previous United States passport, naturalization certificate, driver's license, a government or business identification card or pass. If the manager does not produce any of the above evidence of identity, he or she must have an identifying witness complete an affidavit on the application form. This witness must have known the manager for at least two years and must state under oath that the manager is the person he represents himself to be.
5. The passport fee is $13. A passport is valid for five years after which it is necessary to apply for a new one.
6. A list of the countries he or she is planning to visit.
7. A completed application.

*Obtaining visas.* There are few countries that require the American visitor to obtain a visa. The countries the manager is most likely to visit do *not* require a visa—countries in Western Europe, for example. Be safe, though, and check with your travel agent. Requirements vary from country to country in regard to matters such as vaccinations. Your travel agent will also be able to advise you about this. If a visa is required by a particular country, the manager must present his or her passport at its consulate, fill out a visa form, and (usually) pay a visa fee. The time it takes to process a visa varies with the particular country.

## 10.12. Customs Information

Your travel agent will tell you how much merchandise (in terms of value) purchased abroad can be brought back to the United States duty free. Some items, such as liquor and perfumes, are separately limited as to amount. Most foreign countries also limit the amount of liquor and ciga-rettes-that you can bring *there*.

There are pamphlets put out by the U.S. government that supply the latest United States customs laws and regulations. One is entitled *United States Customs Information for Passengers from Overseas*. Another is called *Customs Hints for Returning Americans—Visitors from Canada, Cuba, Mexico, and Other Western Hemisphere Nations*. These pamphlets are available from the United States Treasury Department, Bureau of Customs, Washington, D.C.

## 10.13. Arranging for Travel Funds

When a businessman travels, either in this country or abroad, he can get along with very little cash. There are substitutes that are safer than money and often just as easy to use.

*Traveler's checks.* Traveler's checks are as negotiable as money, but have the advantage of being replaceable at no monetary loss if they are stolen or misplaced. The most widely used check of this type is put out by American Express. Checks come in $10, $20, $50, and $100 denominations. They can be obtained at banks or directly from the American Express Company.

When the manager buys these checks, he or she will have to sign them in the presence of the teller (which means that you cannot purchase them for the manager). The manager will also sign each check again as he or she uses it, so the person cashing it can compare the signatures. He or she must also make a record of the number of each check (you might do this for the manager), to be able to report the number of any lost or stolen check immediately to American Express.

*Letters of credit.* The manager can purchase a letter of credit from a local bank for funds of $1,000 or more. When traveling, he or she will be able to draw against this letter of credit at banks anywhere in the world until the face value is exhausted. When the letter of credit is issued, the entire amount is charged to the manager's (or the company's) account, but if he or she does not spend the entire value, the letter of credit can be turned in to the bank and the remaining balance will be credited to the account. The manager must appear in person before a representative of the bank to obtain a letter of credit.

*Credit cards.* Many American credit-card systems can be used throughout the world. An American Express credit card, for example, will be honored by airlines and many hotels, restaurants, and nightclubs here and abroad.

### 10.14. Information About Foreign Countries

*Articles, booklets and books.* You can usually get travel folders describing foreign countries from a travel agent. Also, watch for travel articles in current issues of magazines.

Every country that encourages tourist business has a travel bureau in the United States where you can get booklets plus information about special events.

*Bureau of Foreign Commerce.* The Bureau of Foreign Commerce in the Department of Commerce will provide information on economic developments, regulations, and trade statistics on any country. Information is available from the Washington headquarters or any of the bureau's 33 field offices. The bureau can supply names of the key commercial officers to contact, both here and abroad, and will set up overseas appointments for the manager. The bureau also has a trade complaint service with which the manager can communicate if he or she is involved in a dispute with a foreign company. Another service of the bureau is supplying information on industrial property rights to protect patents, trademarks, and copyrights abroad.

*Bureau of Foreign Commerce publications.* 1. *Foreign Commerce Weekly.* Information on economic conditions, market trends, commodity news, and the like.

2. *Trade lists.* Names and addresses of foreign manufacturers, producers, processors, exporters, wholesalers, distributors, sales agents, and service agents.

3. *World Trade Directory Reports.* Name and describe organizational details of individual firms in a given field.

4. *World Trade Information Service Reports.* Detailed, analytical information on trade and investment conditions and developments in individual countries.

# 11

# *THE ART OF WRITTEN COMMUNICATION*

## THE MECHANICS OF LETTER WRITING

A letter's appearance makes the first impact on a reader and can influence his state of mind when he absorbs its contents. Every business office has a preferred style for the letters it sends out; very often the secretary has determined that style. If the choice is up to you, select a style you consider appropriate, neat, efficient, and dignified.

### 11.1. Standard Letter Styles

The four principal styles of letter are the full-block, block, semiblock, and official. For samples, see 14.1, Letter Styles.

*Full-block style.* A letter set in full-block style is distinguished by the absence of any indentations; all structural parts begin flush with the left margin, which gives a neat, uniform appearance. This is a comparatively trouble-free construction because it requires very few typewriter adjustments. It is easier, for example, to have the complimentary close and dateline aligned with the paragraphs at the extreme left than shifted to the right. The full-block style uses open punctuation (see 11.2).

*Block style.* The block style differs from the full-block style in that the date and reference lines are flush with the right margin and the complimentary close begins slightly to the right of the center of the page. Both lines of the signature are aligned with the complimentary close. The inside address and the paragraphs are blocked, flush with the left margin. The salutation and attention line, if any, are also flush left. Open punctuation is commonly used (see 11.2). The block style is probably the most widely used style in a business letter.

*Semiblock style.* The semiblock style is like the block, except that the first word of each paragraph is indented five or ten spaces.

*Official style.* The official style is used by many executives for personal letters written on executive-size letterhead. Here, the inside address, which is written in block form and has open punctuation, goes *below* the signature.

## 11.2. Punctuation in Your Letters

The body of your letter is punctuated according to the standard rules of punctuation. Punctuation for the inside address, salutation, and complimentary close depend, however, on the particular punctuation style you adopt.

*Mixed punctuation* is the most popular style in today's business letters. You use no end-of-line punctuation in the inside address. You do use a colon after the salutation, and a comma after the complimentary close.

*Open punctuation* employs no end-of-line punctuation in the inside address, no punctuation after the salutation, and no punctuation after the complimentary close. Open punctuation is used most often with the full-block letter style.

## 11.3. Parts of Business Letters

*Dateline.* A dateline must appear on every letter you send. Use the date of dictation, not the date the letter is typed (if there is a difference).

The position of the dateline depends on the style and length of your letter. It is usually typed from 2 to 4 spaces below the letterhead; it should go farther down if the letter is short. Whether the date is placed flush at the left or right depends on the style of letter you are writing (see 11.1). The space between the date and the inside address is usually between 2 and 12 spaces, depending on the size of the stationery and the length of the letter; the shorter the letter, the greater the space.

There is only one correct way to write the date in ordinary business correspondence. If, for example, you are writing a letter on the last day in January, you date it this way:

January 31, 19____

Never use *th, d, nd, rd,* or *st* following the day of the month; do not abbreviate the name of the month; do not use a numerical figure for the name of the month. The only time you spell out the day of the month or year is in very formal letters and invitations.

*Inside address.* When addressing an individual in a company, write his or her name followed by the company name. You may also include the individual's business title, such as *Treasurer* or *Secretary.* This would go either on the same line as his name or on the next line, depending on which line is shorter. (See 11.6, Titles.)

Write the name of an individual, his or her firm, and address exactly as the addressee writes it or as it appears on the addressee's letterhead. Observe both his spelling and punctuation; single-space. Never take the liberty of abbreviating business titles or positions. *Mr., Mrs., Miss,* or *Ms.* precede the individual's name, even when the business title is used. (See 11.6-11.9, Forms of Address.)

See section 11.2 for ways to punctuate the inside address and the other parts of business letters.

Begin the inside address at the left margin of the letter. Place it between 2 and 12 spaces below the dateline, depending on the letter's length. If, however, you are writing an official-style letter, you place the inside address 2 spaces below the signature.

*Attention line.* Often, you write a business letter to a company, even though you may know that a particular person in that company will be the one to handle the matter. The use of an attention line (it must be on the envelope as well as on the letter, of course) is one way of assuring that the letter will reach that person promptly while indicating that the letter is not personal. If the person named is not there to open it, someone else in the company will.

The trend is away from the use of attention lines in business letters. Letters are more often addressed directly to individuals.

If the manager does use attention lines, here is the preferred style. Type the words *Attention Mr. John Doe* two spaces below the address and two spaces above the salutation. Do not abbreviate *Attention;* do not punctuate or underscore the attention line. Note that when an attention line is used, the salutation is *Gentlemen,* since the letter is really addressed to the company.

*Salutation.* Type the salutation even with the left margin, two spaces below the inside address. If an attention line is used, type the salutation two spaces below the attention line. Business letters require a colon after the salutation; only personal letters take a comma.

If the letter is addressed to an individual, but the person's name is not known, make the salutation singular; for example, *Dear Sir* or *Dear Madam.* If the letter is addressed to a company, use the plural *Gentlemen.* When the person's name is known, use the title *Mr., Mrs., Miss,* or *Ms.* (See also 14.2, Addressing Officials.)

*Subject line.* A subject line, stating briefly the subject of the letter, is a convenience to both writer and reader. The writer does not have to compose a wordy opening paragraph explaining the purpose of the letter; the reader can conveniently file the letter by subject and can quickly refer to any past correspondence on the same subject.

If your letter is full-block style, place the subject line two spaces below the salutation flush with the left margin. For other styles, center the subject line. The subject line is part of the body of the letter, not of the heading, and therefore is always placed after the salutation.

The subject line in legal letters is prefaced by *In re*—for example, *In re Lewis Estate.* The modern trend in nonlegal correspondence, however, is to omit prefatory words, such as *Subject* or *In re,* from the subject line.

*Body of the letter.* A letter should be single spaced with double spaces between paragraphs—unless the letter is very short and written on a full-sized letterhead, when it is permissible to double-space the body.

When you use semiblock style, indent the first word of each paragraph five or ten spaces. The block style has each line flush with the left margin. When a letter is double spaced, always indent paragraphs.

*Spacing letters properly.* Single spacing is the form most commonly used in a business letter. However, single-spaced letters have double spacing between the paragraphs, thus making a sharper frame and presentation of facts in the finished piece of work.

Let common sense guide you in determining how to space your work. If you are typing a letter that contains so few words that a single-space treatment would make the words look lost on a page, double-space the lines. Generally, letters of 100 words or less look best double spaced. Even when the body is double spaced, however, the inside address is usually single spaced.

*Complimentary close.* The complimentary close is the closing phrase in a letter expressing the regard of the writer for the addressee. The complimentary close varies with the tone of the letter and the degree of acquaintanceship with the addressee. The degree of formality should correspond with that of the salutation.

Type the close two spaces below the last line of the letter. Begin it slightly to the right of the center of the page, except when using the full-block style, where you begin flush with the left margin. Never let your close extend beyond the right margin of the letter. Capitalize only the first word. If mixed punctuation (see 11.2) is used, place a comma after the close.

The preferred forms of complimentary close are *Sincerely yours, Very sincerely yours, Sincerely.* In formal letters to persons of high position, close with *Respectfully yours.* When the correspondents are friends, you may use *Cordially, Best regards,* or *Best wishes.* (See also 14.2, Addressing Officials.)

*Signature.* The signature part of a business letter usually consists of the writer's typed name, business title, and manually written signature. The writer's name is typed because handwritten signatures are often illegible; if his or her name is printed on the letterhead there is no need to type it.

When you include the writer's business title, you are indicating that he or she is writing the letter in an official capacity. A personal letter written on firm stationery has no business title in the signature.

Firms of professional men, such as attorneys or accountants, frequently sign letters manually with the firm name, particularly if the letter expresses a professional opinion or gives professional advice. In some offices the firm name is typed on the letter and the lawyer or accountant who dictated it signs his name, thus:

Forbes, Sandford & Crowe

By *George H. Forbes*

A letter signed in the firm name, whether manually or typed, is written in the first-person plural (*we*), not singular (*I*).

1. *Where to type the signature.* When you include the company name in the signature, type it two spaces below the complimentary close. Type the writer's name four spaces below the firm name, and the writer's position either on the same line or the next line, depending on the length of his name and title. When the firm name is not included, type the writer's name and position four spaces below the complimentary close. Align the signature with the first letter of the complimentary close. A lengthy company name might have to be continued on another line, indented two spaces. No line of the signature should extend beyond the letter's right-hand margin.

Type the signature exactly as the dictator signs his or her name. If he signs his name *Kenneth A. Carroll,* do not type his signature *Kenneth Carroll, K. A. Carroll,* or use any other variation. Never type *Mr.* in the signature line.

If you want to indicate a business title or degree, have it follow the typed signature. The only title that precedes the written or typed signature is *Miss* or *Mrs.* in parentheses (see below). *Ms.* is not used in signature lines.

2. *Signatures of women.* It is important that a woman sign her business correspondence properly to avoid confusion. For example, a woman should sign her letters with her full name, because if she were to use only her initials and surname the reader might assume she was a man. Here are other rules for specific situations.

A single woman may precede her typed signature with the title *Miss* in parentheses. She may also eliminate a title because the absence of one implies that she is unmarried.

*Florence Jackson*

(Miss) Florence Jackson

*Florence Jackson*

Florence Jackson

In business correspondence a married woman has a choice of preceding her typed signature with *Mrs.,* in parentheses, or of using her married name for her typed signature (which is required social usage). She should do one or the other, so it is clear she is married.

*Florence Jackson*

(Mrs.) Florence Jackson

*Florence Jackson*

(Mrs. Thomas P. Jackson)

A widow signs her name as she did before her husband's death.

A woman who is divorced has a choice. If she chooses *not* to use her maiden name, she signs her given name, with or without the initial of her maiden name, and her former husband's surname. The typed signature is the same as the written signature, preceded by *Mrs.* in parentheses. Instead of this, she may combine her maiden name with her former husband's surname in the typed signature.

*Florence L. Jackson*
(Mrs.) Florence L. Jackson

*Florence L. Jackson*
(Mrs. Lowe Jackson)

Note: It is incorrect for a widow to sign her business letters:

*Florence L. Jackson*
(Mrs. Thomas P. Jackson)

3. *When the secretary signs.* When you sign the manager's name to a letter he wrote, simply add your initials below his name, to show that you signed it on his behalf.

*Harvey Reid*
Harvey Reid
Sales Manager

*Note:* A substitute signature indicates a lack of personal attention by the dictator. The procedure should be used only when absolutely necessary to insure prompt mailing.

When you write a letter and sign it with your own name in your official capacity as secretary you have to include the manager's name.

*Alice Pearson*
Secretary to Mr. Reid

Do not include initials unless another man in the company has the same last name.

*Identification initials.* The identification line consists of the initials of a letter's dictator and the secretary who types it. If, however, the dictator's name is typed in the closing lines, his or her initials may be omitted and only the transcriber's initials used.

Most companies place identification initials on carbon copies and the original. Some authorities recommend that initials appear only on the carbons. This can be done simply by shielding the ribbon with a small strip of paper.

Type the identification initials flush with the left margin, one or two spaces below the last line of the signature. If the official style of letter is used (see 11.1), type the identification line two spaces below the address. Lower-case type may be used for the typist's initials. If the dictator's initials are included, they precede the transcriber's. There are no periods separating initials; sets of initials are separated by a colon. When the person who signs the letter has not dictated it, type his initials first and follow with those of the dictator and the transcriber.

When the dictator's name is not included in the typed signature, identify him by typing out the initials of his given names followed by his full surname; then follow with a colon and type your initials.

Identification data are never included in personal letters.

*Enclosure mark.* Even though the presence of an enclosure is men-tioned in the body of the letter, you must still indicate that there is an enclosure by making a notation below the identification initials, if there are any. At the left margin, one or two spaces below the initials, type the word *Enclosures* followed by the number that are inserted. If an enclosure is to be returned, type in parentheses *to be returned* after your indication of the enclosure.

Many typists specifically identify the enclosure, for example, *Enc. Cert. ck. $258.75.*

*Special mailing notation.* If a letter is to be sent special delivery, registered, or by messenger, you indicate it by typing the means of delivery flush to the left and below the identification and enclosure marks. This notation is for the benefit of the company writing the letter and therefore is put only on the carbon. (See section 11.5 for placement on envelopes.)

*Notation for distribution of carbon copies.* If one or more copies are to be sent to someone other than the addressee, it should be noted on the letter. Type the carbon distribution notation—*Copy to Mr. V. R. Kiffney*—flush with the left margin, two spaces below all other notations. The abbreviation *c.c.* may be used instead of *Copy to.*

If you do not want the addressee to know that copies are being sent to others, write a *blind copy notation (b.c.).* You do this by noting the distribu-tion in the upper left corner of the carbon copies and omitting it from the original.

*Postscript.* The postscript is a handy method of adding an extra thought to a letter already typed. You do not have to rewrite your letter if you type your afterthoughts two spaces below the identification line or the last notation on the letter. Indent the left margin of the postscript the same space as you indent your paragraphs—do not indent at all if you use the full-block style. The abbreviation *P.S.* usually precedes the actual text of your postscript, but can be omitted. An additional postscript is usually preceded by *P.P.S.*, if *P.S.* was used for the first one.

*Second page of a letter.* The second page should be a plain sheet of paper—never a letterhead. The paper, however, should be the same size and quality as the letterhead. Write your heading one inch from the top of the paper and leave three spaces between the heading and the text of your continued letter. The heading should contain the name and the address at the left, the page number at the center, and the date at the right. The margins should be exactly the same as those for the first sheet.

A second page should contain more than a mere few lines. Organize your letter so that extra pages are used only when they are really needed. If possible, begin a new page with a new paragraph. If you do carry over a paragraph, try to have at least two lines of it on the second page. There is no need to type "Continued" at the bottom of the first page.

## 11.4. Interoffice Correspondence

Interoffice memoranda are written in a different format from that of business letters going outside the firm. On interoffice memoranda the inside address, salutation, and complimentary close are omitted, but headings are usually used.

An efficient memorandum style commonly used has three headings: *To, From,* and *Subject.* They are typed one under the other at the left margin in capital letters. Each heading is followed by a colon. If the writer's name appears in the *From* line, the writer's initials are either typed or handwritten a few spaces below the last line of the memo's text. If you do not use a *From* heading, type out the full name of the writer instead of his initials.

The date, placed either at the upper right margin or at the lower left margin, should never be omitted.

The name of each recipient of a copy of an interoffice memorandum should be typed on the memorandum, unless it is for general distribution throughout the organization. The letters *F.Y.I.* (For Your Information) after a name means that a copy is sent to that person merely to keep him informed. Make a copy for each recipient and an extra copy for the files.

If a memorandum does not have to go into the recipients' files, you can have one copy routed to many people. Simply write the names of those who are to see it on the memorandum with instructions to "pass it on." Each person receiving the memorandum will strike out his or her name, write the date on which he or she read the memorandum and took action, and see that it is passed to the next name. If you want the memo routed back to you, include your own name after the other names.

Unless the material in an interoffice memorandum is confidential, it is common practice not to use an envelope. You might fold the memo so only the addressee's name shows, if you feel the contents should not be public.

## 11.5. Envelopes

The first line of the address should begin slightly below the center of the envelope. The items in the envelope address are the same as those in the inside address. The U.S. Postal Service, however, requests that you use zip codes and two-letter state abbreviations (see 14.4).

If the address takes up two or three lines, double-space. If it takes up more than three lines, single-space.

If your return address is not printed on the envelope, type it at the upper left corner.

Special mailing instructions, such as *SPECIAL DELIVERY*, should be written at the upper right, beneath the stamps. Type them in capital letters and underscore.

If you write an attention line in your letter, also write one on its envelope. Type it on the lower left-hand corner.

If the contents of your letter are confidential, type the word PER-SONAL in capital letters above the address at the left center.

## FORMS OF ADDRESS

The rules for addressing persons in business correspondence have been changing. The current trend includes not only less formality, but also specific new forms of address, as shown in the sections below. (See also 14.2, Addressing Officials.)

## 11.6. Titles

An individual's business title may be included in the inside address of a business letter (and thus on the envelope). If the title is very short, it can be positioned on the first line, for example:

> Mr. John King, President
> ABC Corporation

If the title is long, place it on the second line, for example:

> Ms. Caroline Adams
> Director of Long-Range Planning
> XYZ Company

However, if the title causes the inside address to run over four lines, omit it.

## 11.7. Degrees

If you place initials or abbreviations for degrees after the name of an individual, use only the person's highest degree. For instance:

> *Wrong:* Jean Davis, B.A., M.A., Ph.D.
>
> *Right:* Jean Davis, Ph.D.

The exception to this rule is that two or more degrees of equal rank may be used, for example, John Howard, LL.D., Ph.D. List the degree pertaining to the individual's principal occupation first. A scholastic title such as professor should not be used when degrees are given, although a business title such as treasurer may be placed on the second line of an address.

## 11.8. Addressing Men

If a man has no other title such as *Dr.*, precede his name with *Mr.* If you are addressing more than one man, use the plural *Messrs.*

*Esquire* or *Esq.* may be used in addressing prominent attorneys and other professional men if the individuals do not have other titles. *Mr.* does not precede the name in that case, and no other title should be used.

See also 11.6, Titles, and 11.7, Degrees.

## 11.9. Addressing Women

Place the title *Miss* or *Ms.* before the name of an unmarried woman and the name of a woman whose marital status is unknown. Use the plural form *Misses* when addressing more than one woman. A married woman is addressed socially by her husband's full name preceded by *Mrs.* In business, however, she may be addressed either by her husband's name or by her given name and her married name preceded by *Mrs.* Some women use their maiden names in business preceded by *Ms.* Use the form she prefers if you know it. Address a woman with a professional title by her title followed by her given and last name.

A widow is addressed socially by her husband's full name preceded by *Mrs.* In business, use either her husband's full name or her given name and her married name preceded by *Mrs.* A divorcee may use either *Miss, Ms.,* or *Mrs.* if she uses her maiden name. *Mrs.* is used if she retains her married name. In business she may be addressed by her given name and her married name or by her maiden and married names (the latter is used socially). Follow the form preferred by the individual when you know it.

See also 14.2, Addressing Officials.

---

## WRITING BUSINESS LETTERS

Although some individuals dictate all but the simplest letters, many entrust the handling of a major portion of outgoing letters to their secretaries. Modern business letters are direct and to-the-point. An effective letter *talks* to the reader. Therefore, write in a conversational tone and avoid trite and stilted phrases. Also avoid unnecessary words and "pet" expressions. Use short words and sentences as often as possible. Adopt a positive tone in your letters and state the *who, what, where,* and *why* of your message right away.

The following sections discuss some of the more common letters you will have to write:

### 11.10. Acknowledgments of Letters Received during the Manager's Absence

You must acknowledge all letters addressed to the manager when he or she is absent for any length of time. Your letter may either (a) acknowledge, but not answer, or (b) acknowledge and answer.

*An acknowledgment without an answer.* For this type of letter you should state that the manager is away; indicate when he or she will return and that the letter will receive appropriate attention then. If the delay will cause the writer inconvenience, add a note of apology. The following is an example of a style you may adapt:

Dear Mr. Carney:

As Mr. Stanley will be away from the office until March 28, I am acknowledging your letter of March 15 concerning the new building specifications. I will bring this to his attention as soon as he returns, and I'm certain he will contact you promptly.

Please accept my apologies for this unavoidable delay.

Sincerely yours,

*Barbara Nelson*

Secretary to Mr. Stanley

*An acknowledgment that also answers.* If you are responding with more than a mere acknowledgment, *know the facts* or else your response will create confusion and chaos. You should always identify the letter, explain that the manager is away, and state the correct facts that answer the letter. If appropriate, say that the manager will write in greater detail when he or she returns. As an example:

Dear Mr. Wagner:

Your letter reminding Mrs. Morse of the Advertising Club dinner on April 24 has arrived during her temporary absence from the office.

Mrs. Morse plans to attend the luncheon and deliver her scheduled twenty-minute talk on "The Plight of Mass Media Magazines." If there are any changes in these plans I know she will contact you promptly upon her return.

Sincerely yours,

*Iris Meade*

Secretary to Mrs. Morse

## 11.11. Letters Calling Attention to Missing Enclosures

When you receive a letter in which the sender has neglected to place an enclosure, notify him or her about it immediately. Your letter should:

1. Identify the incoming letter and enclosure.
2. State that the enclosure was omitted.
3. Ask that the enclosure, or a copy of it, be sent to you.

Dear Mr. LaRue:

In your letter of May 2 to Mr. Harris you mentioned that you were enclosing the proposed plans for the new dormitory; however, they were not enclosed.

As Mr. Harris will need the plans to present to the Board of Trustees on May 10, could you please mail them today? Thank you.

Sincerely yours,

*Martha Green*

Secretary to Mr. Harris

## 11.12. Letters Arranging Appointments

Letters arranging an appointment in the manager's interest can usually follow a definite pattern:

1. Refer to the purpose of the appointment.
2. Suggest the time, place, and date. If that is not possible, be sure to ask the person to whom you are writing to indicate his or her preference to you.
3. Ask for a confirmation of the appointment if time and place are specified.

The following letter has all the elements you should include when arranging an appointment.

Dear Mrs. Harrington:

Mr. Lynch would like to see you on Friday, March 14, at 10 o'clock at his office, Room 714, to go over final details of the building contract.

Please let us know whether this time is convenient for you.

Sincerely yours,

*Alice Horan*

Secretary to Mr. Lynch

## 11.13. Letters Making Plane Reservations

Be sure to include in your letter:

1. Name and position of the person desiring the reservation
2. The flight and date on which space is desired

3. Schedule of flight

4. Credit card number, if any

5. Request for confirmation

Gentlemen:

Mr. Donald Hewitt, president of Hewitt Motors, would like to reserve space to Los Angeles on Jet Flight 422 out of Chicago on Friday, February 27. His air travel card number is 85632.

Our schedule shows that this flight leaves at 11:45 a.m., Central Standard Time, for Los Angeles, and arrives at 4:45 p.m., Pacific Standard Time.

Please confirm this reservation by wire immediately. Thank you.

Sincerely yours,

*Ruth Terry*

Secretary to Mr. Hewitt

## 11.14. Letter Requesting a Refund on Unused Ticket

Mention the date, city of departure, identifying ticket number, the cost, credit card number (if any), and to whom the refund should be sent.

Dear Sir:

Re: Ticket No. 198-92-001
Tulsa to New York City
Flight No. 663

The above ticket was issued to Mrs. Anne Purvis of this company for use on April 19.

Unfortunately, Mrs. Purvis was forced to cancel her reservation and would now like a refund on the ticket. The fare for the ticket was $98.26, paid by Mrs. Purvis's check number 1566, April 14, 1978.

Please make the refund check payable to Anne Purvis. The ticket is enclosed.

Sincerely,

*Doris Trask*

Secretary to Mrs. Purvis

### 11.15. Letters Making Hotel Reservations

When you write for hotel reservations for the manager, include the following information:

1. Accommodations desired
2. Name of person for whom reservation is requested
3. Date and time of arrival
4. Probable date of departure
5. Request for confirmation

Gentlemen:

Please reserve a single room with bath for Miss Lynda Brown, beginning Thursday, January 15. She plans to leave the afternoon of January 23.

Since Miss Brown will not reach Denver until Thursday night, please hold the room for late arrival.

I would appreciate receiving your confirmation of this reservation as soon as possible.

Sincerely yours,

*Barbara Allen*

Secretary to Miss Brown

When you are accompanying the manager on a business trip, you should pattern your letter for reservations after the following:

Gentlemen:

Please reserve a room and bath, together with a large connecting sitting room, for Mr. Harold Mack, beginning Wednesday night, December 5. He plans to leave early December 10.

I will accompany Mr. Mack and would like a single room with bath for myself for the same period. Please have my accommodations on a different floor.

Since our flight does not reach Newark Airport until 9:30 p.m., please hold both reservations for late arrival.

I would appreciate receiving your confirmation as soon as possible.

Sincerely yours,

*Claire North*

Secretary to Mr. Mack

### 11.16. Letter that Calls Attention to an Error in an Account

A secretary is often responsible for keeping up the manager's personal accounts. If you find the accounts are incorrect, you must tactfully call attention to any error. Avoid giving the impression that you are complaining. The most frequent errors that crop up are (1) when the amount of an item is incorrect, (2) when the total is incorrect, (3) when returned merchandise has not been credited, and (4) when an item not purchased is charged to the account.

*When the amount of an item is incorrect.* Here are the points that should be covered in your letter:

1. Give the name and address of the account, along with its number.
2. Describe the incorrect item, and tell why it is not correct.
3. State your version of what the item should be, giving any documentary information you have.
4. Ask for a corrected statement *or* enclose check for the correct amount and ask that the error be rectified on the account.

Gentlemen:

> Account 732-111-413
> James L. Henderson
> Henderson and Mueller, Inc.

Your statement of June 14 charges Mr. Henderson's account for a dinner party at the Greenbrier Lodge in Mt. Evans on May 2 for $98.98.

According to the charge record, the total should be $78.98, or $20 less than the amount on the statement.

Enclosed is Mr. Henderson's check for this month's statement, less the $20 overcharge. Please credit his account accordingly.

Thank you.

> Sincerely yours,
>
> *Norah Black*
>
> Secretary to Mr. Henderson

*When an item not purchased is charged to the account.* Here are the points that should be covered:

1. Name, address, and number of the account
2. Description of the item charged in error, including the price and date charged

3. Any additional pertinent information you have
4. A request that the charge be investigated
5. A request for a corrected statement

Gentlemen:

The October statement for Ms. Janice Dexter's account (number 198-6340-8322) shows a charge of $19.95 for twelve rolls of cellophane tape purchased in September. However, she did not order or receive any tape at that time.

Although Ms. Dexter purchased a dozen rolls of tape in August, the charge for those tapes was properly recorded on her September statement, which was paid by Ms. Dexter's check number 907, September 20, 1978.

I have deducted $19.95 from Ms. Dexter's October statement and am enclosing her check for the balance, $96.50. Please credit her account accordingly.

Thank you.

Sincerely yours,

*Helen Athens*

Secretary to Ms. Dexter

## 11.17. Follow-up Letters

When your follow-up files show that a letter has not been answered or action has not been taken by the desired date, it is time to trace the letter for a reply. You may either enclose a copy of your original letter or simply inquire with adequate reference to it.

1. Describe your original letter.
2. Try to suggest a good reason for the lack of response without criticism.
3. Enclose a copy of your original letter if it was long or contained important details.

*When you do not enclose a copy of your original letter.* The following example would be written for your own signature:

Gentlemen:

On April 5 we ordered six gallons of Mason's one-coat rubber cement, to be delivered to our Art Department. As yet we have not received the material or an acknowledgment of the order.

Our original order may have been lost in the mail, so please consider this a duplicate. As our supply of rubber cement is now running low, we hope you will be able to fill this order immediately. Please let us know if there will be any delay.

Thank you.

Sincerely yours,

*Mary Jane Hart*

Mary Jane Hart

*When you enclose a copy of your original letter.* The following example would be written for the manager's signature:

Dear Miss Jacobs:

Since your busy schedule often keeps you away from your office, you have probably not had time to consider my August 11 request to borrow your beautiful photographic display. In case my original letter did not reach you, I'm enclosing a copy of it.

Our Meetings Committee feels your display would be perfect for our upcoming seminar, October 29. If you have no objection to our using the display, I would appreciate your reply by October 5.

Thank you—and my compliments on your outstanding photographic compositions.

Cordially,

*Harry M. Richards*

Harry M. Richards

---

## WRITING PERSONAL LETTERS

In every business and profession there are occasions when personal letters must be written to business acquaintances. As a secretary, you may have the responsibility of writing many of these letters for the manager.

A personal letter must sound sincere and must be written with the person to whom it will be sent in mind. It should be written on the manager's personal stationery and signed by the manager. Write in a style and tone that the manager would use.

The following sections include examples of the types of personal business letters you may be asked to write.

### 11.18. Letter of Congratulations

The achievements of the manager's business friends and associates provide many opportunities for letters of good wishes and congratulations. Such a letter is best when it is brief, natural, and enthusiastic. Do not be flippant or credit an achievement to mere luck. Recognize that the reader has worked hard and earned his reward. If the letter lacks sincerity or seems to make light of the accomplishment it is acknowledging, it will suggest to the reader that the manager is jealous.

*Upon promotion.* Here is a letter with appropriate tone and content:

Dear Phil:

I just heard about your appointment as head of the West Coast division. Congratulations on your promotion. I know from the example of your previous work that you will do an outstanding job. Your remarkable strides over the past ten years have given us all tremendous satisfaction.

Best wishes for still greater success in the future.

Sincerely,

*Upon receiving an award of honor.* Congratulate the recipient and be sure to tell him the honor is richly deserved.

Dear Dr. Morris:

Congratulations upon being named Philadelphia's *Woman of the Year.* I can think of no other person who deserves the honor more.

In spite of attempts to do your many philanthropic deeds under the cloak of anonymity, word of your activity has finally spread. I cannot say that I am sorry because your wonderful example is bound to inspire others also to take pride in their city and to help improve it by their own generous actions.

All of my colleagues at Bliss & Collins join me in this expression of congratulations and good wishes.

Sincerely yours,

*Upon retirement.* Stress the past achievements of the person who is retiring.

Dear Roy:

I just learned of your resignation from the Tyrrell & Grover Company.

Let me congratulate you on your record of wise leadership, which has given your company the stature it now has.

I'm sure no man, upon retiring from business, ever took with him as high a degree of respect and good wishes from so many devoted friends and associates.

Sincerely,

## 11.19. Letters of Condolence and Sympathy

A letter to express sympathy should be written with tact, sincerity, and brevity. Do not philosophize on the meaning of life and death; it is best not to quote scripture or poetry. Show concern without being maudlin.

*Upon a death in the family.* To show sincerity, be sure to avoid hackneyed, meaningless phrases.

Dear Mrs. Levitan:

It was with deep regret that I learned this morning of the sudden death of your brother. Although I did not have the pleasure of knowing him well, I was keenly aware of the wonderful personal attributes that made him respected and loved by so many people.

Words mean little at such a time as this, but still I want to send you this expression of my deepest sympathy. If there is anything I or my firm can do to help you in the next few weeks, please call on me.

Sincerely,

*Upon personal injury or illness.* Show the reader your sincere concern and hopes for a speedy recovery. Where possible, be optimistic about his quick return to normal activity.

Dear Bruce:

I heard about your unfortunate accident at this morning's meeting of the society. From all reports you are making a speedy recovery and will be back to work in no time; naturally, I am delighted to hear this.

My plans are to be in Hartford on Tuesday. I will stop by at the hospital in the evening, and I hope to find you looking and feeling like your old self.

Cordially,

*Upon material loss or damage.* Express regret and offer to help out if possible.

> Dear Mr. Van Brunt:
>
> I was distressed to learn that you had suffered considerable flood damage during the last storm. News like this is particularly sad when it involves such a good business friend.
>
> The facilities of my company are available to you during this time of stress. Please let me know if I can be of help in any way.
>
> Sincerely yours,

## 11.20. Letters of Appreciation

A letter of appreciation should not have the appearance of something written merely to conform to the rules of etiquette. It should show a *genuine* feeling of gratitude.

You should express yourself with complete naturalness by using an informal style of writing. The degree of informality is determined by the extent of the favor and the relationship with the correspondent.

*For personal favor or service.* A letter like the following shows that the favor was truly appreciated:

> Dear Mr. Martin:
>
> I talked with Senator Ryan shortly after I walked into his reception room, thanks to your letter of introduction. The Senator was very helpful to me and I am deeply grateful to you for arranging the interview.
>
> My sincere thanks to you for your kindness.
>
> Sincerely yours,

*For hospitality.* Make the reader feel his kindness is not taken for granted. The letter should be written no later than a day or so after the visit.

> Dear Mrs. McKay:
>
> Thank you very much for helping to make my stay in Baltimore a pleasant one. The time spent with you and your husband were the highlights of my trip.
>
> I am looking forward to seeing you both in Boston this summer. Regards to Mr. McKay, and again, many thanks.
>
> Sincerely,

*For speaking before a group.* When a person gives his time and energy to speak at a club or association, he deserves a note of appreciation. An oral "Thank you" at the meeting itself is, of course, necessary, but a letter is called for as well.

Dear Mr. Bruan:

This is just a note to tell you again how much we enjoyed hearing your speech at the association dinner earlier this week. The points you made were stimulating. They are being discussed just as much today as they were on the evening of the dinner.

I am particularly appreciative that you were able to come because I know how busy you are at this time of the year. My gratitude is fully shared by the entire membership of the association.

Sincerely yours,

## 11.21. Letters of Invitation

An invitation should carry a degree of natural warmth and enthusiasm. It should also be complete in detail, telling the invitee the scheduled time and place. When the gathering is strictly of a business nature, state the reason for the invitation.

*To attend banquet, lecture, or entertainment.* The letter should show a true desire to have the reader attend. The formality of tone depends, of course, on the nature of the relationship between the reader and writer.

Dear Hal:

I would like very much to have you as my luncheon guest on Tuesday, March 20, at the Country Club. The occasion is an auspicious one for us —Golden Anniversary of Gold Products, Inc.

If it is convenient for you, I will pick you up at your office at noon. I am looking forward to seeing you then.

Cordially,

*To give an address.* Flatter your reader by telling him how eager everyone is to hear what he has to say. State whether there will be a question and answer period at the end. Give the exact details about time and place.

Dear General Chalmers:

The Executive Council of the New York Chamber of Commerce has asked me to extend an invitation to you to be the guest speaker at our annual dinner. The dinner will take place on Monday, December 3, in the Green Room of the Hilton Hotel, at 8 p.m.

The entire postwar history of Southeast Asia is reflected in the story of your unique experiences there. Our membership would be greatly honored if you could find time in your busy schedule to give us your first-hand account. We all are aware of your untiring efforts toward creating lasting peace and harmony in the world, and we would be privileged indeed to meet you and hear you speak at that time.

If it is acceptable to you, I will allot some time for questions and answers at the end of your remarks.

I look forward to hearing from you soon.

Sincerely yours,

*To be an overnight guest.* When inviting a business associate to be a house guest, make sure that the woman of the house joins in extending the invitation.

Dear Tom:

Do you plan to attend the Brokerage Convention in Columbus this year? If so, Mary and I insist that you stay with us during your visit here. You will have a bedroom to yourself and can come and go as you like.

It will be a real pleasure to have you as our guest, and I do hope you will plan to stay with us if you have made no other commitments.

Cordially,

### 11.22. Letters of Acceptance

A letter that accepts an invitation should be graciously appreciative and enthusiastic. If there are any questions about the details of the writer's participation—such as whether to dress formally, or the proposed length of his speech—ask for clarifications in the letter. As in all personal letters, the degree of formality depends on the personal relationship between the reader and writer.

*Of invitation to attend a banquet, lecture, or entertainment.* The following reply will make the reader feel that the invitation was warmly received, and accepted with genuine pleasure.

Dear Stan:

I appreciate very much your inviting me to attend your company luncheon at the Country Club on March 20, and I accept with pleasure.

Instead of having you pick me up at my office, as you suggested, I think it would be best if we met at the club. I have some calls to make late in the afternoon and will have to use my own car.

I am looking forward to seeing you again after much too long a time.

Cordially,

*Of invitation to give an address.* The letter should indicate flattery at receiving such an invitation. It will be appreciated by the spokesman for the group that extended the invitation if he is told the exact topic that will be discussed. This will enable him to give advance publicity and information to the members.

Dear Mr. Buford:

I am deeply honored at receiving your invitation to speak before the Chamber of Commerce on December 3 at the Hilton Hotel. I gladly accept.

If you think it would be suitable, I will give a forty-five minute talk on "Agricultural Reform—What it Means to Asia." I will be very happy to answer any questions at its conclusion.

It will be a pleasure to visit with the members of the chamber, many of whom I know, and I thank you again for your invitation.

Cordially,

*Of invitation to be an overnight guest.* Do not accept what has not been offered. In other words, if the manager is invited to stay overnight, his reply should not indicate that he is looking forward to being a guest for longer than one night. Be sure to let the host know the hour of his expected arrival.

Dear Ray:

I do plan to attend the convention this year and I accept with pleasure the kind invitation of Mary and you to be your house guest during my stay in Columbus. I will arrive at the airport at eight o'clock, Thursday evening, April 24, and I plan to leave on the 26th. I'll see you at your house about nine o'clock on Thursday.

It will be delightful to see you and Mary again. My only hope is that we don't bore Mary too much with reminiscences of our "wild" college days. See you on Thursday.

Cordially,

### 11.23. Letters of Declination

A letter saying that the manager cannot accept an invitation must be written with tact. It should say that he or she is appreciative of the offer but regretfully must decline it. It is usually best to give the reason why the invitation cannot be accepted. However, never offer more than a simple statement of the reason; a lengthy explanation suggests to the reader an excuse rather than a genuine reason.

*Of invitation to attend a banquet, lecture, or entertainment.* Make sure that the refusal does not sound ungrateful.

Dear Marge:

You know how much I always enjoy your company's luncheons. Unfortunately I will have to miss this one because of a sales conference in Chicago on the same day.

I do want to thank you for thinking of me and I hope the gathering will be as much fun and as great a success as always.

Cordially,

*Of invitation to give an address.* When declining an invitation to speak, state the reason for the inability to attend. Do not be coy and imply that it would be impossible to speak on a subject that would interest "such an esteemed and knowledgeable group."

Dear Mr. Buford:

I am deeply honored to receive your invitation to speak before the Chamber of Commerce on December 3 at the Hilton Hotel. It is with sincere regret that I have to decline. Official duties will keep me in Japan through the whole month of December.

Although I know you understand the circumstances, I am extremely sorry they will prevent my being in New York. Thank you again for sending me such a cordial invitation. I do hope to have another chance to meet with you and the entire chamber sometime in the near future.

Sincerely yours,

*Of invitation to be an overnight guest.* The entire household should be thanked for the invitation. The declination should be written promptly so they do not make unnecessary preparations for the expected stay.

Dear Ray:

It was really kind of Mary and you to invite me to stay at your house through the length of the convention. I only wish that my traveling program was such that I could accept. Unfortunately I can stay in Columbus for only a few hours on the sixteenth; I have to be back in Newark on the morning of the seventeenth.

I am sure you can imagine how pleasant it would be for me to visit Mary and you in your home. Although the situation doesn't permit me that privilege, I thank you both most sincerely for your kindness.

Cordially yours,

The person receiving your letter of declination deserves an early reply as well as the tactful and appreciative tone appropriate to this type of response.

# 12

## *USING CORRECT ENGLISH*

### Easy RULES FOR PROPER PUNCTUATION

Punctuation marks give clarity, emphasis, and value to written words, making it easier for the reader to comprehend the exact thoughts of the writer. Incorrect punctuation can convey meanings entirely different from what the writer intended; it can even make a letter or report completely unintelligible. The following sections show you how to use the 12 principal marks of punctuation correctly.

### 12.1. Apostrophe

1. The principal use of the apostrophe is to form the possessive case of nouns.

a. The singular possessive is formed by adding an apostrophe and an *s*. To form the plural possessive when the plural ends in *s*, all you add is an apostrophe; if the plural does not end in *s*, add an apostrophe and an s.

The letter's salutation (the salutation of one letter)
the letters' salutations (the salutations of more than one letter)
the children's shoes

b. If a word ends in *ss,* it is permissible to make it possessive by adding an apostrophe without an additional *s.* This avoids the awkward appearance of three *s*'s in a row.

the boss' desk
the class' teacher

c. The possessive form of most proper names is formed by adding an apostrophe and *s* to a singular or apostrophe alone to a plural. If the name has two or more syllables, the possessive may be formed by using the apostrophe alone—but it is still good form to add an apostrophe and *s.*

Kenneth's
the Harrises'
Adams's (or Adams')

d. Possession is sometimes shown by the use of an *of* phrase. When the thing possessed is a specific number or group belonging to the posessor, the *'s* is also used; this forms a double possessive. *But,* when the thing possessed is not restricted or limited to **a** specific number or group, the *'s* is not used.

Those comments of her employer's were remembered (specific) comments)
The comments of her employer are never forgotten (generally speaking)

e. Indicate joint possession by adding an apostrophe *s* to the final noun. Separate possession is indicated by adding an apostrophe *s* to each noun.

Joan and Carole's room
Joan's and Carole's rooms

f. Form the possessive of singular compound nouns by adding apostrophe *s* to the last word. Form the possessive of plural compound nouns by using the *of* phrase.

The general manager's training
The training of the two general managers

g. Inanimate objects ordinarily take an *of* phrase because they are not thought of as being able to possess anything. *But* usage has made the possessive form correct for various expressions of time and measurement.

a day's pay
six dollars' worth
eleven pounds' weight

h. The possessive may be placed at the end of a name made up of

several words, if the construction remains clear. If it sounds awkward, use
an *of* phrase.

> the American Red Cross' fund drive
> the fund drive of the American Society for the Prevention of
>     Cruelty to Animals

i. Use an apostrophe *s* after indefinite or impersonal pronouns to form
the possessive. *Never* use the apostrophe with a possessive pronoun.

> someone's          hers
> anybody's          yours
> his                its

2. Use the apostrophe in a contracted word to indicate the omission of a
letter, letters, or figures. The apostrophe is also used to indicate the omission of part of a date.

> we're
> it's
> July '62

3. Use the apostrophe *s* to form plurals of numbers, letters, symbols,
and abbreviations unless *s* alone can be added without causing confusion.

> Watch your p's and q's.
> She golfs in the high 80s.
> All c.o.d.'s must be receipted.
> The company profits soared during the 1950s.

4. Omit the apostrophe in names of companies and organizations
where the possessive is already implied.

> Farmers Market
> Lumbermens Mutual Casualty Co.
> Citizens Union

## 12.2. Brackets

Use brackets to enclose comments or explanations in quoted material,
to rectify mistakes, and to enclose parenthetical statements within parentheses. If your typewriter has no bracket key, improvise one by using the
virgule (slant) and underline. (See section 5.2.)

> In his address he stated, "The [American] Civil War was caused
>     by economic factors."
> It was *I* [not *me*] to whom you spoke.
> The modern history of Italy (see *When in Rome* by Benito Condito
>     [2d ed.]) is a history of great men.

## 12.3. Colon

1. The colon is a mark of punctuation that introduces something: a list, series, tabulation, extract, text, or explanation. Do not, however, place a colon after the verbs *are* or *were* unless a formal vertical listing follows.

There are many letter styles:
1. Full Block
2. . . .

The standard styles in which letters are set up are:
1. Full Block
2. . . .

The standard styles in which letters are set up are (1) Full Block, (2) . . .

In his report to the committee, Mr. Jones wrote: . . .

2. A colon is used after the salutation in a business letter.

Dear Sir:
Dear Mr. Carey:

3. Use a colon between the hours and minutes when the time is expressed in figures.

7:20 p.m.

4. Use a colon to separate the chapter and verse in Biblical references.

Luke 3:7

5. Do not put in a dash after the colon. A colon, alone, is sufficient indication of a break in the sentence.

## 12.4. Comma

The comma is used primarily as a mark of separation to clarify the grouping of words and phrases. Some sentences must have commas to be clear. In other cases the comma's proper usage is dictated by the writer's own style. Use the comma when it helps clarify the meaning, but avoid it when it adds nothing and only slows down the reading pace.

1. Use commas to separate more than two words and phrases in a series.
The office needs a new clock, desk, typewriter, and pencil sharpener.

2. Use commas to separate the two main clauses of a compound sentence joined by a coordinate conjunction. The comma may be omitted if

the clauses are short. (Examples of coordinate conjunctions are *but*, *and*, *or*, *for*, *neither*, *nor*, and *either*.) Do *not*, however, separate the parts of a compound predicate with a comma.

> Most of the pages have typographical errors, but some are perfect.
> He typed the manuscript and then he proofread it.
> She went into town and spent the day shopping.

3. Use commas to set off transitional phrases and words, such as *however*, *therefore*, *nonetheless*. Omit the comma if the transition is smooth without it.

> When I travel in the U.S. I go by plane. When I go abroad, however, I travel by ship.
> It's nonetheless a good idea.

4. Words in apposition—that is, words that give additional information about a preceding expression—are usually set off by commas. *But,* an appositive takes no commas when it distinguishes a preceding expression from other persons or things of the same group. In the second example, for instance, *Aida* is distinguished from other operas written by Verdi.

> The stenographer, Miss Smith, is on vacation.
> The opera *Aida* is by Verdi.

5. Use commas to set off parenthetical words when the degree of separation is not great enough to require parentheses or dashes.

> The first thing to do, I believe, is to set your goals.
> The rule, of course, must be obeyed.

6. Do not use a comma between a name and the word *of* indicating position or place.

> Senator Moynihan of New York.
> Mr. Delaney of Smith, Barney & Co.

7. Use a comma when you write numbers with more than three figures, *but* do not insert one when you write street, room, post office box, and telephone numbers.

> 8,975 employees          Box 9874
> 5009 Broadway            LO 7-0796
> Room 7319

8. Use a comma after introductory expressions.

> Yes, Mr. Levinson is on vacation.
> Well, you can't be too sure about it.

9. Use a comma to set off a quoted sentence from the rest of the sentence.

"There will be no bonus," Mr. McPheeters stated, "unless the company shows a profit."

10. Use a comma to indicate the omission of a word or words.

Mr. Husing will be back on Monday; Mr. Swing, on Wednesday.

11. Use a comma to set off a nonrestrictive phrase or clause—one that adds additional information but is not essential to the sentence. Do not set off a restrictive phrase or clause—one that is essential to the meaning of the sentence. (Note: *That* is used to introduce a restrictive clause; *which* is used to introduce a nonrestrictive clause.)

The clothing store that opened recently has a sale today.
The clothing store on the corner, which has excellent apparel, is closed on Mondays.

## 12.5. Dash

1. Use the dash (two hyphens with no space before or after) to emphatically set off explanatory clauses or a change in thought.

We saw a revival last night—it was *A Christmas Carol*—and we enjoyed it.
Give him the first two chapters—no, on second thought you'd better give him the whole book.

2. Use a dash to indicate hesitancy in speech.

I think it was John Adams—or was it John Quincy Adams?—who was our second president.

Note the placement of the question mark in the example above. When the material set off by dashes requires an interrogation (or exclamation) point, retain the punctuation *before* the second dash.

3. Use dashes to set off an appositional phrase when commas mark off words within the appositive, itself.

A box of supplies—pencils, paper, and envelopes—was delivered yesterday.

4. A dash may be used before a clause that summarizes a series of words or phrases.

The Netherlands, Belgium, and Luxemburg—these are known as the Benelux countries.

## 12.6. Ellipsis

When you are quoting and want to extract words, use the *ellipsis* (plural, ellipses)—three consecutive dots or asterisks to indicate the omission of the words. If the words omitted would ordinarily be followed by a period, place a period immediately after the three dots.

The contract stated: "The parties . . . will pay damages."
The contract stated: "The parties of the first part and the second
    part. . . ."

## 12.7. Exclamation Point

Use an exclamation point after a statement to indicate strong feeling, emotion, or irony.

What a beautiful sight!
Great! I don't have to go.

The exclamation point is also used in sales literature for emphasis.

Bargain Prices!
Sale!

## 12.8. Hyphen

1. Use a hyphen as a connecting link in compound terms.

a. A hyphen is used between two or more words serving as a single adjective before a noun. These words are *not* hyphenated when they follow the noun.

two-story house
well-bred person
John is well bred.

b. Do *not* use a hyphen to connect an adverb ending in *ly* and an adjective.

nicely dressed executive

c. A hyphen is used in a compound term consisting of a noun and a prepositional phrase.

son-in-law
blow-by-blow
person-to-person

d. Use a hyphen in compound numbers written as words.

twenty-two
one hundred and twenty-two

e. When writing out a fraction, use a hyphen to separate the numerator and denominator.

five and one-half acres
one-third of the property

f. When describing someone or something by nationality, hyphenate geographically descriptive words. This shows that the person or thing shares the qualities of both parts of the hyphenated word.

German-American
Latin-American
Scotch-Irish

2. Except after the short prefixes *co, de, pre, pro,* and *re,* which are generally printed solid, use a hyphen to avoid doubling a vowel or tripling a consonant.

| | |
|---|---|
| coordinate | semi-invalid |
| deemphasize | micro-organism |
| preeminent | bell-like |

3. Use a hyphen with the prefixes *ex, self,* and *quasi.*

ex-president
self-determination
quasi-contract

4. Use a hyphen to join duplicated prefixes.

super-superlative
re-replace

5. Use a hyphen to prevent mispronunciation or to avoid ambiguity.

co-op
re-mark (mark again)

6. Use a hyphen to join a single capital letter to a noun or a participle.

X-ray
H-bomb
T-shaped

7. The adjectives *elect* and *designate*, as the last element of a title, require a hyphen. (Note that vice-president-elect takes two hyphens.

vice-president-elect
president-elect
ambassador-designate

8. Where two or more hyphenated compounds have a common basic element and that element is only stated once, the hyphens are retained.

two-, four-, and six-story houses
6-, 12-, 24-inch rulers
Anglo- or Franco-American trade

9. Use a hyphen to indicate a span of time.

the 1963-64 season

10. Use a hyphen at the end of a line to show that part of a word is being carried over to the next line. A word must be divided according to its breakdown into syllables; if you do not know a word's proper division into syllables, look up that word in the dictionary. There are, however, a few supplementary rules you should keep in mind.

a. Do not divide words pronounced as one syllable.

walked
meant

b. Do not divide four-letter words.

upon
also

c. Do not separate a one-letter syllable at the beginning of a word from the rest of a word.

against
align

d. Do not divide abbreviations.

UCLA
C.O.D.

e. Do not carry over to the next line a one- or two-letter syllable at the end of a word.

f. Do not divide proper names. Avoid separating initials, titles, or degrees from the name.

g. Do not divide numerical figures.

h. Words that are already hyphenated should be divided only where the hyphen naturally falls.

father-in-law

i. Do not divide a word after a silent consonant.

often
subtle

j. Divide words containing a one-letter syllable after the one-letter syllable.

ele-phant
cara-mel

*Exception:* Divide before the single-vowel syllable when it is the first syllable of a root word.

dis-avow
dis-unite

*Exception:* Divide between the vowels when there are two consecutive single-vowel syllables.

evalu-ation
allevi-ation

*Exception:* Divide before the single-vowel syllable when it is part of one of the suffixes *able* or *ible*. Note, however, that there are many words ending in *able* or *ible* in which the *a* or *i* does not form a syllable by itself. These words, such as *pos-si-ble* and *ca-pa-ble*, are divided after the *a* or *i*.

charge-able
sens-ible

k. Divide a word between the consonants when the final consonant in a word is doubled before a suffix.

occur-rence
compel-ler

l. Divide after the consonants (whether single or double) in a root word. Do not carry them over to the ending.

elop-ing
endear-ing

m. Do not break up words for more than two successive lines.
n. Do not hyphenate the last word on a page.

## 12.9. Leaders

Leaders are a row of dots or hyphens used to lead the eye across a space to a word or a number. Leaders are often used in indexes, tables, and statements of accounts.

## 12.10. Parentheses

1. Use parentheses to set off matter not part of the main statement or not a grammatical element of the sentence, yet important enough to be included.

Man legal sources (see *Black's Law Dictionary*) give the common-law background.

2. Use parentheses to enclose numbers or letters designating items in a series.

Check letters for (1) signature, (2) inclusion of enclosures, and (3) correct address.

3. Use parentheses to enclose a figure when it follows an amount written out in words, or when the American equivalent of foreign currency is given.

Twenty-five (25) dollars.
It cost £3 ($8.40).

*Correct placement of parentheses:* a. A reference in parentheses at the end of a sentence is placed before the period, unless it is a complete sentence in itself.

His reference was the Bible (New Testament).
His reference was the Bible. (See Luke 4:2.)

b. Commas, periods, and other punctuation marks belong within the parentheses if they belong to the parenthetical clause or phrase. They are outside the parentheses if they belong to the words of the rest of the sentence.

>Many reference books (see, for example, Fowler's *Modern English Usage*) prefer open punctuation.

To form the possessive of regular plurals (nouns ending in *s*), add only the apostrophe.

## 12.11. Period

1. Use a period after a declarative sentence that is not exclamatory, or after an imperative sentence.

>I am writing the letter.
>Write the letter.

2. Use a period after a number or letter that precedes part of a series. A period often is used instead of parentheses.

>a. Full-Block Style
>b. Official Style

3. Use a period to separate integers from decimals.

>7.8 percent
>$17.50

4. Use a period after the abbreviation of a word or after a letter or letters representing a word. Do not use a period, however, if the abbreviation is a well-known symbol, such as letters standing for various government agencies.

>Okla.
>qt.
>Mr.
>ICC (Interstate Commerce Commission)

5. Do not use a period after contractions.

>ass'n
>sec'y

6. Do not use a period after shortened forms of names and words in common use.

>Ed
>Ken
>ad
>photo

7. Do not use a period after a letter used in place of a name unless it is the initial of a name.

A met B
A. (Mr. Ajax) met B. (Mr. Brown)

8. Do not use periods after Roman numerals except when enumerating items.

Elizabeth II
III. Forms of Address

## 12.12. Question Mark (Interrogation Point)

1. Use an interrogation point after a direct question.

How are you?

2. Do not use an interrogation point after an indirect question.

He asked me if I needed supplies.

3. Do not use a question mark after sentences that are interrogative in form but declarative in meaning.

May I be so bold as to correct you.
Will you please return it promptly.

4. Use a question mark to express doubt about the accuracy of a fact or figure.

The board is 12 (?) feet long.

5. A question mark may be used after each of several interrogative phrases.

Did we meet in London? In Paris? Rome?

## 12.13. Quotation Marks

1. Use quotation marks to enclose the precise quoted words of a speaker or writer.

"Make two carbons," he said.
"The speech," Mr. Smith remarked, "was much too long."

2. Do not use quotation marks when the name of the speaker or writer immediately precedes the quoted material, such as in question and answer material.

Mr. Abel: On what date was the contract signed?
Mr. Baker: September 12, 1959.

3. A quotation within a quotation should be enclosed in single quotation marks.

> A voice on the radio was heard to say, "The Premier today emotionally proclaimed, 'The war is over!' "

4. Use quotation marks to enclose nicknames.

John Birks "Dizzy" Gillespie
A. B. "Happy" Chandler

5. Do not use quotation marks to enclose slang expressions. In situations where slang is appropriate, quotation marks are out of place.

6. Use quotation marks to enclose the names of books, articles, songs, essays, and art works. Well-known works such as the Bible are not enclosed in quotation marks. In letters or advertising material, the title of a book may be capitalized for emphasis. In printed material the title of a book is italicized; therefore, in preparing material for the printer, underline the title.

"For Whom the Bell Tolls"
"Stardust"
Michelangelo's "Pieta"

*Correct placement of quotation marks:* a. When quoted material is more than one paragraph long, place quotation marks at the beginning of each paragraph, but at the end of the last paragraph only.

b. Place commas and periods inside quotation marks. Place other punctuation marks inside quotation marks only if they are part of the matter quoted.

> "Gone With the Wind," I understand, is due for another revival.
> Mr. Brandt said, "We must all work harder."
> "Nice guys finish last."
> She asked, "Is anyone here going to the office picnic?"

## 12.14. Semicolon

1. You may use a semicolon to separate the parts of a compound sentence when the comma and conjunction are omitted. The semicolon creates a more pronounced break in a sentence than a comma.

> The delegates arrived; the arguments began.
> We sent two packages; the rest will be sent tomorrow.

2. Use a semicolon to separate items in a series when any of the items contain commas.

The committee included Hal Smith of Yonkers, New York; Pete Rosar of Little Rock, Arkansas; and Dr. Alexander Smith from Mayo Clinic.

3. Use a semicolon before an adverb that serves the purpose of a conjunction. The conjunctive adverbs are *accordingly, also, besides, consequently, furthermore, hence, however, indeed, likewise, moreover, nevertheless, otherwise, similarly, so, still, therefore, thus.*

He will attend the meeting; indeed, he will be the main speaker at the meeting.

## GUIDE TO CAPITALIZATION

Although there is no universal set of rules for correct capitalization, the trend is toward more lowercase letters. When authorities differ, the important thing is to be consistent in the method you use. The following rules are appropriate for modern business correspondence and reports.

### 12.15. Biblical References

1. All words denoting the Deity of the Bible should be capitalized, *but* the word *god* is not capitalized when it refers to a pagan god.

| | |
|---|---|
| God | the Almighty |
| our Father | The gods are angry |

2. Pronouns referring to the Deity should be capitalized if they stand for His name.

I pray for His mercy.

3. Capitalize all names for the Bible and its books and divisions.

the Good Book
the Book of Exodus

## 12.16. Education

1. Capitalize names of schools, colleges, and departments. Lowercase them when they are not part of the official title.

Columbia University
the university
Department of Business Education
the business education department

2. Capitalize the names of classes. Lowercase them when the word refers to a member of the class.

Senior Class
a senior

3. Capitalize the titles of courses. Lowercase subjects if they are not derived from a proper name.

I am taking Secretarial Science II
English and history are required for freshmen.

4. Capitalize academic degrees and honors if the full name is given. Lowercase them when they are not part of a name or title.

Jane Jones, Master of Arts          Davis Fellowship
Jane Jones, M.A.                     the fellowship
the degree of master of arts

## 12.17. Geographical Designations

1. Capitalize directions of the compass when they designate definite geographical sections of the country, *but* do not capitalize them when they are used to denote direction.

The South again voted Democratic.
Walk two blocks south, and then bear to the west.

2. Capitalize popular names for regions and localities.

the Loop (Chicago)
the West End (London)
the Battery (New York)

3. Capitalize names of the divisions of the world or of a country.

the Orient
the Atlantic Coast

### 12.18. Governmental and Political Bodies

1. Capitalize the names of legislative, administrative, and deliberative bodies, domestic and foreign. Lowercase *legislature* when it stands alone. Capitalize the words *state* and *commonwealth* when they are part of a name. Lowercase them when they stand alone.

> the legislature
> the Commonwealth of Massachusetts
> The legislatures of those states are controlled by Democrats.
> the state of New York
> New York State

2. Capitalize *federal, government,* and *administration* when they are part of an official title. Otherwise, lowercase them.

> Federal Reserve Bank
> The federal government sent troops.
> Her Majesty's Government

3. Capitalize *city, county, district, ward, precinct, department, committee,* and the like when they are part of a name, *but* lowercase them when they stand alone or are used as general terms.

> Sullivan County
> The country has undergone many changes.
> Second Ward
> this district

4. Capitalize names of political parties and organizations, *but* lowercase their adjectival forms when unrelated to a party. However, the word *party* is always lowercased.

> Republican party
> Democrat
> A democratic form of government

### 12.19. Headings and Titles

In titles of literary works and in names of firms and organizations, capitalize all words, except conjunctions, prepositions, the *to* in an infinitive, and articles. You may, however, capitalize any word if it has more than four letters. But always capitalize the first word after a dash or colon.

> The Way of All Flesh
> How to Succeed in Business Without Really Trying

Americans for Democratic Action
Pioneering Americans: The Voyage to the Moon

## 12.20. Historical Terms

1. Capitalize the names of important events, *but* lowercase *war* unless it is part of the name of a war.

World War II
Battle of Bull Run

2. Capitalize the names of important historical documents.

Declaration of Independence
Magna Charta

3. Capitalize designations of eras of history and periods in the history of a language or literature.

Middle Ages
Elizabethan Age
Atomic Age

## 12.21. Holidays and Seasons

1. Capitalize religious holidays, feast days, and specially designated secular days and weeks. *But* lowercase *election day, primary day.*

Christmas               Thanksgiving Day
Passover                National Tavern Week

2. Lowercase names of seasons: *autumn, fall, spring, summer, winter;* also *springtime, autumnal, summery, midwinter. But* capitalize a season on the rare occasions when the season is personified, that is, when the season is given some attribute of a human being.

If Winter comes, can Spring be far behind?

## 12.22. The Judiciary

1. Capitalize the full title of a court, *but* lowercase *court* when it is standing alone or when it is used in a general descriptive sense.

Domestic Relations Court
In *Jones vs. Smith,* the court held . . .
an appellate court

2. Capitalize *court* when it refers directly to the judge or presiding officer.

The Court overruled the motion.

3. Capitalize titles when they precede a name *but* lowercase *chief justice, associate justice, judge, magistrate, surrogate,* and so on when they stand alone, unless they are used in place of a proper name.

The Judge is in his chambers.
A surrogate is an elected official in New York.

4. Capitalize *bar* and *bench* when they are part of a judicial body, *but* lowercase them in other instances.

American Bar Association
the bar

## 12.23. Legislation

1. Capitalize the official title of specific acts, bills, codes, and laws. Lowercase acts that are only described generally.

Minnesota Mortgage Moratorium Act
Sherman Antitrust Act
the Morse bill
a child-labor law

2. Capitalize *constitution* when it refers to the specific constitution of a country or state, *but* lowercase it as a general term.

the New York State Constitution
the United States Constitution
A constitution is made up of . . .

3. Capitalize *amendments* to the Constitution when they are referred to by number or by full title, *but* lowercase them when they are used as a general term or as part of a general descriptive title.

Fourteenth Amendment
prohibition amendment

## 12.24. Listings

1. When a list of items, each item being a complete sentence, is preceded by a colon, the first word of each formally introduced enumeration

is capitalized. Lowercase brief enumerations that do not make sentences, unless they are itemized one beneath the other.

> A secretary uses the guide under these circumstances: (1) Someone outside her immediate office wants the material. (2) Her employer expects to take the material outside the office. (3) She expects . . .
>
> Her qualifications for the position: (1) initiative, (2) intelligence, (3) tact, (4) charm, (5) . . .
>
> Her qualifications for the position are:
>> 1. Initiative
>> 2. Intelligence
>> 3. Tact
>> 4. Charm
>> 5. . . .

2. Lowercase enumerations that are not preceded by a colon.

> The features to consider in selecting paper for a business letterhead are (1) appearance and feel, (2) workability, (3) permanence, and (4) cost.

## 12.25. Numbers

1. Capitalize sums of money when they are written out in checks, business letters, and legal documents.

> Your contribution of One Hundred and Fifty Dollars is greatly appreciated by the Republican National Committee.

2. Capitalize words that indicate a classification, a division, a listing, or when nouns or abbreviations are used with numbers or letters in a title.

> Form No. 723
> Unit C
> Plan II

3. Spell out and capitalize the numerical names of streets and avenues if they are numbers of 12 or under.

> 20 Fifth Avenue
> 440 West Tenth Street

### 12.26. Personal Titles

1. Capitalize official titles when they precede a name, *but* not when they follow it or are used alone.

> Secretary Paul W. Houts was the toastmaster and President James Hopkins delivered a fifteen-minute speech.
> The officers present were James Hopkins, president, and Paul W. Houts, secretary.

2. Capitalize family titles used with a name or in direct address *but* not when used in other constructions.

> I didn't think Uncle Ralph was there.
> Was he there, Mother?
> He is my favorite uncle.

3. Capitalize *president* when it precedes a proper name. Otherwise lowercase it.

> President Carter
> the president
> the presidency

4. Capitalize titles of cabinet members, heads of government departments, and government dignitaries when the titles are used with proper names; otherwise lowercase them. But the title of *Speaker of the House* is always capitalized to avoid confusion.

5. Capitalize the titles of *governor, lieutenant governor, mayor, borough president*, and the like when they are used with proper names. Otherwise lowercase them.

> Governor Adams will see you now.
> The mayor of a large city has varied and numerous responsibilities.

6. Capitalize the titles of state *senator, assemblyman, alderman*, and the like when they precede proper names *but* lowercase them when they follow names or are used alone.

7. Capitalize titles of heads of state and city departments, such as *police commissioner, commissioner of highways, attorney general, sheriff* when they precede proper names but lowercase them when they follow a name or stand alone.

> Commissioner Jones
> the attorney general

8. Lowercase subordinate titles, such as *deputy sheriff, assistant district attorney,* except when they precede proper names.

The deputy sheriff attended.
At the meeting was Deputy Sheriff Morano.

9. Capitalize *acting* and *under* when they are part of a capitalized title.

Acting Secretary of State Morris
Under Secretary of State Dawson
the acting secretary

10. Capitalize all titles of honor or of nobility when they precede a name. Some British titles are capitalized when used without a personal name as well.

Princess Margaret
the Duchess of Kent
the pope

11. In formal lists, if titles and descriptive designations immediately follow names they should be capitalized.

## 12.27. Personification

Capitalize words that are personified. A word is personified when it is an inanimate object, abstract idea, or general term that has been given some attribute of a human being.

The Chair called the meeting to order.
When Headquarters insisted, we obeyed.

## 12.28. Proper Nouns

1. Capitalize the names of particular persons, places, and things (proper nouns) and adjectives derived from them. *But* lowercase proper nouns and adjectives when they have developed a specialized meaning no longer related to a particular person, place, or thing.

Turkey
Turkish
turkish towel

2. Capitalize common nouns or epithets when they are used with, or as substitutes for, proper names.

the First Lady
Catherine the Great

3. Always capitalize trade names.

Coca-Cola
Paper Mate

## 12.29. Quotations

1. Capitalize the first word of a direct quotation *but* use lowercase when there is an indirect quotation.

> The president stated over the air, "We shall not get involved in a war."
> The president stated over the air that we would not get involved in a war.

2. Do not capitalize the first word in the second part of a broken quotation, *unless* it is a complete sentence.

> "If the contract is not signed by tomorrow," he said, "we will take our business elsewhere."
> "If the contract is not signed by tomorrow we will take our business elsewhere," he said. "This delay is costing us money."

## 12.30. Races and Tribes

Capitalize names of peoples, races, and tribes.

Caucasian
Negro
Iroquois

## DICTIONARY OF CORRECT WORD USAGE

The image of your company is affected by the manner in which thoughts and ideas are communicated to others. The misuse of *one word,* for example, can convey to a customer an impression of poor quality not only in correspondence, but quite possibly in the product as well.

Section 12.31 provides an alphabetical list of words and phrases that frequently cause trouble, with explanations and examples to help you solve your grammatical problems.

### 12.31. One Hundred Commonly Misused Words

*about* If a sentence already indicates that an approximation or estimation is being made, *about* is redundant. Also, never use *at about* in combination. If you are being precise, use *at;* if you are giving an approximation, use *about.*

> We estimate that 500 [not *about* 500] will attend.
> The guests will arrive *about* midnight. (Approximately)
> The guests will arrive *at* midnight. (Precisely)

*adapt, adopt*   *Adapt* means make suitable or adjust to; *adopt* means take as one's own.

> She *adapted* herself to the colder climate by wearing her new sable coat.
> The company *adopted* the suggestions that were made.

*adverse, averse*   *Adverse* means in opposition, unfavorable; *averse* means having a dislike for. *Adverse* refers chiefly to opinion or intention; *averse* to feeling or inclination.

> The outcome was *adverse* to Far Eastern interests.
> They are *averse* to any kind of criticism.

*advise, inform* When you give advice to someone, you *advise* him; when you convey information or facts, you *inform* him.

> An accountant and lawyer should *advise* you when you go into a new business.

*affect, effect* To *affect* is to concern or influence. *Effect* as a verb is to bring about or cause; *effect* as a noun means result or consequence.

> The location of the store will *affect* [influence] sales.
> You can *effect* [bring about] an improvement in sales if you change your approach to customers.
> The *effect* [consequence] of the strike was a raise in salary.

*alike* Never precede with *both.*

> They are *alike* [not *both alike*] in many respects.

*all, all of* When used with a pronoun, *all* is followed by *of.* When *all* is used with a noun, *of* is not needed.

> *All* the workers [noun] attended.
> *All of* them [pronoun] attended.

*all right* This expression would always be written as two words. Any other construction, such as *allright* or *alright,* is incorrect.

> Is everything *all right?*

*allusion, illusion, delusion* An *allusion* is reference to something; an *illusion* is a deceit of the senses or false image; a *delusion* is a false concept.

> In his speech there was an *allusion* [reference] to the plays of Shaw.
> The mirrors gave the *illusion* [false image] of a larger room.
> He has the *delusion* [false concept] that he is the smartest man in the world.

*amounts* Words starting an amount (time, money, measurement, weight, volume, fractions) take a singular verb.

> Thirty-five hours *is* the usual work week.
> Two feet *is* the correct measurement.
> Three pounds *is* plenty.
> Fifty dollars *is* his price.

*anxious, eager* To be *anxious* is to be worried; to be *eager* is to anticipate enthusiastically.

> She was *anxious* [worried] about getting a promotion.
> She was *eager* [anticipating] to get a promotion.

*any time* *Any time* is never written as one word.

> I'll be home *any time* after six o'clock.

*anyone, any one* Use *anyone* when *anybody* can be substituted in the sentence with no change in meaning. In other uses, *any one* is the correct form. (Both forms are singular and should be followed by a singular verb and singular pronoun.)

> *Anyone* you choose *is* [not *are*] acceptable.
> *Any one* of the manuscripts *is* [not *are*] acceptable on the basis of *its* [not *their*] clarity.

*apt. liable, likely* *Apt* means suited to or suggests a habitual tendency; *liable* means exposed to a risk; *likely* means probable or quite possible.

> She is *apt* to forget her umbrella.
> If you leave your purse on the desk it is *liable* to be stolen.
> It is *likely* that I will be asked to work a little later tonight.

*around, about* *Around* refers to circumference. Do not use *around* when you mean approximately; it is preferable to use *about*.

> They marched *around* City Hall.
> *About* 700 men were there.

*as* 1. Use the form *as . . . as* in affirmative statements; *so . . . as* in negative statements.

> Her typewriter is *as* good *as* mine.
> Her machine is not *so* good *as* yours.

2. Use *as* to express comparision when a verb follows; use *like* as a preposition that takes an object.

Do *as* your competitors *do*.
There is no other product *like* ours on the market.

3. Don't use *as to* as a substitute for simple prepositions, such as *about, among, of,* or *upon*.

He was questioned *about* [not *as to*] his past employment.
She has no idea *of* [not *as to*] the whereabouts of the file.

*beside, besides*   *Beside* means next to or near; *besides* means also or in addition to.

When they stood *beside* each other, you couldn't tell them apart.
You can expect a bonus, *besides* your regular salary.

*better, best*   Use *better* when comparing two objects; *best* when comparing more than two. Do not use *better than* for *more than*.

This is the *better* of the two machines.
This is the *best* machine in the office. (More than two machines)
There are *more than* [not *better than*] five machines in the office.

*between, among*   1. Use *between* when reference is made to only two persons or things; use *among* when reference is made to more than two.

The animosity *between* the two partners is distressingly great.
The friendliness *among* the workers is heartening.

2. Use the object case after *between*.

*Between* you and *me* [never *I*].

3. Do not use *each* or *every* after *between* or *among* when *each* or *every* would have a plural sense.

The cast took curtain calls *between* acts [not *between every act*].
Harmony must prevail *among* the partners [not *among every partner*].

*biannual, biennial, semiannual*   *Biannual* means twice a year; *biennial* means once every two years. *Semiannual* is distinguished from *biannual* in that *semiannual* implies an interval of six months. (*Biannual* can mean at six-month intervals, but not necessarily.)

He is responsible for the *biannual* reports. (Two reports a year.)
Congressmen are elected *biennially*. (Every two years.)
The *semiannual* sale occurs every January and July.

*biweekly, bimonthly*   These words are confusing because they can have more than one meaning. *Biweekly* means occurring every two weeks and also means occurring twice a week; *bimonthly* means occurring every two months and also means occurring twice a month. Avoid this confusion by spelling out what you mean—that is, use *once every two weeks, once every two months, twice a week, twice a month.*

*blame* **Blame on** is a colloquialism and should be avoided in business communication. Use a substitute, such as *attribute to,* or change the construction so you can use *blame for.*

> Wrong: He tries to *blame* his own shortcomings *on* me.
> Right: He tries to *blame* me *for* his own shortcomings.
> Right: He *attributes* his shortcomings *to* me.

*both* 1. *Both* is plural and therefore followed by plural verb and plural pronoun.

> Both John and Mary *are* [not *is*] working late and *they collect* [not *collects*] overtime pay.

2. *Both* should not be used with the words *between, alike, at once, equal, or equally.*

> Wrong: *Both* Ralph and Hal are *equally* guilty. (Omit either *both* or *equally.*)

*bring, take* These words have opposite meanings. To *bring* means to *come* with some person or thing to another place. To *take* means to *go* with some person or thing to another place.

> I will *bring* the papers [with me] when I come to court tomorrow.
> I will *take* the papers to court tomorrow.
> Please *bring* the papers with you tomorrow.
> Please *take* the papers to him tomorrow.

*but that* This construction is incorrect when it follows the word "doubt."

> There is no doubt *that* [not *but that*] she is capable.

*capital, capitol* *Capitol* refers to the building in Washington, D.C., where Congress sits or to the building in which a state legislature meets. If the word has any other meaning, it is spelled *capital.* (The U.S. *Capitol* is always spelled with a *capital* C; a state *capitol* building is spelled with a small *c*).

> Albany is the *capital* of New York. The building in which the State Senate sits is the *capitol.*

*censor, censure* As a noun, *censor* means an overseer of morals and conduct who has the power to forbid objectionable publications; as a verb, it means to act as a *censor*. *Censure*, as a noun, is condemnation or disapproval; as a verb, it means to condemn or disapprove of.

> The *censor* stopped the performance.
> They *censored* our mail.
> One derelict in his duty is subject to *censure*.
> His disregard of rules was *censured* by the authorities.

*common, mutual* Use *common* to mean shared by a group of two or more; use *mutual* to designate that something is reciprocally given and received.

> There was a *common* effort to meet the deadline.
> There was a *common* fear of war.
> There is *mutual* respect between the parties.

*compare to, compare with* Use *compare to* when suggesting general similarities or stating that a similarity exists; use *compare with* when describing specific similarities or differences.

> He *compared* the work *to* a masterpiece. (Suggestion of general similarity.)
> He *compared* the copies *with* the original. (Specific comparison.)

*complement, compliment* To *complement* is to add to so as to make whole; to *compliment* is to praise or flatter.

> Accessories *complement* your wardrobe.
> She was *complimented* on her new dress.

*conscious, aware* *Conscious* tends to emphasize inner realization; *aware* emphasizes perception through the senses.

> He became *conscious* of the reason for his failure.
> He was *aware* of the absence of fresh air in the room.

*consensus* *Consensus* means agreement of opinion; the expression *consensus of opinion* is therefore redundant.

> There was a *consensus* [not *consensus of opinion*] to take the day off and have a long weekend.

*consider* Don't follow *consider* with *as*.

> Will I be *considered* [not *considered as*] a candidate?

*contemptible, contemptuous* *Contemptible* means deserving of being despised; *contemptuous* means scornful.

> Lying to a friend is *contemptible*.
> A renegade is *contemptuous* of law and order.

*continual, continuous*  *Continual* means something occurs frequently or in close succession; *continuous* means that something proceeds steadily without interruption.

> There was a *continual* flow of memos from Mr. Smith's office. (Frequent, but not uninterrupted)
> There was a *continous* flow from the faucet. (Uninterrupted)

*council, counsel, consul*  *Council* refers to a board or assembly; *counsel*, as a noun, refers to advice or to a person giving advice, and *counsel*, as a verb, means to advise or to recommend; *consul* is an emissary looking after his country's interests in a foreign country.

> The *council* meets on Thursday.
> He *counseled* patience for all.
> The British *consul* returned to London for consultations.

*credible, creditable, credulous*  Use *credible* to mean believable; *creditable* to mean praiseworthy; *credulous* to mean believing too easily.

> His alibi is *credible*. (Believable)
> She did a *creditable* job in getting the work done on time. (Praiseworthy)
> He is *credulous* enough to buy the Brooklyn Bridge. (Believes too easily)

*dates from*  When tracing back a date use *dates from*; the expression *dates back to* is incorrect.

> American independence *dates from* [not *dates back to*] 1776.

*different*  Don't use *different* to show separate identity that has already been established. When using *different*, follow with the preposition *from*, not *than*.

> Five secretaries [not five *different* secretaries] asked for a July vacation.
> The machine is *different from* [not *different than*] any I have ever seen.

*disinterested, uninterested*  *Disinterested* means impartial; *uninterested* means a lack of interest.

> A referee must be *disinterested*. (Impartial)
> I'm *uninterested* [have no interest] in sports.

*Disorganized, unorganized*  Use *disorganized* to describe a situation where previously existing order has broken down; use *unorganized* when referring to a situation where no order has existed.

> Office routines were *disorganized* by the presence of painters and carpenters.
> *Unorganized* protesters can turn into rioters.

*effect*  See AFFECT.

*either*  1. *Either* is followed by a singular verb.

> Either of these *is* [not *are*] acceptable.

2. *Either* designates one of two persons or things; *any one* designates one of three or more.

> *Either* of the [two] typewriters. . . .
> *Any one* of the [three] secretaries. . . .

*else*  *Else* should not be combined with *but*.

> It was nothing *but* [not *else but*] a bad cold.

*emigrate, immigrate*  You *emigrate* from a country; you *immigrate* to another country.

> Einstein *emigrated* from Germany.
> Einstein *immigrated to* the United States.

*enormity, enormousness*  *Enormity* is generally associated with wickedness; *enormousness* refers to great size.

> The *enormity* of the crime shocked the community.
> The *enormousness* of the office surprised him.

*equally*  The construction *equally as* is incorrect.

> Management is *as* [not *equally as*] guilty as labor.
> Management is *equally* [not *equally as*] guilty *with* labor.

*every*  *Every* is singular and therefore followed by singular verb and singular pronouns.

> *Every* member *votes* for *his* choice.

*every one, everyone*  Use *everyone* when *everybody* can be substituted in the sentence with no change in meaning. In other uses, *every one* is the correct form. (Both forms are singular, followed by a singular verb and singular pronoun.)

> *Everyone* [everybody] attends regularly.
> *Every one* of you should attend.

*farther, further*  Some authorities state that *farther* should refer to distance, and *further* should refer to time, quantity or degree. This distinction, however, is disappearing, with *further* becoming more widely used and *farther* becoming extinct.

*fewer, less*  Use *fewer* when referring to number; *less* when referring to amount or degree.

> We had *fewer* hurricanes this year.
> *Less* work is needed than usual.

*formally, formerly* *Formally* means in a formal manner; *formerly* means previously.

> He was *formally* initiated into the club.
> *Formerly,* he was president of another company.

*former* *Former* may be used to designate the first of two persons or things; it is incorrect when more than two are involved, in which case *the first* should be used.

> Baker and Smith sailed on the Queen Mary; the *former* sat at the Captain's table.

*generally, usually* Use *generally* when you mean in a general sense or as a whole; use *usually* when you mean in the majority of cases.

> It was *generally* felt that the market would rise.
> The market *usually* rises in July.

*help* Do not follow with *but* when used in the sense of avoid.

> I cannot *help feeling* [not *help but feel*] that you blundered.

*him, he* Forms of the verb *to be* (is, are, was, were) do not take an object but are followed by a predicate nominative. A common error is the use of the objective case of a pronoun (*him*, them, me, us, her) as a predicate nominative.

> It was *he* [not *him*[ who won first prize.

*hope* When *hope* is used in the passive voice, *it* is always the subject. When *it* is omitted, the sentence is poorly constructed.

> The company is approaching what, *it is hoped,* [not *what is hoped*] will be a banner year. (*What* is the subject of *will be* and not of *is hoped.*)

*if, whether* *If* is followed by a supposition or condition; *whether* introduces two or more alternatives. Sometimes only one alternative is mentioned because the other one is implied.

> *If* it rains, I won't go.
> I haven't decided *whether* I will stay or go.
> I don't know *whether* to go [or not].

*imply, infer* To *imply* is to insinuate or hint at; to *infer* is to deduce from or conclude from.

> The speaker *implied* that somebody committed an error.
> The listener *inferred* that the criticism was directed towards him.

*in, into, in to*  Use *in* when denoting position or location; use *into* when denoting motion from without or within. Do not use *into* when it is correct to use *in to*.

> He was *in* the other office.
> Put the chair *in* the other room. (The chair cannot move itself from one place to another.)
> He went *into* the dining room.
> He took her *in to* dinner. (You can't go *into* dinner.)

*ingenious, ingenuous*  *Ingenious* means clever, skillful; *ingenuous* means frank, innocent, trusting.

> He devised an *ingenious* [clever] system to trace phone calls.
> He is very *ingenuous* [trusting] for a man who has been fooled so often.

*latter*  *Latter* may be used to designate the second of two persons or things previously mentioned. It is incorrect to use latter when more than two have been mentioned.

> Between Paris and London, I prefer visiting the *latter*.
> Of all the cities I have visited—Vienna, Paris, London—I prefer London [not *the latter*].

*less*  See FEWER, LESS.

*liable*  See APT, LIABLE, LIKELY.

*like*  1. Don't use *like* in place of *such as*.

> There are many advantages, *such as* [not *like*] efficiency and economy.

For the proper use of *as* and *like*, see AS (2).

*majority, plurality*  In a contest a *majority* is a number constituting more than half the votes cast; *plurality* refers to the excess of votes by the leading candidate over another candidate. This distinction is important when there are more than two candidates.

> Moore received 500 votes; Selig 400; Lanin 200. Moore has a *plurality*, but not a *majority* of the votes. Moore's *plurality* is 100 votes.

*mutual*  See COMMON, MUTUAL.

*myself, me*  Do not use *myself* when the sentence requires the objective case. *Myself* is used to call attention to the subject and to emphasize a noun or pronoun.

> *I* endanger *myself* more than you realize.
> *I myself* have seen him.

*number* Follow *number* with a singular verb when used collectively, and with a plural verb when used distributively.

> The *number* of worthy applicants *increases* each year. (Collective because number is thought of as *total*)
> A *number* of worthy applicants *are* turned away. (Distributive because number is thought of as *many*)

*off* It is incorrect to use *off of* in a sentence.

> He was ushered *off* [not *off of*] the train.

*only* The position of the word *only* in a sentence is determined by the intended meaning of the sentence. As a general rule, *only* should be placed near the word or words that it limits. The following examples will illustrate how the placement of *only* can change the stress and meaning of a sentence.

> I *only* saw him in the theatre yesterday.
> I saw *only him* in the theatre yesterday.
> I saw him *only* in the theatre yesterday.
> I saw him in the theatre *only* yesterday.

*over* It is incorrect to use the expression *over with; with* is superfluous.

> Now that the holiday season is *over* [not *over with*], I can relax.

*people, persons* *People* refers to a group of individuals collectively; *persons* refers to certain specific individuals.

> Many *people* lack the initiative to get ahead.
> Two *persons* in this room will get promotions.

*percent, percentage* *Percent* (or *per cent*) is used to express a specific portion and is always preceded by a number. *Percentage* expresses an indefinite portion; it is not preceded by a number, but must be preceded by an adjective to be clear.

> Eighty *percent* (or *per cent*) of our typewriters are electric.
> A *small percentage* of secretaries are unionized.

*practical, practicable* *Practical* means suited and worthwhile for use or action; *practicable* means feasible or capable of being put into practice.

> The plan is *practicable*, but not *practical*. (It is possible to put the plan into action, but for some reason it is not worth the effort.)

*presently, at present* *Presently* means soon; *at present* means now.

> We will start work *presently* [soon].
> *At present* [now] we are working on it.

*principal, principle*   *Principal,* as a noun, has a variety of meanings; as an adjective, it means chief, main, most important. *Principle* is a noun only and cannot be used as an adjective; it means a fundamental or general truth, a rule.

> He is *principal* of a high school.
> An agent may bind his *principal.*
> That one client is our *principal* source of income.
> The Golden Rule is a *principle* you should try to live up to.

*proposition*   A *proposition* is a proposal. The word cannot be used as a verb.

> Right: He received a business *proposition.* (Noun)
> Wrong: He *was propositioned* (Verb)

*refer*   *Refer* is able to stand on its own without the word *back* attached to it.

> I *referred* [not *referred back*] to the World Almanac.

*regardless*   There is no such word as *irregardless.* Misuse might arise from confusion with *irrespective,* which is a legitimate word.

> The World Series is exciting *regardless* of the teams that play.

*same*   Do not use *same* to stand for something previously stated. (This usage was common in business letters many years ago.)

> We have received your order for stationery, and will ship *it* [not *same*] today.

*seldom*   Do not attach *ever* to the word *seldom;* it is a colloquialism that should be avoided in business correspondence. It is proper to use *seldom* by itself, or *hardly ever.*

> I *seldom* [or *hardly ever,* but not *seldom ever*] see a foreign movie.

*somebody, someone*   These words are singular, and any verb or pronoun that follows is also singular. Write *someone* as one word when it is equivalent to *somebody;* otherwise it is two words.

> I heard that only *someone* [or *somebody*] at the top of his [not *their*] class *is* [not *are*] being considered for the appointment.
> If *some one* person was appointed, the announcement of it will be today.

*state, assert, say*   These three words are sometimes used interchangeably in spite of the different shades of meaning. *Say* is the least formal of these words and the most generally used. *State* has a ring of formality and means to set forth in detail. *Assert* means to affirm or maintain a claim to something.

> She *said* she was going to the party.
> He *stated* his objections forthrightly.
> He *asserted* that he owns the property.

*surround*  Use *surround* with *by*, not *with*, when *surrounded* has the passive voice.

> The building *is surrounded by* [not *with*] parks.

*that, which*   Use *that* to introduce a defining or restrictive clause; use *which* to introduce a thought that is additional or parenthetical.

> The park that starts at Fifty-ninth Street is Central Park.
> Central Park, *which* is in the middle of Manhattan, has a fine zoo.

*toward, towards*  Either *toward* or *towards* is correct. *Towards* is the prevailing form in British usage.

*transpire, happen*   *Transpire* means to leak out or become known; its use by some as a synonym for *happen* or *take place* is not approved by most authorities.

> The amount of his salary was allowed to *transpire* [leak out].
> Salary negotiations *took place* [not *transpired*] at union headquarters.

*try*  Follow with an infinitive, rather than with *and* a verb.

> Try *to see* [not *try and see*] me tomorrow.

*uninterested*  See DISINTERESTED, UNINTERESTED.

*unorganized*  See DISORGANIZED, UNORGANIZED.

*us, we*   *Us* is the objective case of *we*, and is sometimes misued for *we*.

> They are not as generous as *we* [are generous] when office collections come around.

*usually*  See GENERALLY, USUALLY.

*very, very much*  Use *very* when it precedes a passive participle that has the force of an adjective. Use *very much* (or *much*) when it precedes a passive participle that has strong verbal force. When it is proper to use *much* as a modifier, it is also proper to use *very much*; if you cannot use *much*, the correct modifier is *very*.

> A *very delighted* [used as an adjective] crowd saw the home team's victory.
> A *very underrated* [adjective] player was the hero.
> I was *very much* [or *much*] *delighted* [used as a verb] that the home team won.
> I was *very much* [or *much*] *pleased* [verb] at the outcome.

*Note:* There are passive participles that are used as verbs but have lost their verbal force by common usage.

> I am *very tired* [not *very much tired*] of hearing about it.
> He is *very* celebrated [not *very much celebrated*].

*we*  See US, WE.

*when, where* 1. *When* should introduce an adverbial clause of time; *where,* an adverbial clause of place.

> *When* [not *where*] there is default in a mortgage payment there may be a foreclosure.
> *Where* the new office is located is a mystery to me.

2. Do not use *when* or *where* when defining a word.

> Wrong: No-par stock is *where* [or *when*] stock has no designated or nominal value in money.
> Right: No-par stock is stock without any designated or nominal value in money.

*whether* See IF, WHETHER.

*which* See THAT, WHICH.

*while* When *while* is used as a conjunction it means as long as or during the time that. Do not substitute *while* for *although, whereas,* or *but.*

> *While* [during the time that] Mr. Bacon was on vacation, Mr. Moss was in charge.
> *Although* [not *while*] the stock has arrived, I cannot distribute it.
> *Whereas* [not *while*] most employees take a summer vacation, some take theirs in the winter.

*who, whom* *Who* is in the nominative case and is principally used as the subject of a sentence or clause. *Whom* is in the objective case and is principally used as an object of a preposition or as an object of a verb.

> He is the man *who* does the hiring. (Subject of the verb *does*)
> *Who* has authority here? (Subject of the verb *has*)
> Dr. Brown is the person *who* I believe is best qualified to give an opinion. (Subject of the verb *is qualified. I believe* is parenthetical and does not change the case of *who.*)
> She is the person to *whom* I report in the morning. (Object of preposition *to*)
> *Whom* do you wish to see? (Object of the verb *see*)
> Mrs. Shilling is the only one *whom* I know well. (Object of the verb *know*)

---

## A REVIEW OF THE PARTS OF SPEECH

The following definitions of the parts of speech and examples of their usage along with some rules of grammar will help you understand sentence construction and, therefore, to write better letters and to speak with more effectiveness.

### 12.32. Adjective

An adjective is a word that is used to modify a noun or pronoun. The degree of an adjective is usually changed by adding *-er* or *-est*. However, if the adjective is a long word or if the suffix makes it sound awkward, the adjective is generally compared by the use of *more* or *most*.

short, shorter, shortest
awkward, more awkward, most awkward

### 12.33. Adverb

An adverb is used to modify a verb, an adjective or another adverb. Most adverbs end in *-ly*, although an adverb can also add *-er* or *-est* and be preceded by *more* or *most, less* or *least*.

It is a common grammatical error to confuse the proper uses of adverbs and adjectives. Remember that an adjective describes the subject (noun), and that an adverb describes the action (verb).

I was *really* [not *real*] saddened by what happened. (The adverb *really* is the correct modifier of the verb *saddened*. The adjective form *real* cannot modify a verb.)

Qualify an adjective with an adverb rather than another adjective.

How much abuse can an *ordinarily* [not *ordinary*] *sensitive* man take?

### 12.34. Article

Articles are the words *a, an,* and *the* used before nouns to limit their application. Repeat the article when you are referring to two separate persons or objects.

She has a black and a white Chevrolet (Two cars)
She has a black and white Chevrolet. (One car)

### 12.35. Conjunction

A conjunction is a connective word that joins together sentences, clauses, phrases, or words. Conjunctions are classifiable as *coordinating* (*and, but, or, nor, for, yet, so*) or *subordinating* (*when, though, as, if, since, where*).

## 12.36. Gerund

A gerund is derived from a verb and used as a noun. It always ends in *-ing*.

1. Use the possessive form of nouns, pronouns, or prepositions before gerunds.

> I had not heard of the *company's* [not *company*] *buying* the building.

2. The gerund is identical in form with the present participle (see *participle*) and is often confused with it. The use of the gerund with a possessive may give the sentence a meaning entirely different from that given by the use of a participle.

> I do not approve of the *girl's reading* [I do not approve of the reading] the book. (Gerund)
> I do not approve of the *girl reading* [I do not approve of the girl] the book. (Participle)

3. If a verb has a noun form, use that instead of the gerund.

> *Poor:* Accepting the position was an ill-advised move.
> *Better:* Acceptance of the position was an ill-advised move.

## 12.37. Infinitive

An infinitive is the simple verb form usually preceded by *to* (*to be, to dance*, and so on).

*Tense.* Use the present infinitive, not the perfect, after past conditions, such as *should have liked, would have been possible.*

> It would have been possible *to reduce* [not *to have reduced*] the cost at that time.

*Split infinitives.* The infinitive sign *to* and the verb naturally go together; it is best not to split the infinitive by placing a word or words between *to* and the verb, but split infinitives are preferable to ambiguity or awkwardness.

> *Wrong:* He told us *to* accurately *alphabetize* the index.
> *Right:* He told us *to alphabetize* the index accurately.
> *Awkward:* Efforts *to unite* firmly bolters from the party were a failure.
> *Improved:* Efforts *to* firmly *unite* bolters from the party were a failure.

### 12.38. Modifier Placement

The construction of a sentence gives it its meaning. If you misplace even one word you can change the whole sense of a sentence. Here are some common errors in the placement of modifiers—errors that should not crop up in your writing.

*Misplaced modifiers.* Modifiers that apply to specific expressions in a sentence are in fixed positions. They are usually placed immediately before or after the expressions they modify. If you change the fixed position of the modifier you change the meaning of the sentence.

> *Wrong:* I saw the new file cabinet *walking down the stairs.*
> (This phrase modifies *I* and should be immediately preceding it or following it. The file cabinet was not walking down the stairs.)
> *Right: Walking down the stairs*, I saw the new file cabinet.

*Ambiguous or "squinting" modifiers.* When a modifier is placed between two words, and can logically modify either one, the meaning of the sentence is obscured. A modifier so placed is called a "squinting" modifier.

> *Ambiguous:* That man I see frequently walks to the station.
> (Does frequently refer to seeing, or to walking?)
> *Clear:* That man I frequently see walks to the station.
> *Clear:* That man I see walks to the station frequently.

### 12.39. Noun

A noun is the name of a person, place, or thing. It can be the subject of a sentence (nominative case), the object of a verb or of a preposition (objective case), or it can show possession (possessive case). The possessive is formed by adding *'s*.

My *employer's hobby* helps take his *mind* off his *worries.*

*Employer's* is a noun showing possession; *hobby* is a noun and the subject of the sentence; *mind* is a noun and the object of the verb; *worries* is a noun and the object of a preposition.

*Collective nouns.* A collective noun (committee, Senate, membership, and the like) is treated as singular if you are referring to the group as such, plural if you are referring to the individual persons or things of which the group is composed. The number of the verb and pronoun depends on whether the collective noun is used in the singular or plural. A common error in the use of collective nouns is the failure to abide by the choice of number once it has been made.

> The council *meets* twice a week to discuss *its* town's problems. *It* meets on Tuesday and Thursday evenings. (Meaning the council as a unit.)
> The council *are* disagreeing about how *they* will raise money. (Meaning that the members disagree among themselves.)

*Predicate nouns.* A noun or pronoun following a verb and representing the subject is always in the nominative case.

> It is *she* (not *her*) who made the decision.

## 12.40. Participle

A participle is formed from a verb but is used as a modifier in a sentence. The active participle always ends in -*ing*. It cannot be used as a noun or pronoun but must modify either; if it does not, it is a "dangling" participle. (See also *gerund*.)

> *Wrong:* When *writing* this book, an attempt was made to organize the material to best advantage. (What does *writing* modify?)
> *Right:* When *writing* this book, the *author* attempted to organize the material to best advantage.

## 12.41. Preposition

A preposition shows the relationship between a noun or pronoun and other parts of the sentence. Some of the more familiar prepositions are *above, after, before, during, for, in, off, through, to, under, upon, with, without.*

Although authorities discourage the placement of a preposition at the end of a sentence, they do not forbid it. It is better to end a sentence with a preposition than to use an awkward, stiff construction.

> *Right:* She is the woman whose house I went *to.*
> *Awkward:* She is the woman *to* whose house I went.

### 12.42. Pronoun

A pronoun is a word that is used instead of a noun. There are two types of pronouns: personal (*I, me, we, us, you, he, she, it,* and *they*) and relative (*who, whom, which,* and *that*). Personal pronouns may be subjects, predicate nouns, or objects; relative pronouns are used to refer to persons, animals, or things.

*Agreement of pronoun with alternative subjects.* When alternative subjects, usually separated by *or* or *nor*, are logically singular they require a singular pronoun. When alternative subjects differ in person and number the pronoun takes its number from the part of the subject nearest the pronoun.

Neither the manager nor his assistant submitted *his* [not *their*] files.

Neither the manager nor his assistants submitted *their* [not *his*] files.

*Agreement of indefinite pronouns.* Indefinite pronouns (*everybody, anybody, anything,* and the like) are always singular and are followed by singular verbs and singular pronouns.

Everyone *was* [not *were*] trying to advance *his* [not *their*] cause.

*Ambiguous reference of pronouns.* Make sure that a pronoun clearly refers to the noun for which it stands.

The assistant personnel manager hired a new employee even though *he* is not a high school graduate. (It is not clear whether *he* refers to the assistant personnel manager or the new employee.)

The assistant personnel manager hired a man who is not a high school graduate. (This is just one of the ways you can clear up the ambiguity of the previous sentence.)

### 12.43. Sentence Structure

Ideas used exactly the same way in a sentence (parallel ideas) require similar kinds of words or structures. They are usually joined by one of the coordinating conjunctions (*and, or, nor, but* or *for*). Following are some common errors in the use of parallelism.

*Compounds.* The words used in parallel structure must be the same parts of speech.

> *Wrong:* Today a secretary has to be *attractive* in appearance and a high *intelligence.* (*Attractive* is an adjective and *intelligence* is a noun.)
> *Right:* Today a secretary must be *attractive* and *intelligent.*

*Inconsistency in series.* When more than two items occupy parallel positions, those late in the series are sometimes carelessly given inconsistent forms.

> *Wrong:* She is pretty, intelligent, generous, and every characteristic of a likable person.
> *Right:* She is pretty, intelligent, generous, and likable.

*Faulty comparisons.* Comparisons require parallel forms and word order. They make sense only if the expressions in parallel positions stand for comparable ideas.

> *Wrong:* The secretary felt that her *job* was harder than a *teacher.* (*Job* and *teacher* are not comparable.)
> *Right:* The secretary felt that her job was harder than that of a teacher.

*False parallelism.* Frequently expressions that should not be parallel are carelessly put into parallel order.

> *Wrong:* The secretaries are in the office and typing at their desks.
> *Right:* The secretaries are in the office typing at their desks.

## 12.44. Verb

A verb is used to show action or state of being. There are two types of verbs: transitive and intransitive. A *transitive verb* is an action verb that takes a direct object. An *intransitive verb* has no object; if it denotes action, the action is limited to the subject.

She *cleaned* her desk. (Transitive verb)
She *lives* in the suburbs. (Intransitive verb)

*Sequence of tenses.* The time relation in a sentence with two or more verbs is indicated by the tense of the verbs; you can show a change in time by using verbs of different tense. The sequence of tenses sometimes causes trouble. The following explanations and examples will help you use the proper tenses.

1. If you are writing in the *past* tense and wish to refer to a preceding event, you must use the *past perfect* tense.

He sold the stock he *had bought* [not *bought*] in April.

2. After a *future* tense in a main clause, use the *present* tense in a dependent clause.

I *will go* home as soon as my replacement *arrives*.

3. A fact that is permanently true is usually put in the *present* tense, even when the main verb is in the *past* tense.

She was taught that crime *does* [not *did*] not pay.

4. The *perfect participle* expresses an action that has been completed at the time indicated by the main verb. A common error is the use of the *present participle* instead of the *perfect*.

He completed the report on schedule, *having worked* [not *working*] unusually long hours.
He will complete the report on schedule, *having worked* [not *working*] unusually long hours.

*The subjunctive mood.* The subjunctive mood of a verb expresses an idea as desirable, possible, or conditional. Although the trend is away from the subjunctive mood, it is necessary in some cases.

1. Use the subjunctive to express a condition contrary to fact. Contrary-to-fact statements are generally introduced by *wish* or *if*. (Not all clauses introduced by *if* express contrary-to-fact conditions; some *if* clauses merely express a condition or a doubt. In these cases the subjunctive is not generally used.)

If I *were* [subjunctive, not the indicative *was*] the boss, I should change things around here. (But I am not the boss.)
I wish he *were* [subjunctive, not the indicative *was*] in a position of authority. (But he is not in such a position.)
If his secretary *was* there, they did not see her. (This is an *if* clause that takes the indicative *was*; it is possible his secretary was there.)

2. Use the subjunctive in clauses introduced by *that* when the main verb expresses necessity, demand, or recommendation.

He demanded that she *resign* [subjunctive, not the indicative *resigns*] from her present position.

3. Use the subjunctive in formal writing to express a motion, resolution, or ruling.

The arbitrator ruled that the injured party *receive* [subjunctive] compensation.

4. Use the past subjunctive to express a supposition or condition in clauses introduced by *as if, as though.*

It appears as though a page *were* [subjunctive, not the indicative *was*] torn out.

*Agreement of subject and verb.* The subject and verb of a sentence should always agree in person and number. The following rules will help you with some of the more troublesome constructions.

1. *Compound subject.* Two or more subjects in the third person joined by *and* take a plural verb. The only exception to this rule is when both nouns refer to the same person or thing.

My mother and father *are* away on vacation.
My good friend and teacher *is* retiring this year. (The friend and teacher is the same person.)

2. *Alternative subjects.* If alternative subjects differ in person and number, the verb takes its number from the part of the subject nearest the verb. Alternative subjects are usually separated by *or* or *nor.*

Neither Jim nor his supervisors *were* [not *was*] aware of the change in plans.

3. *Noun intervening between subject and verb.* Even when separated from the subject by another noun, the verb must agree with the subject.

The president, accompanied by assistants and security guards, *is* [not *are*] in the ballroom.

4. *Subordinate clauses.* A verb in a subordinate clause takes its number from the subject of the clause, not from the subject of the sentence.

My office is one of those that *are* [not *is*] air-conditioned.

5. *Subject following the verb.* When the subject follows the verb, the verb takes the same number as the subject.

Following the dinner *are* [not *is*] the speeches. (*Speeches* is the subject.)

6. *Subject and predicate nominative differing in number.* A *predicate nominative* is a noun or pronoun that follows an intransitive verb and elaborates or modifies the idea expressed in the verb (predicate). As its name implies, a predicate nominative is always in the nominative case. When the subject and predicate nominative differ in number, the verb must agree with the subject.

> The reason for falling behind in the work *is* [not *are*] the many vacations.
> Additional secretaries *are* [not *is*] the answer to our problems.

7. *Subjects that are plural in form but singular in meaning.* Subjects such as *athletics*, *mathematics*, and the like take a singular verb when used strictly as the name of a science or study. However, they take a plural verb when denoting qualities, usually preceded by *his, the, such.*

> Politics *is* forever interesting.
> Such politics always *lose* an election.

8. *Collective nouns.* (See Section 12.39.)

9. *The active and passive voice. Voice* is the quality of a transitive verb that shows when the subject is acting (active voice) or being acted upon (passive voice). The passive voice is less emphatic than the active, and for that reason careful writers avoid its use whenever possible. In business writing, especially, you should use the active. Do not mix voices by shifting from active to passive.

> She *was fired* by her supervisor. (Passive voice, not emphatic.)
> Her supervisor *fired* her. (Active voice, emphatic.)
> The jury *deliberated* for forty-eight hours before the judge *discharged* them [not *before they "were discharged"*].

# 13

# *PREPARING MATERIAL*
# *FOR PUBLICATION*

## Typing the Manuscript

If the manager prepares articles, reports, or other material for publication, it will be your responsibility to type the manuscript. If you observe certain basic rules when typing the manuscript, you can save time, lessen the chances of error, and sometimes reduce typesetting and printing costs.

### 13.1. Typing the Text

Observe the following rules when typing a manuscript.

1. Type all copy on white bond, preferably 8½ by 11 inches.
2. Type on one side of the paper only.
3. Use double spacing.
4. Have a 1¼-inch margin on all four sides of the paper; try to keep the right-hand margin as even as possible.
5. Indent paragraphs at least five spaces.

6. When material is to be copied verbatim from a published source, you may paste the material itself on your white manuscript paper; this saves you the trouble of typing it. Be sure, however, to read the source material carefully so you can correct any typographical errors in it. If you are going to make a lot of changes and the corrected copy will look messy, forget this shortcut and copy it with your typewriter. (Keep in mind that you need permission from the copyright holder to use material verbatim from a printed source.)

7. Make two carbon copies. Always hold on to one of them for reference.

8. Set off quoted material from the rest of the text (a) by single spacing the extracted material or (b) by indenting it from the left margin or from both the left and right margins. A quote within a quote should be indented even further.

9. When typing *footnotes*, double-space and place them at the bottom of the text page. When there are numerous footnotes throughout the text, use superior numbers and number from one on throughout *each* chapter. If there are only a few footnotes, use asterisk and dagger symbols instead of superior numbers. (See 7.17, Footnotes.)

10. Cross-references to material appearing in other parts of the manuscript should read "see page 000," but be sure to put in the correct reference numbers when you receive the final page proofs.

11. Number the manuscript consecutively in the upper right-hand corner, beginning with the first page of text and continuing through the last page of the appendix, including all table pages. Number separately the front-matter pages in small Roman numerals—i, ii, and so on. If you happen to add or remove pages after the manuscript is numbered, you must make the proper indications. For example, if you are adding two pages following page 7, mark them 7a and 7b, and on page 7 make a notation, "Pages 7a and 7b to follow." If you remove two pages following page 7, change the number of page 7 to "7-9" to indicate the deletion.

See also 7.17, Typing the Report, for further instructions on spacing and typing subheads, footnotes, and bibliographies.

## 13.2. Setting Up Tables

When typing a *table*, single-space on a separate page. If, however, your manuscript contains many tables, you may type two or three to a page. Type every table with enough space between columns and around headings to indicate the divisions clearly. Use symbols (such as asterisks) or superior letters (numbers raised above the line of type) to mark footnotes to a table, and place these notes directly beneath the table so that they will not be confused with ordinary footnotes. In the text, refer to *each* table by number—for example, "see Table 6." Do not say "see the table above," for when the printer makes up the type pages he may have to place the table below the reference.

Head each table with a number and title, for example:

Table 4
Sales Volume by Class of Merchandise, 1978

Use only horizontal rules—one after the table head, one after the row of column heads, and one separating the table body from its footnotes. Center column heads above the columns in upper and lowercase. Type stub entries (the items in the first left-hand column) all flush left, each with an initial capital only.

## 13.3. Typing Preliminary and Supplementary Pages

Preliminary pages include the title page and the table of contents (see section 7.17 for typing instructions). Other front-matter material includes the copyright page, dedication page, list of illustrations, preface, and foreword.

*Copyright* details (e.g., Copyright © 1978 by Prentice-Hall, Inc.) may be typed at the bottom of the title page or at the bottom of the following page. (Contact the Register of Copyrights, Library of Congress, Washington, D.C. 20599, for details on securing copyright.) The *dedication* is typed, centered, about a third of the way down on a separate page. The *list of illustrations* should include the table numbers flush left, each followed by the table title, for example:

Table 4   Sales Volume by Class of Merchandise, 1978

The *preface, foreword,* and *introduction* should be typed the same as a text page.

Supplementary pages include bibliography, appendix, and an index. Each should be preceded by an introductory page with the title centered about a third of the way down:

Appendix A
Project Methodology

The body of the *appendix* should be typed the same as a text page. An *index* should be typed with entries flush left, double spaced in single columns. subentries should be indented two spaces. See section 7.17 for details on typing *bibliographies*.

---

## CHECKING MANUSCRIPT AND PROOF

Proofreading is one of the most important stages of production. The secretary must know how to check manuscript copy, galleys, and page proofs, and how to make corrections on each one. (See also 14.7, Proofreading Guides.)

### 13.4. Checking the Manuscript

There are no shortcuts for checking manuscript. The only effective method for finding and correcting errors is to read the manuscript several times very carefully. Do not wait until you get the proof to start checking; late changes are troublesome to the printer and increase your printing costs.

1. Check for any typing errors or omissions.
2. Make sure that capitalization, spelling, and abbreviations are consistent throughout the manuscript.
3. Be sure that all pages are there, in proper sequence, and that all inserts have been numbered and their position noted in the text.
4. See that the table of contents reflects any changes or additions made after it was drawn up.
5. Check to make sure that all necessary permissions for quoted matter or for illustrations have been obtained.
6. Make *short corrections* by crossing out the incorrect word and writing the correction above it, not in the margin.

7. Make *lengthy corrections* on a separate, full-sized sheet and insert it in the manuscript immediately following the page corrected. At the point of correction make a note to "Insert page ____ here"; mark the inserted page, "Insert on page ____ where indicated."

8. Circle anything on the page that you do not want the printer to set in type, such as your instructions to the printer.

9. To start a new paragraph, insert a paragraph sign at the point desired. To run one paragraph into another, draw a line from the conclusion of the first paragraph to the first word of the following paragraph.

10. To separate two words typed as one, draw a vertical line between them.

11. To retain material crossed out, insert a row of dots beneath it and circle the word "stet" in the margin. Be certain the copy is legible; otherwise retype it as an insert (see no. 7 above).

## 13.5. Correcting Galley Proofs

If you are working directly with a printer, he will return galley proofs, with your manuscript, for you to correct. A galley proof contains no illustrations, is not broken up into pages, and contains no running heads (the kind of heading that appears at the top of each page in some books). Printers and typesetters often supply three copies of galleys: one for your files, one to return with your corrections, and one to use in cutting apart and pasting up a dummy of the final publication.

You must read galley proofs carefully and compare them with the original manuscript, make all corrections, and return them to the printer. When correcting galleys, use *proofreaders' marks* (see section 14.7). The printer will then send you corrected proofs to be checked; you will mark them "O.K." when you are satisfied that the proofs are perfect.

When you read galley and page proofs, it is your last chance to make corrections. Changes that are departures from the original manuscript sent to the printer are called *author's alterations*. These corrections are charged for, so the problem is to make such changes as economically as possible and only if necessary. It is less expensive to make a correction on a galley than on a page proof.

In addition to checking the galleys for accuracy of spelling, punctuation, and so on, you should examine the type to be certain the desired typeface has been used in all instances. Check to see if underscored copy has been set in italics; if copy marked with a wavy line beneath it has been set in boldface; and if subheads and titles have been set in the correct typeface and type size. You should also determine if design instructions have been followed: if columns are the correct width, and if spacing and paragraph indention are correct.

### 13.6. Correcting Page Proofs

The printer makes corrections indicated on the galleys and breaks the type up into page lengths. This involves grouping the footnotes where they belong; inserting the illustrations, with appropriate credit and legend lines, as near where you have indicated they should go as is physically possible; adding any hand-set type, such as chapter titles, that may not have been set at the galley-proof stage; and inserting running heads (page headings) and folios (page numbers).

In reading page proofs, first make sure that all corrections indicated on the galleys have been made. Verify the correct position of all tables and illustrations and read all caption and credit lines carefully. Check the page number, and the running head if there is one, on each page. Check to see that facing pages are of equal length. When you have done all this, give the proofs a final critical reading for any possible inaccuracies.

When you make changes on any proof—galley or page—you save money if you can keep the number of characters in the line affected the same after the change as it was before it. If you must make a substantial correction, try to do it at the end of a paragraph and, in page proofs, at the end of a chapter. When the printer makes a correction in a page proof he must disturb the carefully balanced page makeup. A seemingly minor change in a page proof may affect all the pages that follow and result in a staggering bill for alterations.

———————————◆·◀◆▶·◆———————————

## THE STAGES OF PRODUCTION

The secretary is frequently involved in all stages of production, from the preparation of original manuscript to the printing and binding of finished copies. In addition to typing and assembling the manuscript, which includes collecting and arranging photographs and other illustrations, the secretary must be prepared to coordinate and supervise the typesetting, printing, and binding processes.

### 13.7. Copy preparation

It is important to prepare material for typesetting and printing with great care. The penalty for carelessness at this early stage could be a finished product that is not usable—or one that could be corrected only at great expense.

After copy has been written it must be read for accuracy, consistency, clarity, and completeness. If *copyediting* is your responsibility, you will need to correct and polish the copy as necessary. Once this basic work has been completed the copy must be prepared for the typesetter or printer. A final draft must be typed (see 13.1-13.3, Typing the Manuscript) and manuscript copy must then be checked (see 13.4).

If the typed copy is prepared directly for printing, without being typeset, it must be *camera-ready*—in perfect condition for exact duplication. This means corrections must be made so they will not show when photographed, and the material must be typed precisely as you wish it to appear when printed. Instructions to the printer should be written and circled in the margins with a light blue pencil (which will not reproduce).

If you are preparing copy for typesetting before printing, you can mark grammatical corrections and instructions directly on the manuscript (see 13.4), for example, underscoring words to be set in italic (see 14.7). If you wish copy to be typeset in a certain typeface and type size, in columns of a certain width, the manuscript must also be *typemarked* (see 13.8).

### 13.8. Design and Typemarking

Design specifications are usually prepared by a professional artist or designer. If, however, no specifications have been provided, and you are reluctant to leave the matter entirely to the discretion of the typesetter, the manuscript must be typemarked in advance to show your choice of typefaces, type sizes, column widths, spacing, and so on.

*Design* is the shape, appearance, and arrangement of copy and illustrations on a page. One of the best ways to select a design is to look at other publications and borrow ideas from one that seems pleasing and appropriate for your copy. The typesetter will be able to help you determine the right size of type for the text, titles, subheads, tables, and footnotes. Subheads, for example, could be set in a larger size than the text, and might be in a boldface or italic typeface. Indicate words or headings you want emphasized as follows:

1. Underline all words or sections to be set in *italics*.
2. Draw a wavy line under the words or sentences to be set in boldface, or type them in red.
3. Underline with two straight lines all words to be printed in SMALL CAPITALS.
4. Underline with three straight lines all words to be printed in CAPITALS.

*Leading* (the amount of space between lines) will depend upon how much copy you want on a page and how open you want the copy to appear. The dimensions of the finished page and the amount of white space you want for margins will influence your choice of page or column width.

Once all these matters have been settled, and the typesetter has confirmed that he is capable of providing what you want, you must mark sizes, faces, and other specifications on the manuscript, circling such instructions in the margins.

### 13.9. Composition

After a manuscript has been written, edited, typed, checked, and typemarked, it is ready for typesetting (frequently referred to as *composition*). Different types of composition are available, depending upon the method employed, for example, *phototypesetting* (keyboard typesetting that produces a photographic result). Type is most often referred to by the general terms "hot type" and "cold type."

*Hot type* refers to composition by use of hot metal, for example, linotype and monotype. Operators of these machines work at a keyboard similar to that of a typewriter and cast each line of type as a solid metal line. The quality of hot-type composition is often higher than that of cold type.

*Cold type* refers to composition that does not use hot metal, for example, IBM typewriter and Vari-Typer. Phototypesetting machines such as Photon are often included in this category. Speed and economy are principal considerations in the selection of cold type.

When you are ready to order type, it may be wise to compare quality and costs by contacting several compositors and asking for samples of their work along with a quote on setting your material.

See 13.5, Correcting Galley Proofs, and 13.6, Correcting Page Proofs, for instructions on proofreading and correcting galleys and page proofs.

## 13.10. Printing and Binding

You may have your copy typeset and printed by the same firm. At any rate, once the copy is set and galleys and/or pages have been prepared and corrected to your satisfaction, the material is ready for printing. Since it has been typeset, you will be considering offset or letterpress printing (see 4.9 for a description of short-run and low-quality reproduction by copying and duplicating processes).

*Photo-offset lithography* is an economical printing process that uses a plate prepared by a photographic process. Although it is more economical than letterpress when many illustrations are involved, the reproduction of photographs is sometimes inferior.

*Letterpress*, the oldest printing process, uses the relief principle with type and photographs on raised surfaces (*cuts*). The letterpress process is versatile in that it can be used for low-quality work (e.g., newspapers) or very high-quality work (e.g., photographic books).

Before the material is printed, a press proof of the finished product will be presented for you to check things such as the proper order of pages and the position of illustrations. You should take this opportunity to examine each page closely, check running heads, figure captions, folios, length of facing pages, and so on. Typographic errors presumably were caught in the earlier galley and page-proof stages (see 13.5 and 13.6). It would be costly to make type corrections at this point.

After you have approved the press proof, the publication will be printed, collated, bound, and trimmed. Small publications such as magazines are often *saddle-stitched* (two staples at the folded edge). Books commonly use *perfect binding* (with flexible glue on the spine) or they may be *Smyth-sewed* (sewed along the spine so the book will open flat).

Usually the printer handles binding as part of the printing job, although he may not have an in-house bindery, in which case he will subcontract the work to an outside firm. In the beginning, when you request a quote on the proposed job before work begins, be certain that the price you receive covers *all* the stages of production that you will require.

## 13.11. Copyright Procedure

A copyright is a form of protection given by law to the authors of literary, dramatic, musical, artistic, and other intellectual works.

To obtain a copyright, imprint the word "Copyright" and the date (year) of publication and the name of the copyright proprietor on the title page or the page immediately following it (e.g., Copyright © 1978, Prentice-Hall, Inc.). Promptly upon publication, as soon as the first copies are ready for distribution, send two copies of the work, accompanied by application for copyright and the statutory fee to the Registrar of Copyrights, Library of Congress, Washington, D.C. 20599. Of course, if the manager is submitting an article to an outside magazine or other publication, the publisher will take care of the copyright procedures, and will also own the copyright. Complete instructions and applications forms are available free of charge from the Register of Copyrights. Remember to request enough forms so you can make at least one carbon copy for your files.

# 14

# LETTERS, CHARTS, AND TABLES FOR THE SECRETARY

## 14.1. Letter Styles

## Full-Block Style

---

PARKER PUBLISHING COMPANY, INC.

*Executive Offices*

West Nyack, N.Y. 10994                                       914 · EL 8-8800


April 16, 19--


Mrs. Marjorie Hamlett
Training Director
Goodwin Communications
3518 Fremont Avenue
Minneapolis  MN  55405

Dear Mrs. Hamlett:

You have asked me to send you examples of letter styles being used
in offices throughout the country.

This letter is an example of the full block style of letter, which
has been adopted as a standard at Parker Publishing.  We have reproduced it in our Employee Manual so that everyone will be familiar
with the form and the instructions for its use.

Since Parker Publishing is a leading exponent of modern business
methods, we naturally use the most efficient letter form.  This style
saves time and energy.

As you see, there are no indentations.  Everything, including the
date and the complimentary close, begins at the extreme left.  This
uniformity eliminates several mechanical operations in typing letters.

Our dictaphone typists always use this form unless the dictator
instructs otherwise.  The dictator is at liberty to alter the form
if a change is desirable for business reasons.

Since the dictator's name is typed in the signature, it is not
considered necessary to include his initials in the identification
line.

Sincerely yours,


Constance Gibson
Correspondence Manager

dl

## Block Style

---

### PARKER PUBLISHING COMPANY, INC.
#### *Executive Offices*

West Nyack, N.Y. 10994                                    914 · EL 8-8800

April 16, 19--

Your reference 10:4:3

Mrs. Marjorie Hamlett
Training Director
Goodwin Communications
3518 Fremont Avenue
Minneapolis  MN  55405

Dear Mrs. Hamlett:

Probably more business concerns use the block style than any other,
because its marginal uniformity saves time for the typist.  Many
companies are adopting the full block style, however, because it
saves even more time than the block.  This letter is an example of
the block style.

As you can see, the inside address is blocked and paragraph beginnings are aligned with the left margin, as they are in the full
block form.  Open punctuation is used in the address.

The date and reference lines are flush with the right margin.  The
dateline is two spaces below the letterhead, and the reference line
is two spaces below the dateline.  The complimentary close begins
slightly to the right of the center of the page.  Both lines of the
signature are aligned with the complimentary close.

I do not advocate including the dictator's initials in the identification line, because his name is typed in the signature.

Sincerely yours,

Constance Gibson
Correspondence Manager

dl

## Semiblock Style

P A R K E R   P U B L I S H I N G   C O M P A N Y ,   I N C .

*Executive Offices*

West Nyack, N.Y. 10994                                      914 · EL 8-8800

April 16, 19--

Mrs. Marjorie Hamlett
Training Director
Goodwin Communications
3518 Fremont Avenue
Minneapolis MN  55405

Dear Mrs. Hamlett:

    Most companies have a definite preference as to letter
style.  Some leading business corporations prefer that all letters
be typed in semiblock style.  This style combines an attractive
appearance with utility.  Many private secretaries, who are usually
concerned with mass production of correspondence, favor it.

    This style differs from the block in only one respect--
the first line of each paragraph is indented five or ten spaces.
In this example the paragraphs are indented ten spaces.  As in all
letters, there is a double space between paragraphs.

    The dateline is flush with the right margin, two or four
spaces below the letterhead.  The complimentary close begins slightly
to the right of the center of the page.  All lines of the signature
are aligned with the complimentary close.  Open punctuation is used
in the address.

    No identification line is used in this example.  Because
the dictator's name is typed in the signature, her initials are not
necessary.

Sincerely yours,

Constance Gibson
Correspondence Manager

dl

## Official Style

PARKER PUBLISHING COMPANY, INC.

*Executive Offices*

West Nyack, N.Y. 10994                                        914 · EL 8-8800

April 16, 19--

Dear Mrs. Hamlett:

Every correspondence manual should include a sample of the official style. It is used in many personal letters written by executives and professional persons, and looks unusually well on the executive-size letterhead.

The structural parts of the letter differ from the standard arrangement only in the position of the inside address. The salutation is placed two to five spaces below the dateline, depending upon the length of the letter. It establishes the left margin of the letter. The inside address is written block form, flush with the left margin, from two to five spaces below the final line of the signature. Open punctuation is used in the address.

The identification line, if used, should be placed two spaces below the last line of the address, and the enclosure mark two spaces below that. Because the dictator's name is typed in the signature, it is not necessary for the letter to carry an identification line. The typist's initials may be on the carbon of the letter, but not the original.

Sincerely yours,

Constance Gibson
Correspondence Manager

Mrs. Marjorie Hamlett
Training Director
Goodwin Communications
3518 Fremont Avenue
Minneapolis  MN  55405

## 14.2. Addressing Officials

### UNITED STATES GOVERNMENT OFFICIALS

| Personage | Envelope and Inside Address (Add City, State, Zip) | Formal Salutation | Informal Salutation | Formal Close | Informal Close | 1. Spoken Address 2. Informal Introduction or Reference |
|---|---|---|---|---|---|---|
| *The President* | The President The White House | Mr. President | Dear Mr. President: | Respectfully yours, | Very respectfully yours, Very truly yours, or Sincerely yours. | 1. Mr. President 2. Not introduced (The President) |
| *Former President of the United States*[1] | The Honorable William R. Blank (local address) | Sir: | Dear Mr. Blank: | Respectfully yours, | Sincerely yours, | 1. Mr. Blank 2. Former President Blank or Mr. Blank |
| *The Vice-President of the United States* | The Vice-President of the United States United States Senate | Mr. Vice-President: | Dear Mr. Vice-President | Very truly yours, | Sincerely yours, | 1. Mr. Vice-President or Mr. Blank The Vice-President |
| *The Chief Justice of the United States Supreme Court* | The Chief Justice of the United States The Supreme Court of the United States | Sir: | Dear Mr. Chief Justice: | Very truly yours, | Sincerely yours, | 1. Mr. Chief Justice 2. The Chief Justice |
| *Associate Justice of the United States Supreme Court* | Mr. Justice Blank The Supreme Court of the United States | Sir: | Dear Mr. Justice: | Very truly yours, | Sincerely yours, | 1. Mr. Justice Blank or Justice Blank 2. Mr. Justice Blank |

[1] If a former president has a title, such as *General of the Army*, address him by it.

| Personage | Envelope and Inside Address (Add City, State, Zip) | Formal Salutation | Informal Salutation | Formal Close | Informal Close | 1. Spoken Address / 2. Informal Introduction or Reference |
|---|---|---|---|---|---|---|
| *Retired Justice of the United States Supreme Court* | The Honorable William R. Blank (local address) | Sir: | Dear Justice Blank: | Very truly yours, | Sincerely yours, | 1. Mr. Justice Blank *or* Justice Blank<br>2. Mr. Justice Blank |
| *The Speaker of the House of Representatives* | The Honorable William R. Blank Speaker of the House of Representatives | Sir: | Dear Mr. Speaker: *or* Dear Mr. Blank: | Very truly yours, | Sincerely yours, | 1. Mr. Speaker *or* Mr. Blank<br>2. The Speaker, Mr. Blank (The Speaker *or* Mr. Blank) |
| *Former Speaker of the House of Representatives* | The Honorable William R. Blank (local address) | Sir: | Dear Mr. Blank: | Very truly yours, | Sincerely yours, | 1. Mr. Blank<br>2. Mr. Blank |
| *Cabinet Officers addressed as "Secretary"*[2] | The Honorable William R. Blank Secretary of State The Honorable William R. Blank Secretary of State of the United States of America (if written from abroad) | Sir: | Dear Mr. Secretary: | Very truly yours, | Sincerely yours, | 1. Mr. Secretary *or* Secretary Blank *or* Mr. Blank<br>2. The Secretary of State, Mr. Blank (Mr. Blank *or* The Secretary) |
| *Former Cabinet Officer* | The Honorable William R. Blank (local address) | Dear Sir: | Dear Mr. Blank: | Very truly yours, | Sincerely yours, | 1. Mr. Blank<br>2. Mr. Blank |

[2]Titles for cabinet secretaries are Secretary of State; Secretary of the Treasury; Secretary of Defense; Secretary of Agriculture; Secretary of Commerce; Secretary of Labor; Secretary of Health, Education, and Welfare; Secretary of Housing and Urban Development; Secretary of Transportation.

| | | | | | | |
|---|---|---|---|---|---|---|
| *Postmaster General* | The Honorable William R. Blank<br>The Postmaster General | Sir: | Dear Mr. Postmaster General: | Very truly yours, | Sincerely yours, | 1. Mr. Postmaster General *or* Postmaster General Blank *or* Mr. Blank<br>2. The Postmaster General, Mr. Blank (Mr. Blank *or* The Postmaster General) |
| *The Attorney General* | The Honorable William R. Blank<br>The Attorney General | Sir: | Dear Mr. Attorney General: | Very truly yours, | Sincerely yours, | 1. Mr. Attorney General *or* Attorney General Blank<br>2. The Attorney General, Mr. Blank (Mr. Blank *or* The Attorney General) |
| *Under Secretary of a Department* | The Honorable William R. Blank<br>Under Secretary of Labor | Dear Mr. Blank: | Dear Mr. Blank: | Very truly yours, | Sincerely yours, | 1. Mr. Blank<br>2. Mr. Blank |
| *United States Senator* | The Honorable William R. Blank<br>United States Senate | Sir: | Dear Senator Blank: | Very truly yours, | Sincerely yours, | 1. Senator Blank *or* Senator<br>2. Senator Blank |
| *Former Senator* | The Honorable William R. Blank<br>(local address) | Dear Sir: | Dear Senator Blank: | Very truly yours, | Sincerely yours, | 1. Senator Blank *or* Senator<br>2. Senator Blank |

| Personage | Envelope and Inside Address (Add City, State, Zip) | Formal Salutation | Informal Salutation | Formal Close | Informal Close | 1. Spoken Address 2. Informal Introduction or Reference |
|---|---|---|---|---|---|---|
| *Senator-elect* | Honorable William R. Blank Senator-elect United States Senate | Dear Sir: | Dear Mr. Blank: | Very truly yours, | Sincerely yours, | 1. Mr. Blank 2. Senator-elect Blank *or* Mr. Blank |
| *Committee Chairman— United States Senate* | The Honorable William R. Blank, Chairman Committee on Foreign Affairs United States Senate | Dear Mr. Chairman: | Dear Mr. Chairman: *or* Dear Senator Blank: | Very truly yours, | Sincerely yours, | 1. Mr. Chairman *or* Senator Blank *or* Senator 2. The Chairman *or* Senator Blank |
| *Subcommittee Chairman— United States Senate* | The Honorable William R. Blank, Chairman, Subcommittee on Foreign Affairs United States Senate | Dear Senator Blank: | Dear Senator Blank: | Very truly yours, | Sincerely yours, | 1. Senator Blank *or* Senator 2. Senator Blank |
| *United States Representative or Congressman[3]* | The Honorable William R. Blank House of Representatives The Honorable William R. Blank Representative in Congress (local address) (when away from Washington, DC) | Sir: | Dear Mr. Blank: | Very truly yours, | Sincerely yours, | 1. Mr. Blank 2. Mr. Blank, Representative (Congressman) from New York *or* Mr. Blank |

[3]The official title of a "congressman" is *Representative*. Strictly speaking, senators are also congressmen.

| | | | | | |
|---|---|---|---|---|---|
| *Former Representative* | The Honorable William R. Blank (local address) | Dear Sir: *or* Dear Mr. Blank: | Dear Mr. Blank: | Very truly yours, | Sincerely yours, | 1. Mr. Blank 2. Mr. Blank |
| *Territorial Delegate* | The Honorable William R. Blank Delegate of Puerto Rico House of Representatives | Dear Sir: *or* Dear Mr. Blank: | Dear Mr. Blank: | Very truly yours, | Sincerely yours, | 1. Mr. Blank 2. Mr. Blank |
| *Resident Commissioner* | The Honorable William R. Blank Resident Commissioner of (Territory) House of Representatives | Dear Sir: *or* Dear Mr. Blank: | Dear Mr. Blank: | Very truly yours, | Sincerely yours, | 1. Mr. Blank 2. Mr. Blank |
| *Directors or Heads of Independent Federal Offices, Agencies, Commissions, Organizations, etc.* | The Honorable William R. Blank Director, Mutual Security Agency | Dear Mr. Director (Commissioner, etc.): | Dear Mr. Blank: | Very truly yours, | Sincerely yours, | 1. Mr. Blank 2. Mr. Blank |
| *Other High Officials of the United States, in general: Public Printer, Comptroller General* | The Honorable William R. Blank Public Printer The Honorable William R. Blank Comptroller General of the United States | Dear Sir: *or* Dear Mr. Blank: | Dear Mr. Blank: | Very truly yours, | Sincerely yours, | 1. Mr. Blank 2. Mr. Blank |

| Personage | Envelope and Inside Address (Add City, State, Zip) | Formal Salutation | Informal Salutation | Formal Close | Informal Close | 1. Spoken Address 2. Informal Introduction or Reference |
|---|---|---|---|---|---|---|
| *Secretary to the President* | The Honorable William R. Blank Secretary to the President The White House | Dear Sir: *or* Dear Mr. Blank: | Dear Mr. Blank: | Very truly yours, | Sincerely yours, | 1. Mr. Blank 2. Mr. Blank |
| *Assistant Secretary to the President* | The Honorable William R. Blank Assistant Secretary to the President The White House | Dear Sir: *or* Dear Mr. Blank: | Dear Mr. Blank: | Very truly yours, | Sincerely yours, | 1. Mr. Blank 2. Mr. Blank |
| *Press Secretary to the President* | Mr. William R. Blank Press Secretary to the President The White House | Dear Sir: *or* Dear Mr. Blank: | Dear Mr. Blank: | Very truly yours, | Sincerely yours, | 1. Mr. Blank 2. Mr. Blank |

## STATE AND LOCAL GOVERNMENT OFFICIALS

| Personage | Envelope and Inside Address (Add City, State, Zip) | Formal Salutation | Informal Salutation | Formal Close | Informal Close | 1. Spoken Address 2. Informal Introduction or Reference |
|---|---|---|---|---|---|---|
| *Governor of a State or Territory*[1] | The Honorable William R. Blank Governor of New York | Sir: | Dear Governor Blank: | Respectfully yours, | Very sincerely yours, | 1. Governor Blank *or* Governor 2. a) Governor Blank b) The Governor c) The Governor of New York (used only outside his or her own state) |

[1] The form of addressing governors varies in the different states. The form given here is the one used in most states. In Massachusetts by law and in some other states by courtesy, the form is *His (Her) Excellency, the Governor of Massachusetts.*

235

| | | | | | |
|---|---|---|---|---|---|
| *Acting Governor of a State or Territory* | Sir: | The Honorable William R. Blank<br>Acting Governor of Connecticut | Dear Mr. Blank: | Respectfully yours, | Very sincerely yours, | 1. Mr. Blank<br>2. Mr. Blank |
| *Lieutenant Governor* | Sir: | The Honorable William R. Blank<br>Lieutenant Governor of Iowa | Dear Mr. Blank: | Respectfully yours,<br>*or*<br>Very truly yours, | Sincerely yours, | 1. Mr. Blank<br>2. The Lieutenant Governor of Iowa, Mr. Blank<br>*or*<br>The Lieutenant Governor |
| *Secretary of State* | Sir: | The Honorable William R. Blank<br>Secretary of State of New York | Dear Mr. Secretary: | Very truly yours, | Sincerely yours, | 1. Mr. Blank<br>2. Mr. Blank |
| *Attorney General* | Sir: | The Honorable William R. Blank<br>Attorney General of Massachusetts | Dear Mr. Attorney General: | Very truly yours, | Sincerely yours, | 1. Mr. Blank<br>2. Mr. Blank |
| *President of the Senate of a State* | Sir: | The Honorable William R. Blank<br>President of the Senate of the State of Virginia | Dear Mr. Blank: | Very truly yours, | Sincerely yours, | 1. Mr. Blank<br>2. Mr. Blank |
| *Speaker of the Assembly or The House of Representatives*[2] | Sir: | The Honorable William R. Blank<br>Speaker of the Assembly of the State of New York | Dear Mr. Blank: | Very truly yours, | Sincerely yours, | 1. Mr. Blank<br>2. Mr. Blank |

[2] In most states the lower branch of the legislature is the House of Representatives. The exceptions to this are: New York, California, Wisconsin, and Nevada, where it is known as the Assembly; Maryland, Virginia, and West Virginia—the House of Delegates; New Jersey—the House of General Assembly.

| Personage | Envelope and Inside Address (Add City, State, Zip) | Formal Salutation | Informal Salutation | Formal Close | Informal Close | 1. Spoken Address 2. Informal Introduction or Reference |
|---|---|---|---|---|---|---|
| *Treasurer, Auditor, or Comptroller of a State* | The Honorable William R. Blank Treasurer of the State of Tennessee | Dear Sir: | Dear Mr. Blank: | Very truly yours, | Sincerely yours, | 1. Mr. Blank 2. Mr. Blank |
| *State Senator* | The Honorable William R. Blank The State Senate | Dear Sir: | Dear Senator Blank: | Very truly yours, | Sincerely yours, | 1. Senator Blank *or* Senator 2. Senator Blank |
| *State Representative, Assemblyman, or Delegate* | The Honorable William R. Blank House of Delegates | Dear Sir: | Dear Mr. Blank: | Very truly yours, | Sincerely yours, | 1. Mr. Blank 2. Mr. Blank *or* Delegate Blank |
| *District Attorney* | The Honorable William R. Blank District Attorney, Albany County County Courthouse | Dear Sir: | Dear Mr. Blank: | Very truly yours, | Sincerely yours, | 1. Mr. Blank 2. Mr. Blank |
| *Mayor of a city* | The Honorable William R. Blank Mayor of Detroit | Dear Sir: | Dear Mayor Blank: | Very truly yours, | Sincerely yours, | 1. Mayor Blank *or* Mr. Mayor 2. Mayor Blank |
| *President of a Board of Commissioners* | The Honorable William R. Blank, President Board of Commissioners of the City of Buffalo | Dear Sir: | Dear Mr. Blank: | Very truly yours, | Sincerely yours, | 1. Mr. Blank 2. Mr. Blank |

| | | | | | | |
|---|---|---|---|---|---|---|
| *City Attorney, City Counsel, Corporation Counsel* | The Honorable William R. Blank, City Attorney (City Counsel, Corporation Counsel) | Dear Sir: | Dear Mr. Blank: | Very truly yours, | Sincerely yours, | 1. Mr. Blank 2. Mr. Blank |
| *Alderman* | Alderman William R. Blank City Hall | Dear Sir: | Dear Mr. Blank: | Very truly yours, | Sincerely yours, | 1. Mr. Blank 2. Mr. Blank |

## COURT OFFICIALS

| | | | | | | |
|---|---|---|---|---|---|---|
| *Chief Justice[1] of a State Supreme Court* | The Honorable William R. Blank Chief Justice of the Supreme Court of Minnesota[2] | Sir: | Dear Mr. Chief Justice: | Very truly yours, | Sincerely yours, | 1. Mr. Chief Justice *or* Judge Blank 2. Mr. Chief Justice Blank *or* Judge Blank |
| *Associate Justice of a Supreme Court of a State* | The Honorable William R. Blank Associate Justice of the Supreme Court of Minnesota | Sir: | Dear Justice Blank: | Very truly yours, | Sincerely yours, | 1. Mr. Justice Blank 2. Mr. Justice Blank |
| *Presiding Justice* | The Honorable William R. Blank Presiding Justice, Appellate Division Supreme Court of New York | Sir: | Dear Justice Blank: | Very truly yours, | Sincerely yours, | 1. Mr. Justice (*or* Judge) Blank 2. Mr. Justice (*or* Judge Blank) |

[1] If his or her official title is *Chief Judge* substitute *Chief Judge* for *Chief Justice*, but never use *Mr.*, *Mrs.*, *Miss*, or *Ms.* with *Chief Judge* or *Judge*.

[2] Substitute here the appropriate name of the court. For example, the highest court in New York State is called the Court of Appeals.

**COURT OFFICIALS** *continued*

| Personage | Envelope and Inside Address (Add City, State, Zip, or City, Country) | Formal Salutation | Informal Salutation | Formal Close | Informal Close | 1. Spoken Address 2. Informal Introduction or Reference |
|---|---|---|---|---|---|---|
| *Judge of a Court* [3] | The Honorable William R. Blank Judge of the United States District Court for the Southern District of California | Sir: | Dear Judge Blank: | Very truly yours, | Sincerely yours, | 1. Judge Blank 2. Judge Blank |
| *Clerk of a Court* | William R. Blank, Esquire Clerk of the Superior Court of Massachusetts | Dear Sir: | Dear Mr. Blank: | Very truly yours, | Sincerely yours, | 1. Mr. Blank 2. Mr. Blank |

[3]Not applicable to judges of the United States Supreme Court.

## UNITED STATES DIPLOMATIC REPRESENTATIVES

| Personage | Envelope and Inside Address | Formal Salutation | Informal Salutation | Formal Close | Informal Close | 1. Spoken Address 2. Informal Introduction or Reference |
|---|---|---|---|---|---|---|
| *American Ambassador* | The Honorable William R. Blank American Ambassador[1] | Sir: | Dear Mr. Ambassador: | Very truly yours, | Sincerely yours, | 1. Mr. Ambassador *or* Mr. Blank 2. The American Ambassador[2] (The Ambassador *or* Mr. Blank) |
| *American Minister* | The Honorable William R. Blank American Minister to Rumania | Sir: | Dear Mr. Minister: | Very truly yours, | Sincerely yours, | 1. Mr. Minister *or* Mr. Blank 2. The American Minister, Mr. Blank (The Minister *or* Mr. Blank) |

[1]When an ambassador or minister is not at his or her post, the name of the country to which he or she is accredited must be added to the address. For example: *The American Ambassador to Great Britain*. If he or she holds military rank, the diplomatic complimentary title *The Honorable* should be omitted, thus *General William R. Blank, American Ambassador (or Minister)*.

[2]

| | Address | Salutation | | | Introduction / Reference |
|---|---|---|---|---|---|
| *American Chargé d' Affaires, Consul General, Consul, or Vice Consul* | William R. Blank, Esquire[3] American Chargé d'Affaires ad interim (or other title) | Sir: | Very truly yours, | Sincerely yours, | 1. Mr. Blank 2. Mr. Blank |
| *High Commissioner* | The Honorable William R. Blank United States High Commissioner to Argentina | Sir: | Very truly yours, | Sincerely yours, | 1. Commissioner Blank *or* Mr. Blank 2. Commissioner Blank *or* Mr. Blank |

[3]Do not use *Esquire* to refer to a woman in this position.

## FOREIGN OFFICIALS AND REPRESENTATIVES

| | Address | Salutation | | | Introduction / Reference |
|---|---|---|---|---|---|
| *Foreign Ambassador[1] in the United States* | His Excellency,[2] Erik Rolf Blankson Ambassador of Norway | Excellency: Dear Mr. Ambassador: | Very truly yours, | Sincerely yours, | 1. Mr. Ambassador *or* Mr. Blank 2. The Ambassador of Norway (The Ambassador *or* Mr. Blank) |

[1]The correct title of all ambassadors and ministers of foreign countries is *Ambassador (Minister) of* ——— (name of country), with the exception of Great Britain. The adjective form is used with reference to representatives from Great Britain—*British Ambassador, British Minister.*

[2]When the representative is British or a member of the British Commonwealth, it is customary to use *The Right Honorable* and *The Honorable* in addition to *His (Her) Excellency,* wherever appropriate.

**FOREIGN OFFICIALS AND REPRESENTATIVES** *continued*

| Personage | Envelope and Inside Address (Add City, State, Zip, or City, Country) | Formal Salutation | Informal Salutation | Formal Close | Informal Close | 1. Spoken Address 2. Informal Introduction or Reference |
|---|---|---|---|---|---|---|
| *Foreign Minister*[3] *in the United States* | The Honorable George Macovescu Minister of Rumania | Sir: | Dear Mr. Minister: | Very truly yours, | Sincerely yours, | 1. Mr. Minister *or* Mr. Blank 2. The Minister of Rumania (The Minister *or* Mr. Blank) |
| *Foreign Diplomatic Representative with a Personal Title*[4] | His Excellency,[5] Count Allesandro de Bianco Ambassador of Italy | Excellency: | Dear Mr. Ambassador: | Very truly yours, | Sincerely yours, | 1. Mr Ambassador *or* Count Bianco 2. The Ambassador of Italy (The Ambassador *or* Count Bianco) |
| *Prime Minister* | His Excellency, Christian Jawaharal Blank Prime Minister of India | Excellency: | Dear Mr. Prime Minister: | Respectfully yours, | Sincerely yours, | 1. Mr. Blank 2. Mr. Blank *or* The Prime Minister |
| *British Prime Minister* | The Right Honorable Godfrey Blank, K.G., M.C., M.P. Prime Minister | Sir: | Dear Mr. Prime Minister: *or* Dear Mr. Blank: | Respectfully yours, | Sincerely yours, | 1. Mr. Blank 2. Mr. Blank *or* The Prime Minister |
| *Canadian Prime Minister* | The Right Honorable Claude Louis St. Blanc, C.M.G. Prime Minister of Canada | Sir: | Dear Mr. Prime Minister: *or* Dear Mr. Blanc: | Respectfully yours, | Sincerely yours, | 1. Mr. Blanc 2. Mr. Blanc *or* The Prime Minister |

[3]The correct title of all ambassadors and ministers of foreign countries is *Ambassador (Minister) of* _____ (name of country), with the exception of Great Britain. The adjective form is used with reference to representatives from Great Britain—*British Ambassador, British Minister.*

[4]If the personal title is a royal title, such as *His (Her) Highness, Prince,* etc., the diplomatic title *His (Her) Excellency or The Honorable* is omitted.

[5]*Dr., Señor Don,* and other titles of special courtesy in Spanish-speaking countries may be used with the diplomatic title *His (Her) Excellency or The Honorable.*

| | | | | | | |
|---|---|---|---|---|---|---|
| *President of a Republic* | His Excellency, Juan Cuidad Blanco President of the Dominican Republic | Excellency: | Dear Mr. President: | I remain with respect, Very truly yours, *(formal general usage)* Sincerely yours, *(less formal)* | Sincerely yours, | 1. Your Excellency 2. Not introduced (President Blanco *or* the President) |
| *Premier* | His Excellency, Charles Yves de Blanc Premier of the French Republic | Excellency: | Dear Mr. Premier: | Respectfully yours, | Sincerely yours, | 1. Mr. Blanc 2. Mr. Blanc *or* The Premier |
| *Foreign Chargé d'Affaires (de missi)[6] in the United States* | Mr. Jan Gustaf Blanc Chargé d'Affaires of Sweden | Sir: | Dear Mr. Blanc: | Respectfully yours, | Sincerely yours, | 1. Mr. Blanc 2. Mr. Blanc |
| *Foreign Chargé d'Affaires ad interim in the United States* | Mr. Edmund Blank Chargé d'Affaires ad interim[7] of Ireland | Sir: | Dear Mr. Blank: | Respectfully yours, | Sincerely yours, | 1. Mr. Blank 2. Mr. Blank |

[6]The full title is usually shortened to *Chargé d'Affaires.*

[7]The words "ad interim" should not be omitted in the address.

# THE ARMED FORCES/THE ARMY

| Personage | Envelope and Inside Address (Add City, State, Zip) | Formal Salutation | Informal Salutation | Formal Close | Informal Close | 1. Spoken Address  2. Informal Introduction or Reference |
|---|---|---|---|---|---|---|
| *General of the Army* | General of the Army William R. Blank, U.S.A. Department of the Army | Sir: | Dear General Blank: | Very truly yours, | Sincerely yours, | 1. General Blank  2. General Blank |
| *General, Lieutenant General, Major General, Brigadier General* | General (Lieutenant General, Major General, or Brigadier General) William R. Blank, U.S.A. [1] | Sir: | Dear General Blank: | Very truly yours, | Sincerely yours, | 1. General Blank  2. General Blank |
| *Colonel, Lieutenant Colonel* | Colonel (Lieutenant Colonel) William R. Blank. U.S.A. | Dear Colonel Blank: | Dear Colonel Blank: | Very truly yours, | Sincerely yours, | 1. Colonel Blank  2. Colonel Blank |
| *Major* | Major William R. Blank, U.S.A. | Dear Major Blank: | Dear Major Blank: | Very truly yours, | Sincerely yours, | 1. Major Blank  2. Major Blank |
| *Captain* | Captain William R. Blank, U.S.A. | Dear Captain Blank: | Dear Captain Blank: | Very truly yours, | Sincerely yours, | 1. Captain Blank  2. Captain Blank |
| *First Lieutenant, Second Lieutenant* [2] | Lieutenant William R. Blank, U.S.A. | Dear Lieutenant Blank: | Dear Lieutenant Blank: | Very truly yours, | Sincerely yours, | 1. Lieutenant Blank  2. Lieutenant Blank |
| *Chief Warrant Officer, Warrant Officer* | Mr. William R. Blank, U.S.A. | Dear Mr. Blank: | Dear Mr. Blank: | Very truly yours, | Sincerely yours, | 1. Mr. Blank  2. Mr. Blank |
| *Chaplain in the U.S. Army* [3] | Chaplain William R. Blank, Captain, U.S.A. | Dear Chaplain Blank: | Dear Chaplain Blank: | Very truly yours, | Sincerely yours, | 1. Chaplain Blank  2. Captain Blank  (Chaplain Blank) |

[1] *U.S.A.* indicates regular service. *A.U.S.* (Army of the United States) signifies the Reserve.
[2] In all *official* correspondence, the full rank should be included in both the envelope address and the inside address, but not in the salutation.
[3] Roman Catholic chaplains and certain Anglican priests are introduced as *Chaplain Blank* but are spoken to and referred to as *Father Blank*.

## THE ARMED FORCES/THE NAVY

| | | | | | | |
|---|---|---|---|---|---|---|
| *Fleet Admiral* | Fleet Admiral William R. Blank, U.S.N. Chief of Naval Operations, Department of the Navy | Sir: | Dear Admiral Blank: | Very truly yours, | Sincerely yours, | 1. Admiral Blank 2. Admiral Blank |
| *Admiral, Vice Admiral, Rear Admiral* | Admiral (Vice Admiral or Rear Admiral) William R. Blank, U.S.N. United States Naval Academy[1] | Sir: | Dear Admiral Blank: | Very truly yours, | Sincerely yours, | 1. Admiral Blank 2. Admiral Blank |
| *Commodore, Captain, Commander, Lieutenant Commander* | Commodore (Captain, Commander, Lieutenant Commander) William R. Blank, U.S.N. U.S.S. Mississippi | Dear Commodore (Captain, Commander) Blank: | Dear Commodore (Captain, Commander) Blank: | Very truly yours, | Sincerely yours, | 1. Commodore (Captain, Commander) Blank 2. Commodore (Captain, Commander) Blank |
| *Junior Officers: Lieutenant, Lieutenant Junior Grade, Ensign* | (Lieutenant, etc.) William R. Blank, U.S.N. U.S.S. Wyoming | Dear Mr. Blank: | Dear Mr. Blank: | Very truly yours, | Sincerely yours, | 1. Mr. Blank[2] 2. Lieutenant, etc., Blank (Mr. Blank) |

[1] *U.S.N.* signifies regular service; *U.S.N.R.* indicates the Reserve.

[2] Junior officers in the medical or dental corps are spoken to and referred to as *Dr.* but are introduced by their rank.

| Personage | Envelope and Inside Address (Add City, State, Zip, or City, Country) | Formal Salutation | Informal Salutation | Formal Close | Informal Close | 1. Spoken Address 2. Informal Introduction or Reference |
|---|---|---|---|---|---|---|
| *Chief Warrant Officer, Warrant Officer* | Mr. William R. Blank, U.S.N. U.S.S. Texas | Dear Mr. Blank: | Dear Mr. Blank: | Very truly yours, | Sincerely yours, | 1. Mr. Blank 2. Mr. Blank |
| *Chaplain* | Chaplain William R. Blank Captain, U.S.N. Department of the Navy | Dear Chaplain Blank: | Dear Chaplain Blank: | Very truly yours, | Sincerely yours, | 1. Chaplain Blank 2. Captain Blank (Chaplain Blank) |

## THE ARMED FORCES—AIR FORCE

Air Force titles are the same as those in the Army. *U.S.A.F.* is used instead of *U.S.A.*, and *A.F.U.S.* is used to indicate the Reserve.

## THE ARMED FORCES—MARINE CORPS

Marine Corps titles are the same as those in the Army, except that the top rank is *Commandant of the Marine Corps. U.S.M.C* indicates regular service, *U.S.M.R.* indicates the Reserve.

## THE ARMED FORCES—COAST GUARD

Coast Guard titles are the same as those in the Navy, except that the top rank is *Admiral. U.S.C.G.* indicates regular service, *U.S.C.G.R.* indicates the Reserve.

## CHURCH DIGNITARIES/CATHOLIC FAITH

| | Address | Salutation | Salutation (*Always Formal*) | Complimentary Close | Complimentary Close (*Always Formal*) | Introduction |
|---|---|---|---|---|---|---|
| *The Pope* | His Holiness, The Pope *or* His Holiness Pope ——— Vatican City | Your Holiness: Most Holy Father: | *Always Formal* | Respectfully, | *Always Formal* | 1. Your Holiness 2. Not introduced (His Holiness *or* The Pope) |
| *Apostolic Delegate* | His Excellency, The Most Reverend William R. Blank Archbishop of ——— The Apostolic Delegate | Your Excellency: | Dear Archbishop Blank: | Respectfully yours, | Respectfully, | 1. Your Excellency 2. Not introduced (The Apostolic Delegate) |
| *Cardinal in the United States* | His Eminence, William Cardinal Blank Archbishop of New York | Your Eminence: | Dear Cardinal Blank: | Respectfully yours, | Respectfully, *or* Sincerely yours, | 1. Your Eminence *or less formally* Cardinal Blank 2. Not introduced (His Eminence *or* Cardinal Blank) |
| *Bishop and Archbishop in the United States* | The Most Reverend William R. Blank, D.D. Bishop (Archbishop) of Baltimore | Your Excellency: | Dear Bishop (Archbishop) Blank: | Respectfully yours, | Respectfully, *or* Sincerely yours, | 1. Bishop (Archbishop) Blank 2. Bishop (Archbishop) Blank |
| *Bishop in England* | The Right Reverend William R. Blank Bishop of Sussex (local address) | Right Reverend Sir: | Dear Bishop: | Respectfully yours, | Respectfully, | 1. Bishop Blank 2. Bishop Blank |
| *Abbot* | The Right Reverend William R. Blank Abbot of Westmoreland Abbey | Dear Father Abbot: | Dear Father Blank: | Respectfully yours, | Sincerely yours, | 1. Father Abbot 2. Father Blank |

## CHURCH DIGNITARIES/CATHOLIC FAITH continued

| Personage | Envelope and Inside Address (Add City, State, Zip) | Formal Salutation | Informal Salutation | Formal Close | Informal Close | 1. Spoken Address 2. Informal Introduction or Reference |
|---|---|---|---|---|---|---|
| *Canon* | The Reverend William R. Blank, D.D. Canon of St. Patrick's Cathedral | Reverend Sir: | Dear Canon Blank: | Respectfully yours, | Sincerely yours, | 1. Canon Blank 2. Canon Blank |
| *Monsignor* | The Right (or Very)[1] Reverend Msgr. William R. Blank | Right Reverend and Dear Monsignor Blank: *or* Very Reverend and Dear Monsignor Blank: | Dear Monsignor Blank: | Respectfully yours, | Sincerely yours, | 1. Monsignor Blank 2. Monsignor Blank |
| *Brother* | Brother John Blank 932 Maple Avenue | Dear Brother: | Dear Brother Blank: | Respectfully yours, | Sincerely yours, | 1. Brother Blank 2. Brother Blank |
| *Superior of a Brotherhood and Priest*[2] | The Very Reverend William R. Blank, M.M. Director | Dear Father Superior: | Dear Father Superior: | Respectfully yours, | Sincerely yours, | 1. Father Blank 2. Father Blank |
| *Priest* | *With scholastic degree:* The Reverend William R. Blank, Ph.D. Georgetown University | Dear Dr. Blank: | Dear Dr. Blank: | Respectfully, | Sincerely yours, | 1. Doctor (Father) Blank 2. Doctor (Father) Blank |
| | *Without scholastic degree:* The Reverend William R. Blank St. Vincent's Church | Dear Father Blank: | Dear Father Blank: | Respectfully, | Sincerely yours, | 1. Father Blank 2. Father Blank |

[1] Dependent upon rank. See the *Official* (Roman) *Catholic Directory.*
[2] The address for the superior of a Brotherhood depends upon whether or not he is a priest or has a title other than superior. Consult the *Official Catholic Directory.*

| | Address | Salutation | Salutation | Complimentary Close | Complimentary Close | Spoken Address |
|---|---|---|---|---|---|---|
| *Sister Superior* | The Reverend Sister Superior (*order, if used*)[3] Convent of the Sacred Heart | Dear Sister Superior: | Dear Sister Superior: | Respectfully, | Respectfully, *or* Sincerely yours, | 1. Sister Blank *or* Sister St. Teresa  2. The Sister Superior *or* Sister Blank (Sister St. Teresa) |
| *Sister* | Sister Mary Blank St. John's High School | Dear Sister: | Dear Sister Blank: | Respectfully, | Sincerely yours, | 1. Sister Blank  2. Sister Blank |
| *Mother Superior of a Sisterhood (Catholic or Protestant)* | The Reverend Mother Superior, O.C.A. Convent of the Sacred Heart | Dear Reverend Mother: *or* Dear Mother Superior: | Dear Reverend Mother: *or* Dear Mother Superior: | Respectfully, | Sincerely yours, | 1. Reverend Mother  2. Reverend Mother |
| *Member of Community* | Mother Mary Walker, R.S.M. Convent of Mercy | Dear Mother Walker: | Dear Mother Walker: | Respectfully, | Sincerely yours, | 1. Mother Walker  2. Mother Walker |

[3]The address of the superior of a Sisterhood depends upon the order to which she belongs. The abbreviation of the order is not always used. Consult the *Official Catholic Directory.*

## CHURCH DIGNITARIES/JEWISH FAITH

| Personage | Envelope and Inside Address (Add City, State, Zip, or City, Country) | Formal Salutation | Informal Salutation | Formal Close | Informal Close | 1. Spoken Address  2. Informal Introduction or Reference |
|---|---|---|---|---|---|---|
| *Rabbi* | *With scholastic degree:* Rabbi William R. Blank, Ph.D. *or* The Most Reverend John Blank, | Sir: | Dear Rabbi Blank: *or* Dear Dr. Blank: | Respectfully yours, *or* Very truly yours, | Sincerely yours, | 1. Rabbi Blank *or* Dr. Blank 2. Rabbi Blank *or* Dr. Blank |
| | *Without scholastic degree:* Rabbi William R. Blank | Sir: | Dear Rabbi Blank: | Respectfully yours, *or* Very truly yours, | Sincerely yours, | 1. Rabbi Blank 2. Rabbi Blank |

## CHURCH DIGNITARIES/PROTESTANT FAITH

| Personage | Envelope and Inside Address | Formal Salutation | Informal Salutation | Formal Close | Informal Close | 1. Spoken Address  2. Informal Introduction or Reference |
|---|---|---|---|---|---|---|
| *Archbishop (Anglican)* | The Most Reverend Archbishop of Canterbury *or* The Most Reverend John Blank, Archbishop of Canterbury | Your Grace: | Dear Archbishop Blank: | Respectfully yours, | Sincerely yours, | 1. Your Grace 2 Not introduced (His Grace *or* The Archbishop) |
| *Presiding Bishop of the Protestant Episcopal Church in America* | The Most Reverend William R. Blank, D.D., LL.D. Presiding Bishop of the Protestant Episcopal Church in America Northwick House | Most Reverend Sir: | Dear Bishop Blank: | Respectfully yours, | Sincerely yours, | 1. Bishop Blank 2. Bishop Blank |

| | Address | Formal Salutation | Informal Salutation | Formal Close | Informal Close | Spoken/Written Address |
|---|---|---|---|---|---|---|
| *Anglican Bishop* | The Right Reverend The Lord Bishop of London | Right Reverend Sir: | My dear Bishop: | Respectfully yours, | Sincerely yours, | 1. Bishop Blank<br>2. Bishop Blank |
| *Methodist Bishop* | The Very Reverend William R. Blank Methodist Bishop | Reverend Sir: | My dear Bishop: | Respectfully yours, | Sincerely yours, | 1. Bishop Blank<br>2. Bishop Blank |
| *Protestant Episcopal Bishop* | The Right Reverend William R. Blank, D.D., LL.D. Bishop of Denver | Right Reverend Sir: | Dear Bishop Blank: | Respectfully yours, | Sincerely yours, | 1. Bishop Blank<br>2. Bishop Blank |
| *Archdeacon* | The Venerable William R. Blank Archdeacon of Baltimore | Venerable Sir: | My dear Archdeacon: | Respectfully yours, | Sincerely yours, | 1. Archdeacon Blank<br>2. Archdeacon Blank |
| *Dean*[1] | The Very Reverend William R. Blank, D.D. Dean of St. John's Cathedral | Very Reverend Sir: | Dear Dean Blank: | Respectfully yours, | Sincerely yours, | 1. Dean Blank *or* Dr. Blank<br>2. Dean Blank *or* Dr. Blank |
| *Protestant Minister* | *With scholastic degree:* The Reverend William R. Blank, D.D., Litt.D. *or* The Reverend Dr. William R. Blank | Dear Dr. Blank: | Dear Dr. Blank: | Very truly yours, | Sincerely yours, | 1. Dr. Blank<br>2. Dr. Blank |
| | *Without scholastic degree:* The Reverend William R. Blank | Dear Mr. Blank: | Dear Mr. Blank: | Very truly yours, | Sincerely yours, | 1. Mr. Blank<br>2. Mr. Blank |

[1] Applies only to the head of a Cathedral or of a Theological Seminary.

## CHURCH DIGNITARIES/PROTESTANT FAITH *continued*

| Personage | Envelope and Inside Address (Add City, State, Zip) | Formal Salutation | Informal Salutation | Formal Close | Informal Close | 1. Spoken Address<br>2. Informal Introduction or Reference |
|---|---|---|---|---|---|---|
| *Episcopal Priest (High Church)* | *With scholastic degree:*<br>The Reverend William R. Blank, D.D., Litt.D.<br>All Saint's Cathedral<br>*or*<br>The Reverend Dr.<br>William R. Blank | Dear Dr. Blank: | Dear Dr. Blank: | Very truly yours, | Sincerely yours, | 1. Dr. Blank<br>2. Dr. Blank |
|  | *Without scholastic degree:*<br>The Reverend William R. Blank<br>St. Paul's Church | Dear Mr. Blank:<br>*or*<br>Dear Father Blank: | Dear Mr. Blank:<br>*or*<br>Dear Father Blank: | Very truly yours, | Sincerely yours, | 1. Father Blank<br>*or*<br>Mr. Blank<br>2. Father Blank<br>*or*<br>Mr. Blank |

## COLLEGE AND UNIVERSITY OFFICIALS

| President of a College or University | *With a doctor's degree:*<br>Dr. William R. Blank<br>*or*<br>William R. Blank, LL.D., Ph.D.<br>President, Amherst College | Sir: | Dear Dr. Blank: | Very truly yours, | Sincerely yours, | 1. Dr. Blank<br>2. Dr. Blank |

| Position | | | Very truly yours | Sincerely yours | |
|---|---|---|---|---|---|
| | *Without a doctor's degree:*<br>Mr. William R. Blank<br>President, Columbia<br>University<br><br>*Catholic priest:*<br>The Very Reverend<br>William R. Blank,<br>S.J., D.D., Ph.D.<br>President, Fordham<br>University | Sir:<br><br><br><br><br>Sir: | Dear President Blank:<br><br><br><br><br>Dear Father Blank: | Very truly yours,<br><br><br><br><br>Very truly yours, | Sincerely yours,<br><br><br><br><br>Sincerely yours, | 1. Mr. Blank<br>2. Mr. Blank<br>*or*<br>Mr. Blank, President<br>of the College<br><br>1. Father Blank<br>2. Father Blank |
| *University Chancellor* | Dr. William R. Blank<br>Chancellor, University<br>of Alabama | Sir: | Dear Dr. Blank: | Very truly yours, | Sincerely yours, | 1. Dr. Blank<br>2. Dr. Blank |
| *Dean or Assistant Dean of a College or Graduate School* | Dean William R. Blank<br>School of Law<br>*or*<br>(If he holds a doctor's degree)<br>Dr. William R. Blank,<br>Dean (Assistant Dean)<br>School of Law<br>University of Virginia | Dear Sir:<br>*or*<br>Dear Dean<br>Blank: | Dear Dean Blank: | Very truly yours, | Sincerely yours, | 1. Dean Blank<br>2. Dean Blank<br>*or*<br><br>Dr. Blank, the Dean<br>(Assistant Dean) of<br>the School of Law |
| *Professor* | Professor William R. Blar<br>*or*<br>(If he holds a doctor's degree)<br>Dr. William R. Blank<br>*or*<br>William R. Blank, Ph.D.<br>Yale University | Dear Sir:<br>*or*<br>Dear Professo<br>(Dr.)<br>Blank: | Dear Professor<br>(Dr.) Blank: | Very truly yours, | Sincerely yours, | 1. Professor (Dr.)<br>Blank<br><br>2. Professor (Dr.)<br>Blank |

**COLLEGE AND UNIVERSITY OFFICIALS** *continued*

| Personage | Envelope and Inside Address (Add City, State, Zip) | Formal Salutation | Informal Salutation | Formal Close | Informal Close | 1. Spoken Address 2. Informal Introduction or Reference |
|---|---|---|---|---|---|---|
| *Associate or Assistant Professor* | Mr. William R. Blank *or* (*If he holds a doctor's degree*) Dr. William R. Blank *or* William R. Blank, Ph.D. Associate (Assistant) Professor Department of Romance Languages Williams College | Dear Sir: *or* Dear Professor (Dr.) Blank: | Dear Professor (Dr.) Blank: | Very truly yours, | Sincerely yours, | 1. Professor (Dr.) Blank 2. Professor (Dr.) Blank |
| *Instructor* | Mr. William R. Blank *or* (*If he holds a doctor's degree*) Dr. William R. Blank *or* William R. Blank, Ph.D. Department of Economics University of California | Dear Sir: *or* Dear Mr. (Dr.) Blank: | Dear Mr. (Dr.) Blank: | Very truly yours, | Sincerely yours, | 1. Mr. (Dr.) Blank 2. Mr. (Dr.) Blank |

| Personage | Envelope and letter address | Formal salutation | Informal salutation | Formal close | Informal close | Speaking to / Introducing |
|---|---|---|---|---|---|---|
| *Chaplain of a College or University* | The Reverend William R. Blank, D.D. Chaplain, Trinity College or Chaplain William R. Blank Trinity College | Dear Chaplain Blank: or (*If he holds a doctor's degree*) Dear Dr. Blank: | Dear Chaplain (Dr.) Blank: | Very truly yours, | Sincerely yours, | 1. Chaplain Blank  2. Chaplain Blank or Dr. Blank |

## UNITED NATIONS OFFICIALS[1]

| Personage | Envelope and letter address | Formal salutation | Informal salutation | Formal close | Informal close | Speaking to / Introducing |
|---|---|---|---|---|---|---|
| *Secretary General* | His Excellency, William R Blank Secretary General of the United Nations | Excellency:[2] | Dear Mr. Secretary General: | Very truly yours, | Sincerely yours, | 1. Mr. Blank or Sir  2. The Secretary General of the United Nations or Mr. Blank |
| *Under Secretary* | The Honorable William R. Blank Under Secretary of the United Nations The Secretariat United Nations | Sir: | Dear Mr. Blank: | Very truly yours, | Sincerely yours, | 1. Mr. Blank  2. Mr. Blank |

[1] The six principal branches through which the United Nations functions are The General Assembly, The Security Council, The Economic and Social Council, The Trusteeship Council, The International Court of Justice, and The Secretariat.

[2] An American citizen should never be addressed as "Excellency."

**UNITED NATIONS OFFICIALS** *continued*

| Personage | Envelope and Inside Address (Add City, State, Zip, or City, Country) | Formal Salutation | Informal Salutation | Formal Close | Informal Close | 1. Spoken Address 2. Informal Introduction or Reference |
|---|---|---|---|---|---|---|
| *Foreign Representative (with ambassadorial rank)* | His Excellency, William R. Blank Representative of Spain to the United Nations | Excellency: | Dear Mr. Ambassador: | Very truly yours, | Sincerely yours, | 1. Mr. Ambassador *or* Mr. Blank 2. Mr. Ambassador *or* The Representative of Spain to the United Nations (The Ambassador *or* Mr. Blank) |
| *United States Representative (with ambassadorial rank)* | The Honorable William R. Blank United States Representative to the United Nations | Sir: *or* Dear Mr. Ambassador: | Dear Mr. Ambassador: | Very truly yours, | Sincerely yours, | 1. Mr. Ambassador *or* Mr. Blank 2. Mr. Ambassador *or* The United States Representative to the United Nations (The Ambassador *or* Mr. Blank) |

## 14.3. How to Dispatch Mail

ITEM                  HOW TO SEND

Birth Announcements .....................First class
Bonds: negotiable ........................Registered first class
   Nonnegotiable ..........................First class or certified first class
Books ...................................Fourth class
   (Special rates apply to books. The book may be autographed. Mark the package "Special Fourth-Class Rate: Books.")

Catalogs .................................Third, fourth class
   (Special rates apply to printed catalogs individually addressed, consisting of 24 pages or more and not weighing over 10 pounds.
   Each piece must be clearly marked "Catalog.")
Checks, Filled Out.......................First class
   Canceled .............................First class
   Certified.............................Registered first class
   Endorsed in blank ...................Registered first class
Circulars................................Third class
Currency ...............................Registered first class

Documents: No intrinsic value .............Certified mail
   With intrinsic value
   Signed originals......................Registered first class
   Copies ..............................First class
Drawings ...............................Third class

Form letters ............................Third class
   (Check with the post office for the category of third-class mail best suited to your needs.)

Greeting Cards ..........................First class

Jewelry.................................Registered first class
   (Limit of liability is $10,000-$1,000 if commercial or other insurance is also carried.)

Letters
   Carbon copies .......................First class
   Duplicate copies .....................First class
   For delivery to addressee only ...........Registered or certified first class
   Form (see Form Letters)
   Handwritten or typed .................First class

Magazines .............................Second class
Manuscript.............................Fourth class, insured
   (Mark the package "Special Fourth-Class.")
   Accompanied by proof sheets ............Third or fourth class, depending on weight

(Corrections on proof sheets may include insertion of new matter, as well as marginal notes to the printer. The manuscript of one article may not be enclosed with the proof of another unless the matter is mailed at the first-class rate.)

Merchandise (see Packages)

Money Orders . . . . . . . . . . . . . . . . . . . . . . . . . . . . .First class

Newspapers . . . . . . . . . . . . . . . . . . . . . . . . . . . . .Second Class

Packages
    Up to 16 ounces . . . . . . . . . . . . . . . . . . . . . . . .Third class
    16 ounces and over . . . . . . . . . . . . . . . . . . . . . .Parcel post
    (Packages may be sealed if they bear an inscription authorizing inspection by the postmaster. Packages containing articles valued at not more than $200 may be insured, but if they contain articles valued at more than $200, they should be sealed and registered. First-class postage will then apply, and the liability limit is $10,000.)
    Containing personal messages (See *Fourth-class mail, 6. Combination mail.*)

Periodicals . . . . . . . . . . . . . . . . . . . . . . . . . . . . .Second class

Photographs . . . . . . . . . . . . . . . . . . . . . . . . . . . . .Third class
    (Wrap with a cardboard protection and mark the envelope "Photograph Do Not Bend." Photographs may be autographed.)

Postal Cards . . . . . . . . . . . . . . . . . . . . . . . . . . . . .First class

Post Cards . . . . . . . . . . . . . . . . . . . . . . . . . . . . .First class
    (In order to be mailed at post-card rates, cards cannot be smaller than 4¼ by 3 inches or larger than 6 by 4¼ inches. Cards exceeding 6 by 4¼ inches require postage at the first-class rate for letters. If the card is enclosed in an envelope, it cannot be mailed at the post-card rate. Cards carrying a statement of a past-due account are mailed at the card rate because they must be enclosed in an envelope.)

Plants, Seeds, Cuttings, Scions, Bulbs,
Roots . . . . . . . . . . . . . . . . . . . . . . . . . . . . . . . . . .Third class or parcel post
                                           depending on weight

Printed Matter
    Less than 16 ounces . . . . . . . . . . . . . . . . . . . . .Third class
    16 ounces and over . . . . . . . . . . . . . . . . . . . . . .Fourth class

Stock Certificates
    Negotiable . . . . . . . . . . . . . . . . . . . . . . . . . . . . .Registered first class
    Nonnegotiable . . . . . . . . . . . . . . . . . . . . . . . . . .First class or certified

Tapes and Cassettes
    Nonpersonal . . . . . . . . . . . . . . . . . . . . . . . . . . .Special fourth class, marked
                                           SOUND RECORDING
    Personal . . . . . . . . . . . . . . . . . . . . . . . . . . . . . .First class

Typewritten Material (see Manuscript) . . . . . . .First class

## 14.4.  State and Postal Abbreviations

**Traditional and U.S. Postal Service Two-Letter Abbreviations**

| State | Traditional Abbrev. | Postal Abbrev. | State | Traditional Abbrev. | Postal Abbrev. |
|---|---|---|---|---|---|
| Alabama, State of | Ala. | AL | Nebraska, State of | Nebr. | NE |
| Alaska, State of | Alas. | AK | Nevada, State of | Nev. | NV |
| Arizona, State of | Ariz. | AZ | New Hampshire, State of | N.H. | NH |
| Arkansas, State of | Ark. | AR | New Jersey, State of | N.J. | NJ |
| California, State of | Calif. | CA | New Mexico, State of | N.M. | NM |
| Canal Zone | CZ | CZ | New York, State of | N.Y. | NY |
| Colorado, State of | Colo. | CO | North Carolina, State of | N.C. | NC |
| Connecticut, State of | Conn. | CT | North Dakota, State of | N.D. | ND |
| Delaware, State of | Del. | DE | Ohio, State of | Ohio | OH |
| District of Columbia | D.C. | DC | Oklahoma, State of | Okla. | OK |
| Florida, State of | Fla. | FL | Oregon, State of | Oreg. | OR |
| Georgia, State of | Ga. | GA | Pennsylvania, Commonwealth of | Pa. | PA |
| Hawaii, State of | Hawaii | HI | Puerto Rico | P.R. | PR |
| Idaho, State of | Ida. | ID | Rhode Island and Providence Plantations, State of | R.I. | RI |
| Illinois, State of | Ill. | IL | South Carolina, State of | S.C. | SC |
| Indiana, State of | Ind. | IN | South Dakota, State of | S.D. | SD |
| Iowa, State of | Iowa | IA | Tennessee, State of | Tenn. | TN |
| Kansas, State of | Kans. | KS | Texas, State of | Tex. | TX |
| Kentucky, Commonwealth of | Ky. | KY | Utah, State of | Utah | UT |
| Louisiana, State of | La. | LA | Vermont, State of | Vt. | VT |
| Maine, State of | Maine | ME | Virgin Islands | V.I. | VI |
| Maryland, State of | Md. | MD | Virginia, Commonwealth of | Va. | VA |
| Massachusetts, Commonwealth of | Mass. | MA | Washington, State of | Wash. | WA |
| Michigan, State of | Mich. | MI | West Virginia, State of | W.Va. | WV |
| Minnesota, State of | Minn. | MN | Wisconsin, State of | Wis. | WI |
| Mississippi, State of | Miss. | MS | Wyoming, State of | Wyo. | WY |
| Missouri, State of | Mo. | MO | | | |
| Montana, State of | Mont. | MT | | | |

## 14.5. Global Time Chart

To determine STANDARD TIME overseas
add (+) to or subtract (-) from
EASTERN STANDARD TIME as indicated:

| | E.S.T. | | E.S.T. | | E.S.T. |
|---|---|---|---|---|---|
| Afghanistan | +9½ | Finland | +7 | Norway | +6 |
| Albania | +6 | Formosa | +13 | Pakistan | +10 (5)* |
| Algeria | +6 | France | +6 | Panama | 0 |
| Argentina | +2 | Germany | +6 | Paraguay | +1 |
| Aruba | +½ | Ghana | +5 | Peru | 0 |
| Australia | +15 (1)* | Great Britain | +5 | Philippines | +13 |
| Austria | +6 | Greece | +7 | Poland | +6 (6)* |
| Azores | +3 | Guatemala | -1 | Portugal | +5 |
| Belgian Congo | +6 (2)* | Haiti | 0 | Puerto Rico | +1 |
| Belgium | +6 | Hawaii | -5 | Rhodesia | +7 |
| Bermuda | +1 | Hungary | +6 | Roumania | +7 |
| Bolivia | +1 | Iceland | +4 | Salvador (El) | -1 |
| Borneo (Br) | +13 | India | +10½ | Saudi Arabia | +8 (7)* |
| Brazil | +2 (3)* | Iran | +8½ | Singapore | +12½ |
| Bulgaria | +7 | Iraq | +8 | Spain | +6 |
| Burma | +11½ | Irish Republic | +5 | Surinam | +1½ |
| Canal Zone | 0 | Israel | +7 | Sweden | +6 |
| Ceylon | +10½ | Italy | +6 | Switzerland | +6 |
| Chile | +1 | Japan | +14 | Syria | +7 |
| China | +13 (4)* | Korea | +13½ | Thailand | +12 |
| Colombia | 0 | Lebanon | +7 | Tunisia | +6 |
| Costa Rica | -1 | Luxembourg | +6 | Turkey | +7 |
| Cuba | 0 | Madagascar | +8 | Union of South Africa | +7 |
| Curacao | +½ | Malaya | +12½ | USSR | +8 (8)* |
| Czechoslovakia | +6 | Morocco | +5 | Uruguay | +2 |
| Denmark | +6 | Netherlands | +6 | Venezuela | +½ |
| Dominican Republic | 0 | Netherlands Antilles | +½ | Vietnam | +12 |
| Ecuador | 0 | Newfoundland | +1½ | Virgin Islands | +1 |
| Egypt | +7 | New Zealand | +17 | Yugoslavia | +6 |
| Ethiopia | +8 | Nicaragua | -1 | | |

Note: (1)* Brisbane, Canberra, Melbourne,
New South Wales, Sydney, Queensland.
(2)* Leopoldville.
(3)* Rio de Janeiro, Sao Paulo, Santos.
(4)* Hong Kong, Peiping, Shanghai, Tientsin.
(5)* Karachi  (6)* Warsaw  (7)* Djeddah  (8)* Moscow

### 14.6. Common Abbreviations

| | |
|---|---|
| a | ampere |
| a.a. | author's alterations (printing) |
| A.B. | Bachelor of Arts |
| ABA | American Bar Association; American Bankers Association |
| A/C | account current |
| a/c | account |
| A/cs Pay. | accounts payable |
| A/cs. Rec. | accounts receivable |
| a/d | after date |
| ad loc. | to *or* at the place |
| ad. val. | according to value (*ad valorem*) |
| AEC | Atomic Energy Commission |
| AFL-CIO | American Federation of Labor and Congress of Industrial Organizations |
| a-h | ampere-hour |
| amp. | ampere(s) |
| anon. | anonymous |
| a/o | account of |
| AP | Associated Press |
| ARC | American Red Cross |
| ASTA | American Society of Travel Agents, Inc. |
| at. vol. | atomic volume |
| at. wt. | atomic weight |
| a/v | according to value (*ad valorem*) |
| av., avdp. | avoirdupois |
| B.A. | Bachelor of Arts |
| bbl. | barrel(s) |
| B/C | bill of collection |
| B/D | bank draft; bar draft (grain trade) |
| B/E | bill of exchange; bill of entry |
| Bev. | billion electron volts |
| B/F | brought forward (bookkeeping) |
| bf. | boldface |
| b.f. | board foot or feet |
| b.o. | buyer's option; back order |
| B/P | bills payable; bill of parcels, blueprint |
| B.Pay. | bills payable |
| B/R | bills receivable; builders' risks |
| B/S | bill of sale; bill of store |
| B.S. | Bachelor of Science |
| Bs/L | bills of lading |
| B/St | bill of sight |

| | |
|---|---|
| Btu | British thermal unit(s) |
| B/v | bill of value; book value |
| c. | cent(s); carat; chapter(s) |
| C. | Celsius; centigrade; Congress |
| C/A | capital account; credit account; current account; commercial agent; close annealed |
| CAB | Civil Aeronautics Board |
| C a/c | current account |
| c.a.f. | cost, assurance, freight |
| CAP | Civil Air Patrol |
| C/B | cash book |
| cc. | cubic centimeter; carbon copy |
| CCC | Commodity Credit Corporation |
| ccm. | centimeter(s) |
| C/D | certificate of deposit; commercial dock; consular declaration |
| CEA | Council of Economic Advisers |
| cf. | compare |
| c/f | carried forward (bookkeeping) |
| c.f.i. | cost, freight, and insurance |
| c.ft. | cubic foot (or feet) |
| cg. | centigram(s) |
| CIA | Central Intelligence Agency |
| C/L | cash letter |
| cl. | centiliter (metric) |
| c.l. | carload |
| clt | collateral trust (bonds) |
| cm. | centimeter(s) |
| C/N | credit note; consignment note; circular note |
| C/O | cash order; certificate of origin; case oil |
| c/o | in care of; carried over (bookkeeping) |
| C.O.D., c.o.d. | cash, or collect, on delivery |
| C.P.A. | Certified Public Accountant |
| C.R. | class rate; current rate; company's risk; carrier's risk |
| c/s | cases |
| CSC | Civil Service Commission |
| cu. | cubic |
| cu.cm. | cubic centimeter(s) |
| cu.in. | cubic inch(es) |
| cu.mi. | cubic mile(s) |
| c.v. | chief value |
| c.w.o. | cash with order |
| cwt. | hundredweight(s) |
| d. | pence |
| d/a | days after acceptance |

| | |
|---|---|
| D/A | deposit account; documents against acceptance; discharge afloat |
| D/D | demand draft; delivered at destination; delivered at docks; docks due |
| D/d | days after date |
| dd. | delivered |
| decim. | decimeter(s) |
| d.f. | dead freight |
| dg. | decigram(s) |
| dkg | dekagram (metric) |
| dkl | dekaliter (metric) |
| dkm | dekameter (metric) |
| dl | deciliter (metric) |
| D/L | demand loan |
| d.l.o. | dispatch loading only |
| D.L.O. | dead-letter office |
| dm, decim. | decimeter(s) |
| D/N | debit note |
| do. | ditto (the same) |
| D/O | delivery order |
| D/R | deposit receipt |
| dr. | debtor; debit; drawer |
| D/s | days after sight |
| d.w. | dead weight |
| d.w.c. | dead-weight capacity |
| dwt. | pennyweight(s) |
| D/y | delivery |
| ed. | editor; edition(s); education |
| e.g. | *exempli gratia* (for example) |
| e.m.p. | end-of-month payment |
| enc., encl. | enclose; enclosure(s) |
| end. | endorse; endorsement(s) |
| eng. | engineer; engineering; engine; engraved |
| e.o. | *ex officio* (by virtue of an office) |
| e.o.m. | end of the month (payments) |
| et al. | *et alii* (and others) |
| etc. | *et cetera* (and so forth) |
| et seq. | *et sequens* (and the following) |
| et ux. | and wife |
| et vir. | and husband |
| ex | out of *or* from; without *or* not including |
| f. | following (used after a numeral); feminine |
| F., Fahr. | Fahrenheit |
| FAA | Federal Aviation Agency |
| f.a.a. | free of all averages (insurance) |

| | |
|---|---|
| f.b. | freight bill |
| FBI | Federal Bureau of Investigation |
| FCC | Federal Communications Commission |
| f.d. | free delivery; free discharge; free dispatch |
| FDA | Food and Drug Administration |
| FDIC | Federal Deposit Insurance Corporation |
| ff. | following (used after a numeral); folios |
| FHA | Federal Housing Administration; Farmers Home Administration |
| fl. oz. | fluid ounce(s) |
| fm. | fathom(s) |
| FMC | Federal Maritime Commission |
| fn. | footnote |
| F.O.B., f.o.b. | free on board |
| F.P. | floating (or open) policy; fully paid |
| f.p.s. | feet per second |
| F/R | freight release |
| FRS | Federal Reserve System |
| FTC | Federal Trade Commission |
| fwd. | forward |
| F.X. | foreign exchange |
| F.Y.I. | for your information (interoffice use) |
| GAO | General Accounting Office |
| g.gr. | great gross (twelve gross) |
| gi | gill(s) |
| GI | government issue; general issue |
| gm. | gram(s) |
| GNP | gross national product |
| GPO | Government Printing Office (U.S.) |
| gr. | gross (twelve dozen); gram(s); grain |
| g.s. | ground speed (aviation) |
| GSA | General Services Administration |
| HF | high frequency |
| Hg | hectogram |
| hl | hectoliter (metric) |
| Hz. | hertz |
| ibid. | *ibidem* (in the same place) |
| ICC | Interstate Commerce Commission |
| id. | *idem* (the same) |
| i.e. | *id est* (that is) |
| i.p.s. | inches per second |
| IRS | Internal Revenue Service |
| i.v. | invoice value; increased value |
| j. | joule (electricity) |

| | |
|---|---|
| J/A | joint account |
| k. | carat; karat; knot |
| kc. | kilocycle(s) |
| kg., kgm. | kilogram(s) |
| kl. | kiloliter(s) |
| km. | kilometer(s) |
| kV | kilovolts |
| kVA | kilovoltampere |
| l. | liter(s); line |
| L/A | letter of authority; landing account; Lloyd's agent |
| l.c. | lowercase; in the place cited |
| L/C | letter of credit |
| l.c.l. | less than carload lot |
| lf. | lightface |
| l.f. | ledger folio |
| LL | leased line (securities) |
| LL.B. | Bachelor of Laws |
| LL.D. | Doctor of Laws |
| loc. cit. | *loco citato* (in the place cited) |
| log. | logarithm |
| long. | longitude |
| l.t. | long ton |
| m. | meter(s); masculine; married |
| M, M. | thousand; monsieur (*pl.* MM.); noon (*meridie*) |
| ma | milliampere |
| m/a | my account |
| M.A. | Master of Arts |
| mb | millibar |
| M/C | marginal credit |
| mc | megacycle |
| m/d | months after date |
| mg., mgm. | milligram(s) |
| min. B/L | minimum bill of lading |
| mm. | millimeter(s) |
| M/O, M.O. | money order |
| M.P. | Member of Parliament; military police; mounted police |
| m.p.h. | miles per hour |
| mr | milliroentgen |
| ms.(s) | manuscript(s) |
| M/s | months after sight |
| M.S. | Master of Science |
| m.v. | market value |
| n/a | no account (banking) |
| NASA | National Aeronautics and Space Administration |
| NATO | North Atlantic Treaty Organization |
| N.B., n.b. | *nota bene* (note well) |

| | |
|---|---|
| NBS | National Bureau of Standards |
| n.e. | not exceeding |
| N.G., ng. | no good (colloquial) |
| N.L. | night letter (telegraph) |
| NLRB | National Labor Relations Board |
| non seq. | does not follow (*non-sequitur*) |
| n/p | net proceeds |
| n.r. | no risk; net register |
| NCS | National Security Council |
| NSF | National Science Foundation |
| nt.wt. | net weight |
| nth | indefinite |
| nv | nonvoting (stocks) |
| o/a | on account of |
| OAS | Organization of American States |
| o/c | open charter; old crop; open cover; overcharge(s); over the counter |
| o/d | on demand |
| o.e. | omissions excepted |
| OECD | Organization for Economic Cooperation and Development |
| O/o | order of |
| op. cit. | *opere citato* (in the work cited) |
| o.r. | owner's risk |
| o/s | out of stock |
| O/S | on sample; on sale or return |
| o.w. | one way (fare) |
| p. | page |
| p.a. | *per annum* (by the year; each year); private account |
| P/A | purchasing agent; power of attorney; private |
| P/Av. | particular average |
| PBX, P.B.X. | private branch exchange (telephone) |
| P/C | percent; petty cash; price current |
| pct. | percent |
| pfd. | preferred |
| PHA | Public Housing Administration |
| Ph.D. | Doctor of Philosophy |
| PHS | Public Health Service |
| P/N | promissory note |
| P.O.D. | pay on delivery |
| P.O.R. | pay on receipt |
| pp. | pages |
| ppd. | prepaid; postpaid |
| P.P. | parcel post |
| pr.(s) | pair(s); price(s) |
| pro tem. | *pro tempore* (for the same being) |
| P.S. | postscript |

| pwt. | pennyweight |
|---|---|
| P.X. | please exchange; post exchange |
| q | quintal (metric) |
| Q.E.D. | *quod erat demonstrandum* (which was to be proved or demonstrated) |
| q.v. | which see (*quod vide*) |
| R/A | refer to acceptor |
| R/C | reconsigned |
| re | about; in regard to |
| REA | Rural Electrification Administration |
| rev. A/C | revenue account |
| r.f. | radio frequency |
| rhp. | rated horsepower |
| rm. | ream (paper); room(s) |
| r.m.s. | root mean square |
| R.O.G. | receipt of goods |
| ROTC | Reserve Officers' Training Corps |
| r.p.m. | revolutions per minute |
| r.p.s. | revolutions per second |
| R.S.V.P. | *Respondez s'il vous plait* (please reply) |
| rva | reactive volt-ampere |
| S | stere (metric); seconds |
| s/a | subject to approval; safe arrival |
| S/B | statement of billing (transp.) |
| SBA | Small Business Administration |
| Sc.D. | Doctor of Science |
| S/D | sight draft |
| SEC | Securities and Exchange Commission |
| Sh.p. | shaft horsepower |
| Sic | so; thus (to confirm a word that might be questioned) |
| S/N | shipping note |
| S.O. | seller's option; shipping order; ship's option |
| ss | namely |
| SSA | Social Security Administration |
| s.v.p. | if you please |
| t. | metric ton(s) |
| t.a.w. | twice a week (advertising) |
| t.b. | trial balance |
| T/C | until countermanded |
| T/D | time deposit |
| tf., t.f. | till forbidden (advertising) |
| T/L | time loan |
| T/O | transfer order |
| T/R | trust receipt |
| TVA | Tennessee Valley Authority |

| | |
|---|---|
| TWX | teletypewriter exchange |
| u.c. | uppercase |
| ult. | *ultimo* (of the last month) |
| UPI | United Press International |
| u.s. | as above (*ut supra*) |
| USIA | United States Information Agency |
| U/w | underwriter |
| v. | volt; versus |
| V. | value; velocity; volt |
| va | volt-ampere (electricity) |
| VA | Veterans Administration |
| v.f., VF | video frequency (TV) |
| VHF | very high frequency (TV) |
| v.i. | see below (*vide infra*) |
| viz. | namely; that is (*videlicet*) |
| vs. | versus |
| v.v. | vice versa |
| w. | watt (electricity) |
| w.a. | with average (insurance) |
| w/d | warranted |
| w.f. | wrong font (typeface) |
| wh | watt-hour (electricity) |
| w.i. | when issued (stock exchange) |
| w.l. | wave length |
| W/M | weight and/or measurement |
| w.o.c. | without compensation |
| W.R. | warehouse receipt |
| W.W., ww | with warrants (securities) |
| W/W | warehouse warrant |
| x-c., x-cp. | ex-coupon |
| x-d., x-div. | ex-dividend |
| x-i., x-in., x-int. | ex-interest |
| z. | zone; zero |

## 14.7. Proofreading Guides

| | |
|---|---|
| ∧ | Make correction indicated in margin. |
| *Stet* | Retain crossed-out word or letter; let it stand. |
| *Stet* | Retain words under which dots appear; write "Stet" in margin. |
| X | Appears battered; examine. |
| ═ | Straighten lines. |
| ✓✓✓ | Unevenly spaced; correct spacing. |
| ‖ | Line up; i.e., make lines even with other matter. |
| *run in* | Make no break in the reading; no paragraph. |
| *no ¶* | No paragraph; sometimes written "run in." |
| *Out— see copy* | Here is an omission; see copy. |
| ¶ | Make a paragraph here. |
| *tr.* | Transpose words or letters as indicated. |
| ℐ | Take out matter indicated; delete. |
| ℐ | Take out character indicated and close up. |
| ⁄ | Line drawn through a cap means lower case. |
| ⊘ | Upside down; reverse. |
| ⌒ | Close up; no space. |
| # | Insert a space here. |
| ⊥ | Push down this space. |
| ⊏ | Indent line one em. |
| [ | Move this to the left. |
| ] | Move this to the right. |
| ⌐ | Raise to proper position. |
| ⌐ | Lower to proper position. |

| | |
|---|---|
| ⫽⫽ | Hair space letters. |
| *wf.* | Wrong font; change to proper font. |
| *Qu?* | Is this right? |
| *lc.* | Set in lowercase (small letters). |
| *s.c.* | Set in small capitals. |
| *Caps* | Set in capitals. |
| *c&sc* | Set in caps and small caps. |
| *rom.* | Change to roman. |
| *ital.* | Change to italic. |
| ≡ | Under letter or word means caps. |
| ═ | Under letter or word means small caps. |
| ── | Under letter or word means italic. |
| ∿ | Under letter or word means boldface. |
| ∧ | Insert comma. |
| ⸴ | Insert semicolon. |
| ⦂ | Insert colon. |
| ⊙ | Insert period. |
| /?/ | Insert interrogation mark. |
| /!/ | Insert exclamation mark. |
| ⁃⁄ | Insert hyphen. |
| ⩗ | Insert apostrophe. |
| ⩒⩒ | Insert quotation marks. |
| ⩔ | Insert superior letter or figure. |
| ⩘ | Insert inferior letter or figure. |
| [/] | Insert brackets. |
| (/) | Insert parentheses. |
| ⁓ | One-em dash. |
| ⁓ | Two-em parallel dash. |
| ⓢⓟ | Spell out. |

## HOW TO CORRECT PROOF

It does not appear that the earliest printers had any method of correcting errors before the form was on the press. The learned learned correctors of the first two centuries of printing were not proof readers in our sense, they were rather what we should term office editors. Their labors were chiefly to see that the proof corresponded to the copy, but that the printed page was correct in its latinity, that the words were there, and that the sense was right. They cared but little about orthography, bad letters or purely printers' errors, and when the text seemed to them wrong they consulted fresh authorities or altered it on their own responsibility. Good proofs, in the modern sense, were impossible until professional readers were employed, men who had first a printer's education, and then spent many years in the correction of proof. The orthography of English, which for the past century has undergone little change, was very fluctuating until after the publication of Johnson's Dictionary, and capitals, which have been used with considerable regularity for the past 80 years, were previously used on the miss or hit plan. The approach to regularity, so far as we have, may be attributed to the growth of a class of professional proof readers, and it is to them that we owe the correctness of modern printing. More errors have been found in the Bible than in any other one work. For many generations it was frequently the case that Bibles were brought out stealthily, from fear of governmental interference. They were frequently printed from imperfect texts, and were often modified to meet the views of those who published them. The story is related that a certain woman in Germany, who was the wife of a Printer, and had become disgusted with the continual assertion of the superiority of man over woman which she had heard, hurried into the composing room while her husband was at supper and altered a sentence in the Bible, which he was printing, so that it read Narr instead of Herr, thus making the verse read "And he shall be thy fool" instead of "And he shall be thy lord." The word not was omitted by Barker, the King's printer in England in 1632, in printing the seventh commandment. He was fined £3,000 on this account.

## 14.8. Interest Tables

### Exact Interest Table

### Interest on $100 at Various Rates for Various Periods

|      | 5%      | 6%      | 7%      | 8%      | 9%      | 10%     | 11%     | 12%     |
|------|---------|---------|---------|---------|---------|---------|---------|---------|
| 1    | .01389  | .01667  | .01944  | .02222  | .02500  | .02778  | .03056  | .03333  |
| 2    | .02778  | .03333  | .03888  | .04444  | .05000  | .05556  | .06111  | .06666  |
| 3    | .04167  | .05000  | .05833  | .06666  | .07500  | .08333  | .09167  | .10000  |
| 4    | .05556  | .06667  | .07778  | .08888  | .10000  | .11111  | .12222  | .13333  |
| 5    | .06945  | .08333  | .09722  | .11111  | .12500  | .13889  | .15278  | .16667  |
| 6    | .08333  | .10000  | .11666  | .13333  | .15000  | .16666  | .18334  | .20000  |
| 7    | .09722  | .11667  | .13611  | .15555  | .17500  | .19445  | .21389  | .23333  |
| 8    | .11111  | .13334  | .15555  | .17778  | .20000  | .22222  | .24445  | .26666  |
| 9    | .12501  | .15000  | .17500  | .20000  | .22500  | .25000  | .27500  | .30000  |
| 10   | .13889  | .16667  | .19444  | .22222  | .25000  | .27778  | .30556  | .33333  |
| 20   | .27778  | .33334  | .38888  | .44444  | .50000  | .55556  | .61112  | .66666  |
| 30   | .41667  | .50001  | .58332  | .66666  | .75000  | .83334  | .91668  | .99999  |
| 40   | .55556  | .66668  | .77776  | .88888  | 1.00000 | 1.11112 | 1.22224 | 1.33332 |
| 50   | .69445  | .83335  | .97220  | 1.11110 | 1.25000 | 1.38890 | 1.52780 | 1.66665 |
| 60   | .83333  | 1.00002 | 1.16664 | 1.33332 | 1.50000 | 1.66668 | 1.83336 | 1.99998 |
| 70   | .97223  | 1.16669 | 1.36108 | 1.55554 | 1.75000 | 1.94446 | 2.13892 | 2.33331 |
| 80   | 1.11112 | 1.33336 | 1.55552 | 1.77776 | 2.00000 | 2.22224 | 2.44448 | 2.66664 |
| 90   | 1.25010 | 1.50003 | 1.74996 | 1.99998 | 2.25000 | 2.50002 | 2.75004 | 2.99997 |
| 100  | 1.38890 | 1.66670 | 1.94440 | 2.22220 | 2.50000 | 2.77780 | 3.05560 | 3.33330 |

### Time in Which Money Doubles Itself at Interest

| Rate percent | Simple Interest | Compound Interest |
|--------------|-----------------|-------------------|
| 2            | 50 years        | 35 years    1 day |
| 2½           | 40   "          | 28    "     26 days |
| 3            | 33   "    4 months | 23  "     164   " |
| 3½           | 28   "    208 days | 20  "      54   " |
| 4            | 25   "          | 17   "     246   " |
| 4½           | 22   "    81 days | 15   "     273   " |
| 5            | 20   "          | 14   "      75   " |
| 6            | 16   "    8 months | 11   "     327   " |
| 7            | 14   "    104 days | 10   "      89   " |
| 8            | 12   "    6 months | 9   "       2   " |
| 9            | 11   "    40 days | 8   "      16   " |
| 10           | 10   "          | 7   "     100   " |

| Prefixes | Meaning | | Units |
|---|---|---|---|
| milli- | = one-thousandth . . . . | .001 | |
| centi- | = one-hundredth . . . . . | .01 | |
| deci- | = one-tenth . . . . . . . | .1 | "meter" for length |
| . . . | Unit = one . . . . . . . | 1. | "gram" for weight or mass |
| deka- | = ten . . . . . . . . | 10 | "liter" for capacity |
| hecto- | = one hundred . . . . . | 100 | |
| kilo- | = one thousand . . . . . | 1000 | |

### LENGTH

| unit | abbreviation | number of meters | approximate U.S. equivalent |
|---|---|---|---|
| myriameter | mym | 10,000 | 6.2 miles |
| kilometer | km | 1,000 | 0.62 miles |
| hectometer | hm | 100 | 109.36 yards |
| dekameter | dam | 10 | 32.81 feet |
| meter | m | 1 | 39.37 inches |
| decimeter | dm | 0.1 | 3.94 inches |
| centimeter | cm | 0.01 | 0.39 inch |
| millimeter | mm | 0.001 | 0.04 inch |

### AREA

| unit | abbreviation | number of square meters | approximate U.S. equivalent |
|---|---|---|---|
| square kilometer | sq km or km$^2$ | 1,000,000 | 0.3861 square mile |
| hectare | ha | 10,000 | 2.47 acres |
| are | a | 100 | 119.60 square yards |
| centare | ca | 1 | 10.76 square feet |
| square centimeter | sq cm or cm$^2$ | 0.0001 | 0.155 square inch |

### VOLUME

| unit | abbreviation | number of cubic meters | approximate U.S. equivalent |
|---|---|---|---|
| dekastere | das | 10 | 13.10 cubic yards |
| stere | s | 1 | 1.31 cubic yards |
| decistere | ds | 0.10 | 3.53 cubic feet |
| cubic centimeter | cu cm or cm$^3$ also cc | 0.000001 | 0.061 cubic inch |

### CAPACITY

| unit | abbreviation | number of liters | approximate U.S. equivalent | | |
|---|---|---|---|---|---|
| | | | cubic | dry | liquid |
| kiloliter | kl | 1,000 | 1.31 cubic yards | | |
| hectoliter | hl | 100 | 3.53 cubic feet | 2.84 bushels | |
| dekaliter | dal | 10 | 0.35 cubic foot | 1.14 pecks | 2.64 gallons |
| liter | l | 1 | 61.02 cubic inches | 0.908 quart | 1.057 quarts |
| deciliter | dl | 0.10 | 6.1 cubic inches | 0.18 pint | 0.21 pint |
| centiliter | cl | 0.01 | 0.6 cubic inch | | 0.338 fluid ounce |
| milliliter | ml | 0.001 | 0.06 cubic inch | | 0.27 fluid dram |

### MASS AND WEIGHT

| unit | abbreviation | number of grams | approximate U.S. equivalent |
|---|---|---|---|
| metric ton | MT or t | 1,000,000 | 1.1 tons |
| quintal | q | 100,000 | 220.46 pounds |
| kilogram | kg | 1,000 | 2.2046 pounds |
| hectogram | hg | 100 | 3.527 ounces |
| dekagram | dag | 10 | 0.353 ounce |
| gram | g or gm | 1 | 0.035 ounce |
| decigram | dg | 0.10 | 1.543 grains |
| centigram | cg | 0.01 | 0.154 grain |
| milligram | mg | 0.001 | 0.015 grain |

## 14.10.  Tables of Weights, Measures, and Values

Tables of Weights, Measures, and Values (United States Standard)

### LONG MEASURE

| | |
|---|---|
| 12 inches | 1 foot |
| 3 feet | 1 yard |
| 5½ yards, or 16½ feet | 1 rod |
| 320 rods, or 5,280 feet | 1 mile |
| 1,760 yards | 1 mile |
| 40 rods | 1 furlong |
| 8 furlongs | 1 statute mile |
| 3 miles | 1 league |

### SQUARE MEASURE

| | |
|---|---|
| 144 square inches | 1 square foot |
| 9 square feet | 1 square yard |
| 30¼ square yards | 1 square rod |
| 272¼ square feet | 1 square rod |
| 40 square rods | 1 rood |
| 4 roods | 1 acre |
| 160 square rods | 1 acre |
| 640 acres | 1 square mile |
| 43,560 square feet | 1 acre |
| 4,840 square yards | 1 acre |

### SOLID OR CUBIC MEASURE (VOLUME)

| | |
|---|---|
| 1,728 cubin in. | 1 cubic foot |
| 27 cubic feet | 1 cubic yard |
| 128 cubic feet | 1 cord of wood |
| 24¾ cubic feet | 1 perch of stone |
| 2,150.42 cubic in. | 1 standard bushel |
| 231 cubic in. | 1 standard gallon |
| 40 cubic feet | 1 ton (shipping) |

### DRY MEASURE

| | |
|---|---|
| 2 pints | 1 quart |
| 8 quarts | 1 peck |
| 4 pecks | 1 bushel |
| 2,150.42 cubic inches | 1 bushel |
| 1.2445 cubic feet | 1 bushel |

### LIQUID MEASURE (CAPACITY)

| | |
|---|---|
| 4 gills | 1 pint |
| 2 pints | 1 quart |
| 4 quarts | 1 gallon |
| 31½ gallons | 1 barrel |
| 2 barrels | 1 hogshead |
| 1 gallon | 231 cubic inches |
| 7.4805 gallons | 1 cubic foot |
| 16 fluid ounces | 1 pint |
| 1 fluid ounce | .1.805 cubic inches |
| 1 fluid ounce | .29.59 cubic centimeters |

### SURVEYORS' LONG MEASURE

| | |
|---|---|
| 7.92 inches | 1 link |
| 25 links | 1 rod |
| 4 rods, or 100 links | 1 chain |
| 80 chains | 1 mile |

### SURVEYORS' SQUARE MEASURE

| | |
|---|---|
| 625 square links | 1 square rod |
| 16 square rods | 1 square chain |
| 10 square chains | 1 acre |
| 640 acres | 1 square mile |
| 36 square miles | 1 township |

### CIRCULAR OR ANGULAR MEASURE

| | |
|---|---|
| 60 seconds (60″) | 1 minute (1′) |
| 60 minutes (60′) | 1 degree (1°) |
| 30 degrees | 1 sign |
| 90 degrees | 1 right angle or quadrant |
| 360 degrees | 1 circumference |

*Note:* One degree at the equator is approximately 60 nautical miles.

### COUNTING

| | |
|---|---|
| 12 units or things | 1 dozen |
| 12 dozen, or 144 units | 1 gross |
| 12 gross | 1 great gross |
| 20 units | 1 score |

### PAPER MEASURE

| | |
|---|---|
| 24 sheets | 1 quire |
| 20 quires | 1 ream |
| 2 reams | 1 bundle |
| 5 bundles | 1 bale |

*Note:* Although a ream contains 480 sheets, 500 sheets are usually sold as a ream.

### UNITED STATES MONEY

| | |
|---|---|
| 10 mills | 1 cent |
| 10 cents | 1 dime |
| 10 dimes | 1 dollar |
| 10 dollars | 1 eagle |

### MARINERS' MEASURE

| | |
|---|---|
| 6 feet | 1 fathom |
| 100 fathoms | 1 cable's length as applied to distances or intervals between ships |
| 120 fathoms | 1 cable's length as applied to marine wire cable |
| 7½ cable lengths | 1 mile |
| 5,280 feet | 1 statute mile |
| 6,080 feet | 1 nautical mile |
| 1.152⅔ statute miles | 1 nautical or geographical mile |
| 3 geographical miles | 1 league |
| 60 geographical miles, or 69.16 statute miles | 1 degree of longitude on the equator, or 1 degree of meridian |
| 360 degrees | 1 circumference |

*Note:* A knot is not a measure of distance but a measure of speed. Current usage makes a knot equivalent to a marine mile per hour (properly it is $^1/_{120}$ of a marine mile). Hence, when the speed of vessels at sea is being measured, a knot is equal to a nautical mile, or 6,080 feet, or 2,026.66 yards, *per hour*.

### UNITED STATES AND BRITISH WEIGHTS AND MEASURES COMPARED

| | |
|---|---|
| 1 British Imperial bushel | 1.03205 United States (Winchester) bushels |
| 1 United States bushel | .96895 British Imperial bushel |
| 1 British quart | 1.03205 United States dry quarts |
| 1 United States dry quart | .96895 British quart |
| 1 British quart (or gallon) | 1.20094 United States liquid quarts (or gallons) |
| 1 United States liquid quart (or gallon) | .83268 British quart (or gallon) |

### AVOIRDUPOIS MEASURE (WEIGHT)
(Used for weighting all ordinary substances except precious metals, jewels, and drugs)

| | |
|---|---|
| 27$^{11}/_{32}$ grains | 1 dram |
| 16 drams | 1 ounce |
| 16 ounces | 1 pound |
| 25 pounds | 1 quarter |
| 4 quarters | 1 hundredweight |
| 100 pounds | 1 hundredweight |
| 20 hundredweight | 1 ton |
| 2,000 pounds | 1 short ton |
| 2,240 pounds | 1 long ton |

### TROY MEASURE (WEIGHT)
(used for weighing gold, silver, and jewels)

| | |
|---|---|
| 24 grains | 1 pennyweight |
| 20 pennyweights | 1 ounce |
| 12 ounces | 1 pound |

### *Comparison of Avoirdupois and Troy Measures*

| | |
|---|---|
| 1 pound troy | 5,760 grains |
| 1 pound avoirdupois | 7,000 grains |
| 1 ounce troy | 480 grains |
| 1 ounce avoirdupois | 437½ grains |
| 1 karat, or carat | 3.2 troy grains |
| 24 karats | pure gold |

### APOTHECARIES' MEASURE (WEIGHT)

| | |
|---|---|
| 20 grains | 1 scruple |
| 3 scruples | 1 dram |
| 8 drams | 1 ounce |
| 12 ounces | 1 pound |

### APOTHECARIES' FLUID MEASURE
(CAPACITY)

| | |
|---|---|
| 60 minims | 1 fluid dram |
| 8 fluid drams | 1 fluid ounce |
| 16 fluid ounces | 1 pint |
| 8 pints | 1 gallon |

## 14.11. Mathematical Signs and Symbols

+ . . . . . . . . .Plus, the sign of addition
− . . . . . . . . .Minus, the sign of subtraction
± . . . . . . . . .Plus or minus
× . . . . . . . . .The sign of multiplication
÷ . . . . . . . . .The sign of division
: . . . . . . . . .Is to ⎫       The signs of
:: . . . . . . . . .As   ⎬        proportion.
: . . . . . . . . .Is to ⎭     Thus 3:6::4:8.
∵ . . . . . . . . .Because
∴ . . . . . . . . .Therefore
= . . . . . . . . .Equals, the sign of equality
> . . . . . . . . .Greater than
< . . . . . . . . .Less than
≤ . . . . . . . . .Less than or equal to
≥ . . . . . . . . .Greater than or equal to
≈ . . . . . . . . .Nearly equal to
∼ . . . . . . . . .Difference
Σ . . . . . . . . .Summation of
| . . . . . . . . .Bond
√ . . . . . . . .Square Root
∛ . . . . . . . .Cube Root ∜ Fourth Root. ∜ Fifth Root, etc.
() [] {} . . . . .Indicate that the figures enclosed are to be taken together
        Thus $10 \times (7+4)$; $8 - [9 \div 3]$;

$$30 \left\{ \frac{7+3}{4-2} \right\}$$

° ′ ″ . . . . . . . .Degrees, minutes, seconds. Thus $25° \ 15' \ 10''$ represents 25
        degrees, 15 minutes, 10 seconds.
′ ″ . . . . . . . .Feet, inches. Thus $9' \ 10'' = 9$ feet 10 inches.
∞ . . . . . . . . .Infinity
⊥ . . . . . . . . .Perpendicular to
∥ . . . . . . . .Parallel to
# . . . . . . . .Number; numbered
° . . . . . . . . .Degree
○ . . . . . . . .Circle
∠ . . . . . . .Angle
∟ . . . . . . .Right-angle
□ . . . . . . . .Square
▭ . . . . . . .Rectangle
▱ . . . . . . .Parallelogram
Δ . . . . . . . .Triangle
0 . . . . . . . .The cipher, zero
% . . . . . . . .Percent

## 14.12. Roman Numerals

| | | | | | | | |
|---|---|---|---|---|---|---|---|
| I | 1 | XI | 11 | XXX | 30 | CCC | 300 |
| II | 2 | XII | 12 | XL | 40 | CD | 400 |
| III | 3 | XIII | 13 | L | 50 | D | 500 |
| IV | 4 | XIV | 14 | LX | 60 | DC | 600 |
| V | 5 | XV | 15 | LXX | 70 | DCC | 700 |
| VI | 6 | XVI | 16 | LXXX | | DCCC | 800 |
| VII | 7 | XVII | 17 | or XXC | 80 | CM | 900 |
| VIII | 8 | XVIII | 18 | XC | 90 | M | 1000 |
| IX | 9 | XIX | 19 | C | 100 | MM | 2000 |
| X | 10 | XX | 20 | CC | 200 | | |

Notes: 1. Repeating a letter repeats its value: XX=20; CCC=300.
2. A letter placed after one of greater value adds thereto: VIII=8; DC=600.
3. A letter placed before one of greater value subtracts therefrom: IX=9; CM=900.
4. A dash line over a numeral multiplies the value by 1,000: $\overline{X}$=10,000; $\overline{L}$=500,000; $\overline{C}$=100,000.

## 14.13. Wedding Anniversary List

| | | | |
|---|---|---|---|
| First | *Paper* | Thirteenth | *Lace* |
| Second | *Cotton* | Fourteenth | *Ivory* |
| Third | *Leather* | Fifteenth | *Crystal* |
| Fourth | *Linen* | Twentieth | *China* |
| Fifth | *Wood* | Twenty-fifth | *Silver* |
| Sixth | *Iron* | Thirtieth | *Pearls* |
| Seventh | *Wool or copper* | Thirty-fifth | *Coral or jade* |
| Eighth | *Bronze* | Fortieth | *Rubies* |
| Ninth | *Pottery* | Forty-fifth | *Sapphires* |
| Tenth | *Tin* | Fiftieth | *Gold* |
| Eleventh | *Steel* | Fifty-fifth | *Emeralds* |
| Twelfth | *Silk* | Sixtieth | *Diamonds* |

Note: Merchants' associations revise the list from time to time.

## 14.14. Birthstones

| | | | |
|---|---|---|---|
| January | *Garnet* | July | *Ruby* |
| February | *Amethyst* | August | *Sardonyx* |
| March | *Bloodstone* | September | *Sapphire* |
| April | *Diamond* | October | *Opal* |
| May | *Emerald* | November | *Topaz* |
| June | *Pearl* | December | *Turquoise* |

## 14.15. State Information

| State | Official Abbrev. | Legislative Body | Capital | Flower | Nickname |
|---|---|---|---|---|---|
| Alabama, State of | Ala. | Legislature | Montgomery | Camellia | Cotton State, Yellow-hammer State |
| Alaska, State of | Alas. | Legislature | Juneau | Forget-me-not | |
| Arizona, State of | Ariz. | Legislature | Phoenix | Saguaro Cactus | Grand Canyon State |
| Arkansas, State of | Ark. | General Assembly | Little Rock | Apple Blossom | Land of Opportunity |
| California, State of | Calif. | Legislature | Sacramento | Golden Poppy | Golden State |
| Colorado, State of | Colo. | General Assembly | Denver | Columbine | The Centennial State |
| Connecticut, State of | Conn. | General Assembly | Hartford | Mountain Laurel | The Constitution State; Nutmeg State |
| Delaware, State of | Del. | General Assembly | Dover | Peach Blossom | The Diamond State |
| Florida, State of | Fla. | Legislature | Tallahassee | Orange Blossom | Sunshine State |
| Georgia, State of | Ga. | General Assembly | Atlanta | Cherokee Rose | Peach State |
| Hawaii, State of | Hawaii | Legislature | Honolulu | Red Hibiscus | Paradise of the Pacific |
| Idaho, State of | Idaho | Legislature | Boise | Syringa | Gem State |
| Illinois, State of | Ill. | General Assembly | Springfield | Violet | Prairie State |
| Indiana, State of | Ind. | General Assembly | Indianapolis | Peony | Hoosier State |
| Iowa, State of | Iowa | General Assembly | Des Moines | Wild Rose | Hawkeye State |
| Kansas, State of | Kans. | Legislature | Topeka | Sunflower | Sunflower State |
| Kentucky, Commonwealth of | Ky. | General Assembly | Frankfort | Goldenrod | Bluegrass State |
| General Assembly | Frankfort | Goldenrod | Bluegrass | State wealth of Magnolia | |
| Louisiana, State of | La. | Legislature | Baton Rouge | Magnolia | Pelican State; Creole State |
| Maine, State of | Maine | Legislature | Augusta | Pine Cone | Pine Tree State |
| Maryland, State of | Md. | General Assembly | Annapolis | Black-eyed Susan | Old Line State |
| Massachusetts, Commonwealth of | Mass. | General Court | Boston | Mayflower | Bay State |
| Michigan, State of | Mich. | Legislature | Lansing | Apple Blossom | Wolverine State |
| Minnesota, State of | Minn. | Legislature | St. Paul | Moccasin Flower | Gopher State |
| Mississippi, State of | Miss. | Legislature | Jackson | Magnolia | Magnolia State |
| Missouri, State of | Mo. | General Assembly | Jefferson City | Hawthorn | Show-me State |

| State | Abbr. | Legislature | Capital | Flower | Nickname |
|---|---|---|---|---|---|
| Montana, State of | Mont. | Legislative Assembly | Helena | Bitterroot | Treasure State |
| Nebraska, State of | Nebr. | Legislature | Lincoln | Goldenrod | Cornhusker State |
| Nevada, State of | Nev. | Legislature | Carson City | Sagebrush | Silver State |
| New Hampshire, State of | N.H. | General Court | Concord | Purple Lilac | Granite State |
| New Jersey, State of | N.J. | Legislature | Trenton | Violet | Garden State |
| New Mexico, State of | N.M. | Legislature | Santa Fe | Yucca | Land of Enchantment |
| New York, State of | N.Y. | Legislature | Albany | Rose | Empire State |
| North Carolina, State of | N.C. | General Assembly | Raleigh | Dogwood | Tar Heel State |
| North Dakota, State of | N.D. | Legislative Assembly | Bismark | Wild Prairie Rose | Flickertail State |
| Ohio, State of | Ohio | General Assembly | Columbus | Scarlet Carnation | Buckeye State |
| Oklahoma, State of | Okla. | Legislature | Oklahoma City | Mistletoe | Sooner State |
| Oregon, State of | Oreg. | Legislative Assembly | Salem | Oregon Grape | Beaver State |
| Pennsylvania, Commonwealth of | Pa. | General Assembly | Harrisburg | Mountain Laurel | Keystone State |
| Rhode Island and Providence Plantations, State of | R.I. | General Assembly | Providence | Violet | Little Rhody |
| South Carolina, State of | S.C. | General Assembly | Columbia | Yellow Jessamine | Palmetto State |
| South Dakota, State of | S.D. | Legislature | Pierre | American Pasque Flower | Coyote State |
| Tennessee, State of | Tenn. | General Assembly | Nashville | Iris | Volunteer State |
| Texas, State of | Tex. | Legislature | Austin | Bluebonnet | Lone Star State |
| Utah, State of | Utah | Legislature | Salt Lake City | Sego Lily | Beehive State |
| Vermont, State of | Vt. | General Assembly | Montpelier | Red Clover | Green Mountain State |
| Virginia, Commonwealth of | Va. | General Assembly | Richmond | Dogwood | Old Dominion |
| Washington, State of | Wash. | Legislature | Olympia | Western Rhododendron | Evergreen State |
| West Virginia, State of | W.Va. | Legislature | Charleston | Big Rhododendron | Mountain State |
| Wisconsin, State of | Wis. | Legislature | Madison | Violet | Badger State |
| Wyoming, State of | Wyo. | Legislature | Cheyenne | Indian Paintbrush | Equality State |

## 14.16. Parliamentary Procedure: Table of Motions

### Parliamentary Procedure: TABLE OF MOTIONS

(Y=Yes; N=No; ?=Depends upon circumstances or necessity; †=If put to vote; M=Majority)

| | Recognition of Chair Required | In Order if Another Has the Floor | Second Required[1] | Requires Immediate Decision | Debatable[2] | Debate May Extend to Main Question | Amendable | Two-Thirds Vote Required[5] | May Be Reconsidered |
|---|---|---|---|---|---|---|---|---|---|
| To fix the time to adjourn | Y | N | Y | N | N[3] | · | Y | M | N |
| To adjourn | Y | N | Y | Y | N | · | N | M | N |
| Questions of privilege | N | & | N | Y | N | · | N | · | ·[9] |
| Order of the day | N | Y | N | Y | N | · | N | Y | Y |
| To lay on the table | Y | N | Y | Y | N | · | N | M | N |
| Previous question | Y | N | Y | N | N | · | N | Y | Y |
| To postpone to a certain time | Y | N | Y | N | Y | N | Y | M | Y |
| To commit | Y | N | Y | N | Y | N | Y | M | Y |
| To amend | Y | N | Y | N | Y | Y | Y | M | Y |
| To postpone indefinitely | Y | N | Y | N | Y | N | N | M | N[6] |
| Appeals | N | Y | N | Y | N | · | N | Y | Y |
| Objection to consideration | N | N | Y | Y | Y[4] | N | N | M | N[6] |
| Withdrawal of a motion | N | N | Y | N | N | · | N | M | N |
| Division of a question | Y | N | Y | Y | Y | N | Y | Y | N |
| Suspension of the rules | Y | N | Y | N | N | · | N | M | N |
| To fill blanks | Y | N | Y | N | Y | · | Y | M | Y |
| To read papers | Y | N | Y | N | N | Y[4] | N | M | N[8] |
| To reconsider | Y | N | Y | N | Y[4] | Y | N | M | N[8] |
| To rescind | Y | N | Y | N | Y | N | Y | M[7] | Y |
| To substitute | Y | N | Y | N | Y | N | Y | M | Y |
| Main, or principal, motion | Y | N | Y† | N | Y | · | Y | M | N† |
| Point of order | N | Y | Y† | Y | N | · | N | M† | Y† |
| Inquiry | N | ? | Y | Y† | N | · | N | M† | Y† |
| Division of house | N | Y | Y | Y | N | · | N | M | N |

[1] It may be advisable in stockholders' meetings to eliminate entirely requirements for a seconding of motions, since practically every stockholder, except a holder of a single share, has more than one vote, and in effect, therefore, has the right to second his own motion.

[2] Even where a question is not debatable, the chairman may desire debate or tolerate it to facilitate business or to preserve unity, but he is always justified in terminating debate; and he should terminate it if a point of order is raised as to the propriety of debate. Under parliamentary procedure, the minority has the right to deliberate and, if possible, to convince those not in agreement; this right the majority cannot take away. It would seem, however, that this applies only to questions that are debatable.

[3] If no other question is on the floor, it is debatable.

[4] This motion is debatable only if all or any part of the original question is debatable.

[5] In spite of what may be said in the table as to a majority being sufficient, special rules of the corporation or of the statutes may require a two-thirds or any other vote. Unless otherwise stated in a rule or in a statute, a percentage required to carry a question means a percentage of the voting strength present.  [6] The answer applies to negative vote on the question only.

[7] If previous notice of intent to rescind has not been given, a two-thirds vote is required.  [8] A negative vote may be reconsidered.

[9] A question of privilege is decided by the chair, but the decision is subject to appeal.

## 14.17. Glossary of 100 Common Business Terms

*Account.* A record of transactions entered in a ledger as money or some other unit; also, an accounting record containing entries posted from journals (books of original entry).

*Acknowledgment.* A formal declaration before an authorized officer, such as a notary public, that one has signed (or executed) an instrument as a free act and deed.

*Adjusting entry.* An entry made in a journal at the close of an accounting period to assign income and expense to the proper period; also, to correct errors and enter supplementary information.

*Amortization.* The gradual reduction of a debt by making periodic payments to the creditor, which cover interest and principal, and, in the case of real property, may also include taxes and insurance.

*Annuity.* A contract that calls for periodic payments to a specified party for a fixed period or for life; payments may be made monthly, semiannually, annually, or at some other interval.

*Asset.* An item or a right owned by a business or an individual that has present value or future worth, for example, property or a claim against another party.

*Assignment.* The transfer of property, or the right to or interest in property, to another party.

*Attachment.* The legal process used by a creditor to take possession of a debtor's property under court order.

*Auditing.* The examination of accounting records and supporting documents to determine whether the recorded transactions are correct and reported in an acceptable manner.

*Automatic data processing (ADP).* The receipt and transformation of information by means of a machine or group of interconnected machines, with a minimum of human intervention.

*Automation.* The advanced mechanization and implementation of processes by automatic means; a self-acting and reacting system that performs precise operations and requires a minimum of human effort.

*Bailment.* The delivery of personal property for a specific purpose, with the express or implied provision that it will be returned later.

*Balance of payments.* The sum of all visible and invisible (e.g., insurance) payments made to foreign creditors less the amount received from foreign debtors during a designated period.

*Balance sheet.* A statement of an organization's assets, liabilities, and capital accounts that shows the financial position of the owners on a specific date.

*Bank draft.* The order drawn by one bank against another bank to pay a stated sum of money to the party named on the draft, upon demand.

*Bank reconciliation.* A comparison of the checking-account balance shown on the bank statement with the general ledger's cash-account balance; also, the adjustment of the depositor's record of deposits and withdrawals to correspond to the bank's record.

*Bankruptcy.* A condition of insolvency, whereby the available assets of a person or organization are distributed to the creditors (voluntary bankruptcy is declared by a debtor; involuntary bankruptcy is brought about by the action of creditors).

*Beneficiary.* The person or entity, usually a third party, designated to receive the benefits or profits from a transaction or contract.

*Bill of exchange.* A draft drawn by one person ordering another person to pay a specified sum of money to a third party; the recipient may be required to pay on sight (*sight draft*) or at a future date (*time draft*).

*Bill of lading.* A contract between a common carrier and a shipper that acknowledges receipt of certain goods and agrees to transport and deliver those goods to a certain place.

*Bill of sale.* A legal document by which a seller transfers the title to or right or interest in specific personal property to a buyer.

*Binder.* A temporary agreement that provides for the terms of a contract to be in effect until the execution of the formal contract.

*Blue-chip stock.* Common stock that is well known and widely accepted for its earning power and ability to yield dividends under varying economic conditions.

*Bond.* An interest-bearing certificate of debt in which the issuer promises to pay a specified sum of money (principal) at a future date, with a fixed rate of interest payable at certain dates.

*Book value.* The value of a company's assets as carried on the books; also, the book value of a company's common or capital stock, determined as assets less liabilities divided by the number of shares of outstanding stock.

*Capital (assets).* The total tangible assets of organization, for example, money and equipment, plus its intangible resources, for example, patents and goodwill.

*Capital stock.* Shares of common and preferred stock issued to stockholders that represent the aggregate, proprietary interest of those stockholders in the corporation (preferred stock takes precedence over common stock in the distribution of earnings).

*Cashier's check.* A check drawn by a bank against itself and signed by an authorized officer of the bank rather than by the drawer; cashier's checks are used by banks to make payments and transfer funds and are issued to individuals for a nominal fee for their use in making remittances.

*Certificate of deposit.* A document that shows a bank has received a sum of money from a depositor, which the bank agrees to redeem on demand or on a specified date.

*Certified check.* A depositor's check, for which a bank, for a nominal fee, has guaranteed both amount and signature, thereby immediately making the check an obligation of the bank.

*Closing entry.* A journal entry made at the end of an accounting period to close the nominal accounts and transfer the balances to the balance-sheet accounts.

*C.O.D. (cash on delivery).* A condition of sale whereby the bearer of goods must collect payment from the buyer upon delivery and forward it to the seller.

*Collateral.* The asset that is pledged as security by a borrower with a creditor to secure payment of an obligation.

*Collator.* A machine that mechanically or automatically assembles cards or sheets of paper in proper sequence.

*Common law.* A system of law, which originated in England, that is based upon customs and traditions derived from previous court decisions.

*Conditional sale.* A credit transaction whereby the title to goods that are delivered to a buyer remains with the seller until some condition has been met.

*Contract.* A formal or informal, legally binding agreement between two or more parties who agree to do or not to do something.

*Copyright.* The exclusive legal right provided by the government to authors, composers, artists, and others that covers the production, publication, and sale of their works.

*Credit.* The provision that goods or services may be obtained and used, with payments deferred until a future time; also a bookkeeping entry on the right side of a ledger account that signifies an increased liability or decreased asset.

*Data processing.* The receipt and rearrangement of raw data, manually or automatically, into some form suitable for future use.

*Debit.* A bookkeeping entry on the left side of a ledger account that signifies an increased asset or a decreased liability.

*De facto (in fact).* The exercise of power by an entity, such as a corporation or government, as if it were legally constituted; existing in fact (de facto), if not in law (de jure).

*De jure (in law).* The exercise of power by right, such as a de jure corporation that exists in law (de jure) as well as in fact (de facto).

*Demand deposit.* A deposit in a checking account at a commercial bank that may be withdrawn without prior notice (on demand).

*Depreciation.* The reduction in value or expiration of utility of a fixed asset due to wear and tear through use, disuse, obsolescence, inadequacy, and the like.

*Dividend.* A share of the profits of a corporation; the distribution of net earnings paid to stockholders in proportion to their holdings.

*Downtime.* The time during which a machine or worker is unable to perform as a result of equipment breakdown or other operating problem.

*Due process of law.* The regular course of legal proceedings in accordance with established rules and principles.

*Electronic data processing (EDP).* The use of electronic equipment to receive, refine, and convert data into another form for further use.

*Eminent domain.* The right of a government or other legally constituted governing body to take possession of private property for the public good upon payment of just compensation.

*Equity.* The value of an owner's interest in property less obligations against it; also, unwritten law that aims to provide justice according to natural law or right.

*Exchange rate.* The rate or price at which a country can exchange its money for that of another country.

*Escrow.* The security deposited with a third party who will deliver it to the grantee upon fulfillment of certain conditions.

*Financial statement.* A summary of financial data derived from accounting records that shows the financial condition of a business.

*Fixed assets.* The assets of a business that are of a permanent nature, such as land and equipment, that could not be disposed of without affecting business operations.

*Goodwill.* An intangible asset represented by the value of future business profits over and beyond the return normally realized; also, the benefits a company derives from a favorable reputation.

*Gross profit.* The excess of income from sales over the cost of goods sold plus operating expenses.

*Income statement.* A summary of the income and expenses of a business for a specified period; also called profit and loss statement.

*Information-processing system.* A combination of components that interact to receive and refine information to achieve some desired result.

*Information retrieval.* The search and recovery of data from stored records on demand.

*Installment credit.* The provision that goods or services may be obtained and used, with payments or principal and interest charges made at periodic intervals.

*Interest.* The amount (or percentage) paid to another party for the use of borrowed money or credit.

*Journal.* A book of original entry in which business transactions are recorded.

*Ledger.* A book of final entry in which business transactions are transferred from the journals to individual ledger accounts.

*Letter of credit.* An instrument issued by a bank providing for a specified amount of credit in the name of the buyer.

*Liability.* A debt or obligation owed by a person or business to another party.

*Libel.* A written or oral statement that tends to damage the reputation of another.

*Machine language.* The symbols used to enter instructions and information in a computer for processing.

*Media.* Channels of communication, such as magazines or television stations, that carry advertising.

*Merit rating.* A method for evaluating and scoring the performance of employees.

*Microfilming.* A process that reduces data in scale and reproduces it on film.

*Middleman.* A person or organization that provides a service or function in the flow of goods from producer to consumer.

*Money order.* An instrument, which represents money, that can be purchased for a fee to use in making remittances in place of a check or currency.

*Note.* A written promise to pay a specific sum of money on demand or at a specified future date.

*Operations research.* The use of scientific and mathematical procedures to study and solve complex problems.

*Par value.* The principal or face value of a security when issued.

*Petty cash.* A sum of money kept on hand and used for immediate, small payments.

*Policy.* An insurance contract that provides protection as specified by its terms; also, the philosophy of an organization and the manner in which it conducts its business.

*Portfolio.* The list of total security holdings of an individual or institutional investor.

*Posting.* The bookkeeping process of transferring entries from journals to the ledger accounts.

*Power of attorney.* A written document that authorizes one person to act as agent or attorney for another.

*Premium.* A consideration or amount over and above the regular price paid for something; also, a reward or recompense.

*Profit sharing.* An arrangement whereby employees receive a percentage of their company's profits.

*Program.* A plan designed for the solution of problems; also, a set of instructions for computer operations.

*Programming.* The process of preparing a program with machine instructions.

*Proxy.* The authorization given to one person to act for another person in his absence.

*Puts and calls.* The option to buy or sell shares of stock for a specified price within a specified time.

*Real property.* The land, buildings, and man-made improvements attached to it (considered real as opposed to personal).

*Rights (stocks).* The privilege granted by a corporation to stockholders to subscribe to additional shares of stock at a specified (usually below-market) price within a specified time.

*Slander.* The defamation of another person's reputation by making false and damaging oral statements.

*Statute of frauds.* A statute that requires certain contracts and other agreements to be signed and in writing to be enforced.

*Statute of limitations.* A statute that limits the time within which legal action may be instituted.

*Straight loan.* A loan for a specific number of years at a specific rate of interest, with the principal payable in full at maturity and interest payable periodically during the period of the loan.

*Tickler file.* A file or record organized by date to serve as reminder of action to be taken on future dates.

*Time deposit.* A deposit made for a specified period that is not subject to withdrawal by check and on which the bank may require advance notice of intended withdrawal.

*Time sharing.* An arrangement permitting the use of computer time by more than one user.

*Trademark.* The name or symbol that identifies a particular business or product.

*Transcript.* An official copy of court proceedings; also, any written, typed, or printed copy or record.

*Usury.* An interest rate over and above the legal rate.

*Workmen's compensation.* State laws that provide for insurance payments to employees for illness, injury, or fatality occurring on the job.

# INDEX

# INDEX

**N**